IN
SECURITY

WHY A FAILURE TO ATTRACT AND
RETAIN WOMEN IN CYBERSECURITY
IS MAKING US ALL LESS SAFE

JANE FRANKLAND

R3THINK PRESS

First published in Great Britain 2017 by Rethink
Press (www.rethinkpress.com)

To

MY CHILDREN
Who have put up with me working tirelessly,
and pursuing something I believed in.

THE STRONG WOMEN AND MEN IN MY FAMILY
Who have given me the inspiration, courage, and determination
to overcome adversity and believe I could achieve anything.

MY SUPPORTERS
Who have backed me and cheered me on.

Contents

Contents

Challenge Three: Retention

Introduction

If you only read one chapter in this book, make it this one. It's important for it explains how the book came about, the significance of it, and the golden rules you must abide by if you're going to attract and retain more women in cybersecurity. These rules aren't a secret, but they're hidden from most people. When they become obvious to you, it's likely that you'll feel more enlightened, energised, and happier. Importantly, when it comes to women in cybersecurity, and increasing the numbers, you'll know what to do, when to do it, and how to do it. If you implement the changes I recommend and abide by the rules, there's also a good chance you'll positively impact your whole team's performance, your bottom line and the industry at large.

I hope you're ready to get started, and for your thinking to be challenged. This book will most likely do that. Although you'll be rewarded for reading it, in places you may find it an uncomfortable read, for you may discover, like I did, the extent of your prejudices and the mistakes you've been inadvertently making, despite believing in gender equality. Please forgive yourself. This is where you're at now, but I hope not where you'll remain.

The book may also anger you, for gender diversity is a complex and emotive subject. I can only prepare you for this, and apologise in advance for any offence I may cause. This is not intentional. Rather, my aim is to dissect the problem and give you solutions so effective change can be implemented, results measured, and progress made.

All the data I've used stems from a multitude of blogs, books, studies, and conversations that I've had with leading experts on the subject of gender diversity and cybersecurity. I've referenced everything, so you can explore these resources in more depth should you want to. I've also created fresh data, some of which is used. Two hundred and nine women and three hundred and fifty men from all over the world completed a short ten question survey. This data is still being analysed, and a report will be released in the forthcoming months.

Importantly, I've spoken to thousands of men and women in cybersecurity from all over the world, and throughout the whole of our ecosystem. Many of their stories are contained within this book. Sometimes I've referred to the individuals by their real names, and at other times, at their request, I've changed their names so they can't be identified. If I've referred to them by name, the opinions they express are their own and not necessarily those of their employers.

I've tried to provide you with as good a cross section of the industry as I can, from professionals who are just starting out to those who are more seasoned or at the height of their careers, plus representatives from the Lesbian, Gay, Bisexual and Transgender (LGBT) community. I've also worked hard to give cybersecurity professionals from other countries a voice, as our problems are not all the same. Other worldviews are important, particularly as we work globally. Although I couldn't include stories from as many countries as I would have liked, given my time limitations, I've managed to obtain feedback from the USA, Canada, the UK, Ireland, France, Austria, Germany, Spain, Belgium, Switzerland, Finland, Sweden,

Israel, the Middle East, Japan, Singapore, India, Australia, South Africa, Nigeria, and Ethiopia.

How this book came about

It all began with a blog. I felt an urge to write about something, and that week it centred on women, specifically in cybersecurity, and how we could increase the low numbers. I was aware that much had been written about women already, for example, are there enough women in the industry? Are women the future? Are women paid more than men? Are women under-represented? However, I was totally unprepared for the extent of the problem until I read a report by (ISC)^2 entitled 'Women in Security: Wisely Positioned for the Future of InfoSec'. Having surveyed nearly 14,000 information security professionals worldwide, the report discovered that only 10% were female. To make matters worse, the figures were declining year upon year despite increasing cybercrime, public awareness, and the growing demand for more cybersecurity professionals.

As a woman who's built a successful career in cybersecurity that's spanned two decades and knows lots of other women in the industry, I was shocked. I just thought women were doing what they normally did – keeping a low profile, not making a fuss, and getting on with the job. But, I was wrong, and I knew something had to be done about it, so I set about writing. I wanted to provide my view on what I'd seen over the past two decades, and offer value to the InfoSec community by proposing pragmatic solutions.

Now, there are few things I do without having an objective, as like most people, I'm short on time, but ironically this was one of them. As far as I was concerned I was taking some time out to write about something I believed in. But, life has a funny way of steering you in the right direction just when you think you've got everything worked out. All I knew was that I had to be a voice. So, one day in November 2015, I began writing.

I started with three main problems.

The problems

First, cyberattacks are growing exponentially. For years cybercrime has delivered a higher return on investment than the drugs trade, with reports speculating that it could grow from $3 trillion in 2015 to $6 trillion annually in 2021.[1] And, according to the World Economic Forum (WEF) these figures could actually be higher, for a significant portion goes undetected, particularly industrial espionage where access to confidential information is difficult to detect. As attack vectors are becoming more sophisticated, better thinking is required to defend against them. Like in times of war, where it takes all resources to win, women can act as an effective battalion by joining and remaining in our workforce.

Secondly, as cyberattacks increase, so does awareness, and it's a drain on our talent pool. Cybersecurity job postings are growing three and a half times faster than other technology jobs, and the media reports there are 1 million vacant cybersecurity jobs globally, which will rise to 6 million by 2020. Then the industry will need an extra 1.8 million cybersecurity professionals in order to plug the skills shortage gap.[2] As women make up about half of the workforce in the world, the industry has failed to harness a massive amount of the prospective talent pool.

Thirdly, cybersecurity has an identity problem and is misunderstood. It's viewed as being incredibly technical, yet it's inherently interdisciplinary and diverse. It involves knowledge in technology, psychology, finance, business, risk, law, and regulation. Whether a person is skilled with people, administration, management, education, or technology, there is something for everyone.

Having outlined the problems, I then went on to explain that the reason why we need to reverse the gender gap issue in cyber-

---

1. http://securityaffairs.co/wordpress/50680/cyber-crime/global-cost-of
-cybercrime.html
2. https://www.isc2cares.org/IndustryResearch/GISWS/

security is because of economics. It's straightforward, not sexist or politically motivated. When we close the gender gap there are huge implications for our global economy. According to a report by McKinsey & Co. entitled 'The Power of Parity', full gender equality would add 26%, or $28 trillion, to global gross domestic product (GDP) in 2025. Companies would have higher equity, operating results and stock-price growth.[3]

Other studies also show that gender-diverse teams are more productive, innovative and able to stay on schedule, and within budget, compared to homogeneous teams.[4] Furthermore, when women are at the helm of business, in leadership roles, not only does Gross Domestic Product (GDP) improve, but also there's more diversity in the workforce, contributions to charities and support of local businesses. And, when women are politically and economically empowered, societies are more stable.

The blog contained many stories, backed up with data. As soon as it was released, I was inundated with comments and private messages. Many had a lot to say about what I'd written and shared stories, which were insightful.[5]

One male cybersecurity professional spoke of his frustration. He told me that he'd spent almost two decades trying to get women to move into technology and advance their careers. In his role as a trouble-shooter he'd told CEOs off for not promoting women who were capable of the job. However, he'd also repeatedly witnessed even the cleverest of women choosing other subjects, such as law, geography, and so on, in preference to a career in cybersecurity. He believed it was because women have different life aims, and

---

3. http://www.mckinsey.com/insights/growth/how_advancing_womens
_equality_can_add_12_trillion_to_global_growth
4. http://www.ncwit.org/sites/default/files/resources/impactgenderd
iversitytechbusinessperformance_print.pdf
5. https://www.linkedin.com/pulse/future-women-cyber-security-how-
do-we-increase-jane-frankland/?trk=pulse_spock-articles

that instead of trying to attract a diverse range of professionals, for example, those who are more arts based, we should be spending our time and money on the women who choose Science, Technology, Engineering and Mathematic (STEM) subjects, ensuring they don't leave the industry upon joining.

Another man relayed how a single mother raised him back in the days when this was a rarity. Reading my article, he realised how large an untapped talent pool – single mothers working remotely – we have. He then went on to tell me how he successfully managed teams around the world, whilst never meeting them face-to-face. Not once was there an issue with the quality of the work his teams produced. He proposed that the industry should become more creative in terms of how it resources cybersecurity professionals, pointing out how many of the duties don't need a degree and could suit flexible home-working environments, thereby lifting many out of poverty.

On the subject of STEM, a woman from Australia agreed that more collaboration was needed if we're going to reverse the situation. She believed that a focus on promoting STEM and cybersecurity in schools and universities would go a long way to improving the low numbers. She told me how she'd worked as a mentor twelve years ago, and went into high schools to promote the take up of STEM subjects to students. There, she found that the girls in the class would refer to computing and electronics as 'boys' stuff'. Having daughters now, she's careful to educate them that there is no such thing as boys' toys and girls' toys. Instead, they are just toys and anyone can play with them.

These are just a handful of stories from conversations that I had. Although the blog resonated with many, it missed one vital message, which is what this book is all about.

The message

In the late 1990s, writer, cryptographer, computer security and privacy specialist Bruce Schneier popularised a concept that became known as the golden triangle. This approach ran on the premise that operational effectiveness could only be achieved if the relationships between people, process and technology were optimised. However, within cybersecurity there's always been a huge tendency to rely on technology, and it's often been used as a silver bullet to try to eliminate cyberattacks and compliance failures. Whilst people have been used to implement the technology and develop processes to support it, there's been a fundamental failure. When it comes to people, the same type has mainly been sought. Typically these people have been male and had a military, mathematical, or science background.

Although people from these backgrounds do worthy work, and are immensely valued, just having the same types of people within cybersecurity has limited our thinking capacity, and made us more siloed. As cyberattacks have become more creative, and hackers have become more collaborative and business-like in their approach, we need better thinking capabilities – people who can see things in different ways, and help us to not be blindsided. We can't expect to solve our problems with the same level of thinking that created them. We need a new approach, and I believe that women can play a significant part in mitigating this risk.

Women are fundamentally different to men. They're different versions of the same species – look in the mirror when you're stark naked, and it's obvious. The not so obvious thing is how men's and women's brains differ, and when it comes to cybersecurity and building better defence strategies and tactics, brainpower matters.

Whilst past research has indicated that men's and women's brains are wired differently, for example, men have better connectivity within each hemisphere, and women have stronger connections between the hemispheres, new research suggests that the degrees to which our brains are male or female may be more complex.[6]

In 2015, when Israeli researchers looked at the hippocampus, the part of the brain that's responsible for memory and emotions, and assessed the brain features that were more common in one sex than the other, and some that were typically found in both, they discovered that almost everyone has a unique range of male and female structures.[7] UK researchers also concluded that there are more similarities between male and female brains than differences. When they performed the largest brain study of its kind in 2017, they found that on average, women had significantly thicker cortices (the part of the brain that's been linked to higher scores on cognitive and IQ tests) than men. However, men showed higher brain volumes than women in every subcortical region, including the hippocampus, the amygdala (emotions, memory, and decision-making), striatum (learning, inhibition, and reward-processing), and thalamus (processing and relaying sensory information to other parts of the brain). Their brains were also more variable than females'.[8]

When it comes to hormones, women and men differ, as both sexes produce the same hormones but to varying levels. The main sex hormonal driver for women is oestrogen, and this encourages bonding, cooperation, collaboration and relationships. It also supports the part of the brain that involves social skills and observations, plus it helps women to determine how they perceive risk and avoid conflict. Serotonin is the hormone that's responsible for stabilising moods and regulating anxiety. According to researchers women produce 52% less serotonin than men, which may indicate

6. http://www.livescience.com/41619-male-female-brains-wired-differently
.html

7. http://www.webmd.com/brain/features/how-male-female-brains-dif
fer#1

8. http://www.sciencemag.org/news/2017/04/study-finds-significant
-differences-brains-men-and-women

why they have more of a tendency to worry than men. Then, there's testosterone, the main sex hormone for men, which is associated with aggression, impulsivity, single mindedness, independence, a lack of cooperation, power, winning, and risk taking.

The latter is obviously of great significance to us in cybersecurity. Countless studies have shown that women and men gauge risk differently. Women are far better at assessing odds than men, and this often manifests itself as an increased avoidance of risk. As women are typically more risk averse, their natural detailed exploration makes them more attuned to changing pattern behaviours – a skill that's needed for correctly identifying threat actors and protecting environments.

When the Norwegian company CLTRe and Gregor Petric, PhD, Associate Professor of Social Informatics and Chair of the Centre for Methodology and Informatics at the Faculty of Social Sciences, University of Ljubljana (Slovenia) studied more than 10,000 employees across five verticals in two countries within the Nordics, they found women to be complying with rules, and embracing organisational controls and technology more than men. Additionally, whilst men rated their knowledge and awareness of IT security, controls and behaviours much more highly than women, men reported higher levels of risky behaviours, both on their own part and that of their colleagues. [9]

These findings correlate with other reports that detail gender differences in regards to compliance and trust online. When HMA, a virtual private network service provider, commissioned a study of Internet users in the USA, they found more women considered what they shared online more than men; were more unlikely to give away personal information such as their birth date, real-world address or social security number on a social media profile than men; and

---

9. https://get.clt.re/report/

were more unlikely to offer this information while chatting online with a friend than men.

They also found that men reported their accounts being compromised or hacked, or accidentally installing spyware, malware or a virus more often than women. Yet, they found that after women experienced a security problem, women were more likely than men to make lasting changes to their online behaviour in order to protect themselves from future problems. Men, on the other hand, tended to fall back on technical means of protection.[10]

In addition to these traits, women are acknowledged to be highly intuitive too. Men, on the other hand, tend to be more pragmatic with their thinking. Whether or not you believe it's because women were withheld information over the centuries and had to develop intuitive skills is immaterial. What matters is their capacity to think differently, because when two sets of people are attacking a problem, they're able to solve it uniquely, and much faster. As not all risk is the same, the dialogue about how to approach it is also richer.

Women score highly when it comes to emotional and social intelligence, which brings about many benefits, including the ability to remain calm during times of turbulence – a trait that's required when breaches and major incidents occur.[11] Furthermore, in a world that values speed and agility, the ability to use intuitive thinking and make good decisions quickly without having all of the information is becoming more of a necessity.[12]

Whilst this book is certainly not about one gender being better than another, it is about playing to our strengths as men and

---

10. https://www.forbes.com/sites/kevinmurnane/2016/04/11/how-men
-and-women-differ-in-their-approach-to-online-privacy-and-security/#4f
65099c7d88
11. http://www.kornferry.com/press/new-research-shows-women-are
-better-at-using-soft-skills-crucial-for-effective-leadership/
12. https://www.cpni.gov.uk/system/files/documents/63/29/insider-data
-collection-study-report-of-main-findings.pdf

women, how both genders complement one another, and how we can become more effective in cybersecurity by working together. It's about it being OK to be different, and celebrating diversity as a strength. Lengthy training courses can't compensate for things that women and men do well naturally, and it's time to value this by strategically building more gender diverse teams.

Having a wide range of perspectives and thought leadership throughout the whole cybersecurity industry, not merely token representation from women, is critical to managing risk effectively. Cybersecurity is not a job just for men, and the industry can reap the rewards when more women are included.

How to read this book

I've broken the book into three parts, and each chapter starts with a story, which typically has been taken from my life. I then link these to the theme of the chapter, weave in more stories from others in the industry, and include data. Finally, the chapter is summarised with learning lessons: the Golden Rules.

The first part is about assumptions. It's about dealing with the elephants in the room – the big problems that are being talked about, but aren't being dealt with. It includes seven chapters:

1. Women cost more
2. Prove it
3. Mind the gap
4. Qualifications don't make a hacker
5. STEM is a red herring
6. Educate the educators
7. HR is holding us back.

The second part of the book is about the challenges, and what we can do to address them. There are three main chapters, which concentrate on attracting, identifying, and retaining female cybersecurity talent:

1. Challenge One
   - Hoot the horn
   - Seeing is believing
2. Challenge Two
   - Recruiting the X factor
   - Enter the dragon
3. Challenge Three
   - Cultivating workplace culture
   - Career navigation
   - Personal branding
   - Personal growth.

Each challenge ends with a checklist, so you'll obtain practical strategies for dealing with the topic that's under discussion. Each one focuses on doing things pragmatically, and levelling the playing field as far as gender goes. Sometimes they'll involve using a technology or people solution, and at other times it may be a process, or a combination of both.

The final part is about what I've seen during the course of writing this book and the next steps. It includes:

- Through the looking glass
- A call to arms
- Acknowledgements
- My sponsors.

The chapters have been written in a specific order. Whilst you can always read any chapter that takes your liking, I'd advise you stick to the order I've presented.

The objective of this book

This book is for all sizes of business and is fundamentally about performance and working to a higher standard in cybersecurity. By increasing diversity within our talent pool, via women we can be more innovative, better problem solvers and more thorough in our approach to risk. Cybersecurity is, after all, a people problem, and only when people are regarded as being the strongest shield throughout our whole ecosystem and given the opportunity to fulfil their potential will we become more resilient in our defence.

To do this we need to integrate teams of cybersecurity specialists across industries and operations, as attacks become more intense, sophisticated and threaten every layer of business and government. We need multiple skillsets, from penetration testers, security auditors, analysts and compliance officers, to systems testers, developers, risk consultants, policymakers, and incident responders. We need people with deep analytical skills so they can spot anomalies and non-compliance issues. We also need good communicators so we can drive collaboration, and creative thinkers so we can solve problems. With this diversity of talent spread, our odds of challenging conventional thinking and staying one step ahead of our attackers increases.

The aim of this book is, therefore, to effect positive change in the way that we're operating as an industry, and to get more women into, remaining in, and playing a bigger part in cybersecurity. It's not necessarily about getting more women into positions at the top, although if that happens it would be fantastic. Rather it's about helping women in cybersecurity to move up and create satisfying careers that meet their life objectives. Not every woman wants to be a CISO, manager, or subject matter expert and it's important we acknowledge this. Many are quite content operating as consultants, project managers, or researchers, or at a mid-level position and that's OK for they're of huge value to the industry.

Who this book is for?
The book is for all to read, and it should appeal to as many men as women. Men are a vital component to reversing the gender diversity gap in cybersecurity. Furthermore, most men want to be part of this

movement, to take an active role in bringing more women into the industry, and women want to include men too. Men want to ensure equal opportunities in the workplace for their female family members so they can fulfil their potential in their chosen careers. They also want to change for themselves the way we're working. They want more of a work-life balance, to be around for their children, and to stop being penalised for wanting to take paternity leave, or taking time off with their children or families.

This book will therefore be of interest to:

- C-levels (CISOS, CIOS, CTOS, CDOS, CEOS) or any cybersecurity leader who has females within his or her team, and wants to attract and retain more
- Any woman in cybersecurity who's interested in gender diversity and wants to be empowered
- Any woman who wants to get into cybersecurity and learn more about our industry
- Any man in cybersecurity who wants to understand the gender dynamics better, create equality in the workforce, and improve performance.

In summary

I hope you'll be engaged throughout this book and become more educated on the challenges surrounding women in cybersecurity. Furthermore, I hope you'll want to implement the recommendations and be an ambassador for cybersecurity. I believe passionately in improving our industry, in combatting cyberattacks, and making businesses, countries, and individuals safer. I also hope that this book, whilst it only deals with gender, will lead the way for all diversity and improvements that we need to make as an industry in order to be more effective.

Being around people who are different to us can cause discomfort, rougher interactions, a lack of trust, greater perceived interpersonal conflict, lower communication, less cohesion, more concern about disrespect, and lots of other problems. However, the upside is that it can enable more creativity, more diligence, and tenacity. Simply interacting with those who are different forces people to prepare better, anticipate alternative viewpoints, and expect that reaching consensus will take effort. It encourages people to search for novel information and perspectives, leading to better decision-making and problem solving.

Finally, I hope that this book inspires you to create a more forward-thinking, progressive, and inclusive industry, where gender equality is demanded, and welcomed. Cybersecurity is a young profession, and we have a real opportunity to create something special. By getting it right, at an early stage of our evolution, we can greater impact the world and lead the way for other professions.

PART ONE

The Assumptions

1. Women Cost More

- Women and discrimination
- Prejudice in the workplace
- The cost of maternity leave

Picture the scene. I'd just delivered a keynote speech to about 120 cybersecurity professionals at an ISSA UK event in London. My presentation was controversial, yet well received. I'd started with the five challenges that I believed we had in regards to gender diversity in cybersecurity – attracting talent, marketing, defining the industry, recruiting, and offering workplace flexibility and recalibrating culture. Then I set out how to overcome them. The audience was fired up. Heavy debate ensued straight after, and the event organisers were happy.

As usual, numerous attendees approached me to discuss the topic further, and right at the end a young woman advanced. I was unprepared for the sentence she delivered.

'Jane, I can't believe what that man has just said.' She pointed to the owner of a recruitment business, whom I'd been introduced to earlier. I was intrigued to find out more, and quickly discovered that he'd been bragging to her about how he'd never employ a woman of childbearing age.

The man then appeared, proceeded to tell me why he stood by his remark, and looked to me for justification. I was dismayed. In fact, as a mother of three children who's worked for my entire career, I was outraged. I replied as follows:

'As you know, over the last two decades I've interviewed and employed hundreds of cybersecurity professionals. I've also owned and built a seven-figure business from the ground up, without investment, and I've had all the pressures associated with being a small business. Whenever I'm interviewing a woman of childbearing age, of course I think, *Are you going to have children whilst working for me? How am I going to manage whilst you're on maternity leave? How long will you be away for? Will you return to work after having your baby, and what will it cost me?* But, I can tell you this. If I've got the right person sitting in front of me, applying for a job, I will bend over backwards to ensure that they're on my team irrespective of their gender. Together, we will find a way to make it work.'

He wasn't happy with my brutal response, especially as a crowd had formed to witness the whole affair. Nor was I happy, and I couldn't stop thinking about what he'd said for days after, for he'd simply voiced what a lot of employers think but are reluctant to talk about – women are more expensive to employ than men. It's a fact. Data supports this. Women take time off to have children. Women take more sick leave than men. And, women move jobs more frequently, so often the learning and development investment made in them is wasted. However, as employers and employment bodies have avoided performing meaningful studies into the costs of women in the workplace, let alone as cybersecurity professionals, I decided to investigate further, and sought evidence from wherever I could.

Women and discrimination

In 2005, Croner Consulting (now owned by Peninsula) published the results of an online poll of 110 HR professionals. It suggested that four fifths of employers instinctively thought twice about employing women of 'childbearing age'; in other words, those between sixteen and forty-nine years of age. The findings reinforced those of a larger report, published the same year by the Equal Opportunities Commission (EOC). When it surveyed 441,000 women in the UK, it found that employers were selective against pregnant employees. Furthermore, discrimination may even start prior to pregnancy. It estimated that 30,000 women in the UK were being pushed out of their jobs due to pregnancy each year, and as only 3% of cases went to tribunal it remained a hidden problem.

In 2014, law firm Slater and Gordon surveyed 500 hiring managers to gauge attitudes and discovered that over a third (40%) were wary of hiring a woman of childbearing age or a woman who has already had a child for a senior role. A quarter said they would rather hire a man to get around the issues of maternity leave and childcare when a woman does return to work, with just under a half (44%) saying the financial costs to their business because of maternity leave were a significant concern. Finally, a third claimed that women were not as good at their jobs when they returned to work from maternity leave.

The results revealed so much. Although the media reports statistics that highlight the profits businesses make when they employ more women, particularly in management, prejudice in the workplace is clearly rife. Whether it's accurate or not, women are still seen to be more expensive to employ than men.

Now, it would be tempting to think that practices like these don't occur in cybersecurity, and that we're above this given the dire shortage of women in our profession, but unfortunately, they do. One of my friends, Sarah, worked for a research and development company as a manager. She had two children whilst working at her previous company, and as we've worked together, I know the quality of her work – it's exemplary. She'd always returned to work straight after her statutory maternity leave, but when she fell pregnant with her third child and informed her new employer, they immediately made her redundant.

Their reasoning didn't stack up. Most women are wary of fighting a discrimination battle in court, particularly whilst pregnant, but Sarah proved an exception. She represented herself, and even though the company played hardball, she held her nerve. She felt she owed it to other women who'd experienced the same injustice, at that organisation and elsewhere, to pursue it. Their case was based on lies and inconsistencies and she settled out of court for a hefty sum two days before the tribunal.

Monique, a senior cybersecurity leader at a large company that is listed on the top 100 global market stock indices, had a different story. She told me how hard she'd worked to climb the ranks and how she'd returned to work after giving birth to her second child only to discover that her job had been given to another employee. Her team had been taken away from her too, she had little influence within her department and her new responsibilities were dull. Stuck in a job she didn't enjoy, and with HR unable to effect change, she knew she could either accept it and remain, or look for another job. She chose the latter.

The more I asked cybersecurity women from around the world about their experiences, the more I discovered a pernicious trend. Just like Sarah and Monique, many women in senior roles, particularly in large organisations, had unacceptable experiences. Many were forced to accept lower pay grades in order to return to work after maternity leave, or if they'd agreed to come back part-time, they found they had no reduction in responsibilities or job sharing opportunities, yet were expected to miraculously perform their full-time role. Increasingly employers appeared to be manipulating the situation until these women were unable to cope and either dismissed for ineffectiveness, forced to resign, or made redundant.

In June 2016, I decided to dig a little deeper and conducted a small, informal focus group with female cybersecurity professionals, aged twenty-four to thirty-five, from financial services and consulting firms in London.

During that session, a young woman named Rachel, who worked at one of the consulting firms, remarked, 'This is the third company I've worked for, and even though my firm is working hard on gender diversity, I've yet to see an older, more senior woman whose career and home life I'd actually want.' She went on to explain, 'I know many driven women who are climbing the ladder, but most are single, divorced or don't have children. I know a handful of working mothers who are working reduced hours so they can spend time with their family, but they don't get the good projects and miss out on bonuses. They're also subjected to negative comments, from both men and women, which thankfully they don't hear, for example, "If she's not prepared to put the time in and work the client's hours, she can't be serious about her career and she shouldn't be working here."'

In March 2016, *The Telegraph* reported that three in four mothers in the UK were subjected to a negative or possibly discriminatory experience in the workplace.[1] Far from showing signs of improvement, the second report from the Equality and Human Rights Commission (EHRC) showed that attitudes towards pregnant women and women returning from maternity leave have deteriorated significantly. In 2015, it reported that 11% of mothers per year, roughly 54,000, who were returning to work subsequently felt forced to leave their job. Furthermore, one in five mothers said they'd experienced harassment or negative comments related to pregnancy or flexible working from their employer or colleagues.

In any country, sexist attitudes and practices such as these undermine the economy and cause unnecessary costs. The lack of flexible working means that women are not using their full skills

---

1. http://www.telegraph.co.uk/women/work/maternity-discrimination-is
-pushing-women-out-of-work---and-its/

and experience. Moreover, discrimination is affecting not just women of childbearing age, but everyone. Studies show that if we address these issues and make men's and women's productivity and employment equal, it will add billions to an economy.

Prejudice in the workplace

Considering the era we're living in, it's astonishing to discover that incidents of prejudice don't just occur once women are in the workplace. Many start during the recruitment phase. I was shocked to learn that many women upon interview are still being asked about their marital status, whether they intend to have children, and if they do have them what their childcare arrangements will be.

I've first-hand experience of this. Early in 2014, I was interviewed by one of the world's top ten accounting and advisory firms about heading up their cybersecurity practice. When the interviewers discovered I had children, they asked what my childcare provisions were. Having started my career as a recruitment consultant, I was outraged by the director who'd asked the question. Knowing that he'd previously worked in recruitment, I thought he should have known better.

Since 1975 it's been illegal to ask these questions in the UK. Twenty years ago, if you asked a woman these types of questions during an interview, you'd have to ask every man the same questions too, otherwise you'd be risking legal action. As a result, we were always instructed, as best practice, never to stoop so low as to ask.

Now I know I'm not the only woman in cybersecurity to have been asked questions such as these. I was discussing it recently with a friend who's a senior risk officer, and who has a daughter. When we compared notes, we discovered that our experiences were identical. However, when she asked her husband, who's also a senior cybersecurity executive, if he'd ever been asked the same question during an interview, he couldn't think of a single incident where it had happened.

Despite these wrongdoings, I've spoken to companies that employ large teams of cybersecurity professionals and they've told me how almost half of the women they employ who fall pregnant and take maternity leave either return to their jobs late, or not at all. Being a business owner, I understand their pain. Career interruptions and turnover, whilst normal, are expensive for all companies, and regrettably, many report that the money invested in recruitment, training and development for women is less likely to produce top executives compared to men. Additionally, the valuable company experience that talented, budding female cybersecurity professionals acquire as they move up through the ranks is more often than not lost.

The cost of maternity leave

Roughly 95% of developed countries have 14-weeks or more paid maternity leave, as do about 50% of African countries, 30% of Asian-Pacific countries, and about 25% of Latin American and Caribbean countries. Whilst the cost of maternity leave in many countries differs, it's generally regarded as an unnecessary expense. In the UK, Statutory Maternity Pay (SMP) is paid for up to thirty-nine weeks. Women get 90% of their average weekly earnings (before tax) for the first six weeks and then £140.98 or 90% of their average weekly earnings (whichever is lower) for the next thirty-three weeks. Tax and National Insurance are deducted, holiday is accrued at a rate of 1.6 days per month, and then there's the cost of benefits, for example, company car, smartphone, pension contribution and healthcare. Large companies typically find replacements to cover maternity leave, but smaller companies usually try to cope by redistributing work throughout the business. It's tough, and the problem is compounded as current rules mean women don't have to commit to when they're coming back to work, so planning is difficult.

We know that Nordic countries rank highest regarding gender equality at work and occupy high employment rates. Speaking recently to senior female cybersecurity professionals, mostly CISOs, in Finland, I discussed this in detail. Johanna Kinnari, an Information-tion Security Manager from one of the largest financial services companies in Finland, told me how she believed that the reason why these countries had better equality in the workplace, better provisions for childcare, was simply because they had a lack of resources. The countries couldn't survive unless everyone pulled their weight in the workforce. As a result, children were welcomed in the workplace, and both genders took turns to share the childcare responsibilities when the children were sick. Her grandmother, who's in her eighties, said it had always been like that.

Looking beyond maternity leave, as I mentioned earlier, women take more time off work. In fact, women are a third more likely to be off sick than men despite returning to the workplace faster. Published by the Office for National Statistics, the survey questioned more than 13,000 Brits and more than 200,000 people throughout Europe.[2] The analysts of the European Health Interview Survey believed that the primary reason for women taking more sick leave than men was because they needed to care for their ill children, but were unlikely to admit that this was the real reason for their absence. The analysts also suggested that mothers might be more likely to stay off work when their child was ill and off school than fathers.

There's a saying 'perception is reality', and as a woman, it's painful to acknowledge that on balance, the data appears to support the case for women being more costly to employ than men. Women do have greater tendencies to plateau or interrupt their careers in ways that limit their personal growth and career development. They do take more time off work and they do change jobs more often.

However, here's the truth bomb. Whilst you could argue that women need to acknowledge this because they know that their value

---

2. http://www.thedrum.com/profile/news/227802/survey-finds-women-take-more-time-sick-men

to employers exceeds the additional cost, and because changing attitudes and practices in the workplace and at home can reduce the additional cost dramatically, you could also argue that women don't cost more to employ than men because of their gender differences. Although women are different to men, what increases the costs to employers is the conflict of their perceptions, attitudes and behaviour with those of men. Women are governed by male-led rules of engagement and forced to conform. The workplace has a system with fundamental rules of design that were created when women weren't there. It was engineered by men and for men, and today, we're effectively trying to shoehorn women in.

As Mary Beard, the English scholar and classicist, points out: women globally are still perceived as belonging to the outside of power. This is evident in the words that we use – shared metaphors, like 'knocking on the door', 'storming the citadel' or 'smashing the glass ceiling', and so on. Phrases like these undermine women's efforts, as they imply that women have to break down barriers, or alternatively that they have to take something that doesn't quite naturally belong to them.

Certainly when it comes to women in cybersecurity we must change the way we're working. We can't expect to attract and retain women in the workplace, and reap all the benefits until the system evolves.

Finally, although this chapter focuses predominantly on working mothers in cybersecurity, I want to bring in women without children, as they too suffer unfairness in the workplace and wage penalties. A British study found that although men with children put in the highest levels of overtime, it was women without children who worked the most unpaid overtime. And whilst mothers face a wage penalty as their managers assume their family responsibilities take precedence over their careers, the assumption for women without children is that they don't have responsibilities outside of the office. One woman, now a senior cybersecurity leader, told me

11

how she was bypassed for promotion by a new male hire. She'd been at the organisation for years, working diligently and had considerably more experience than him. When she queried why he was promoted instead of her, she was told – even though this practice is illegal – that it was because he had a family to look after and she didn't.

In summary, if we're to address this, we need to design a better system and track meaningful data and metrics. We need to learn how to reduce the expense (if any occur); how to change workplace culture, policies and legislation; how to stop wasting the investments we make in talented cybersecurity women; and how to become more responsive to the needs of the women that businesses must employ if they're to benefit from having a gender diverse cybersecurity workforce.

The Golden Rules

- Choose the right person for your team and work around any obstacles such as family commitments
- Watch out for discrimination amongst women in your team, and stamp it out if you notice it occurring
- If a woman is off on maternity leave, make sure she has the job she left to return to
- Be conscious of the words you use, like 'smashing the glass ceiling', 'knocking on the door', and so on
- Design a better workplace system and track meaningful data and metrics

2. Prove It

- Social bias
- The hidden tax of being a woman
- Stepping outside of gender norms
- The trade-off women face
- The relevance of system 1 and system 2 thinking
- Three studies that examine gender bias
- How men and women are judged
- The additional major bind women face

I remember that day vividly. I was bored. I was fifteen years old and sitting in school on a sunny day. My Headmistress was lecturing sixty girls like me, and desperately trying to sell us on why we should stay for the Sixth Form.

I knew that my parents had invested in one of the top girls' schools in England, had paid thousands of pounds out in school fees, and had sacrificed so much for my education since I was five years old. I was the third generation of women to be privately educated at an all-girls school. My mother had been educated at a convent with my grandmother's hard earned savings during World War II, and my grandmother, who'd been raised by her mother and aunt after her father had died in World War I, and was considered gifted, poor, but from a 'respectable family', had received a school bursary. Yet, despite knowing how privileged I was, I'm ashamed to say bored was exactly how I felt.

As my Headmistress droned on, trying to influence us, I reluctantly listened. It was the era of Thatcher. She spoke about how we were going to be the 'next leaders of industry', and of the discrimination we'd face if we chose to leave after our O Levels and be educated with boys in a mixed-sex environment. She talked in great detail about the pressures we'd face not just from the teachers who'd be favouring boys in lessons, but also from boys outside the classroom, and how we'd be ostracised if we chose to study as opposed to party, with them.

I was astounded at what she'd said. Whether she was right or wrong at that time made no difference. I was beginning to rebel, and I wasn't buying into her story. My mind was made up: I was leaving. I was ready for a change, and to mix with boys.

Fast-forward thirty years and I was back at my school, standing in front of 116 seventeen-year-old girls, presenting on women in business and entrepreneurship. No one could have prepared me for that. I retold my story of how I'd graduated in art and design, fallen pregnant soon after, raised my son alone, and then in my twenties, with a partner, built a global cybersecurity company that turned over millions. I spoke about all the firsts, spectacular failures and cockups I'd encountered along the way; the courage you needed as a woman in business; the importance of women helping women; and the effectiveness of personal branding and networking. And lastly, I brought up environment, as it dictates performance. Whilst I didn't regret the decision I'd made to leave the confines of an all-girls school at sixteen, how astute that Headmistress had been all those years ago.

Social bias

Social bias is rife, and few dare to prepare you, like my Headmistress did, for the inequality a woman is invariably going to face as she progresses through life, or the sting of pain that she'll receive when she realises that she's not only going to be party to gender bias, but also guilty of it.

The first time I discovered my own unconscious bias was not too long ago, when I read an old riddle. I then discovered the depth of the bias when I retold it to thousands of cybersecurity professionals at conferences around the world, and also to any passing teenager I encountered. If you've not heard it, give yourself a moment to solve it.

A father and son are driving in a car. They're involved in an accident. The father doesn't survive and the son is badly injured. An ambulance arrives and takes the son to hospital, where the surgeon cries out, 'I cannot operate because this boy is my son!'

Who is the surgeon?

Two things became apparent whenever I asked what the answer was. The first was confusion. Interestingly, those who tended to be more language, social science, or arts based than technical came up with all sorts of imaginative stories to solve the riddle. The second was disbelief at the ease of the riddle from professionals who tended to be more technical or well-travelled as they solved it straight away. Upon reflection, they knew that the scenario was completely viable – the surgeon was in fact the boy's mother.

About 11% of consultant surgeons in the UK and 19% in the USA are female so it's hardly surprising that those who solved it used their experience to help guide them to the answer. Economists refer to this as statistical discrimination: whenever people don't have enough information on someone, they intuitively base their assessment on group averages. Without consideration, we all use group characteristics when judging individuals, and these judgements have consequences. Statistical discrimination is hard to escape, and the cost, or hidden tax, of being a woman serves as a perfect example.

15

The hidden tax of being a woman

Meet Vivienne Ming. She's an entrepreneur, theoretical neuroscientist and big data specialist. She became a trans woman in her thirties, and has calculated the cost of being different – in other words, how much harder you have to work as a woman, ethnic minority or gay man to get the same jobs and promotions as a heterosexual white man.

Her interest in assessing the costs, or tax, as she puts it, started when she was a Chief Scientific Officer at Gild, a company that provides technology recruiting solutions. There, she and her team made a data set of 122 million professionals and compared the career paths of specific populations so they could determine what made a successful programmer.[1]

They examined all sorts of variables: for example, whether code based on gender got reused, how other programmers rated it, what motivated people, what sort of jobs they got, and what people were being paid. Then they used this data to assess how people were being recruited: for example, was it on account of their competence or qualifications? They also considered promotions and what it took for a female programmer to have the same opportunity as a male programmer for the same quality of work.

Through modelling scenarios, such as how good people were at jobs they'd never had, they were able to work out the lifetime opportunity cost of lost work, the bill for extra degrees, or the extra experience women needed to have the same opportunities as white heterosexual men. The actual cost or tax for being different. Give or take exchange rates, they discovered that it costs about £38,000 to be a gay man in England; between $100,000 and $300,000 to be a women in the tech sector in the USA; and $800,000 to $1.5 million to be a woman in the tech sector in Hong Kong or Singapore. If

---

1. http://www.nytimes.com/2013/04/28/technology/how-big-data-is -playing-recruiter-for-specialized-workers.html?_r=1

you're different, Vivienne says, 'You have to go to better schools for longer, and you have to work for better companies to get the same promotions, to get the same quality of work.'[2]

Another study is illuminating. When a group of Computer Science students believed women programmers were more likely than men to suffer prejudice when submitting code for review, they decided to investigate. Like cybersecurity, the numbers of women programmers are low, and rest at about 5.8% according to a survey by Stack Overflow that studied over 26,000 programmers from 157 countries in 2015.[3] However, when the researchers scrutinised approximately 3 million 'pull requests' submitted on GitHub, one of the world's largest open-source software communities, their hypothesis proved false.[4] Surprisingly, they found that code written by women was actually more likely to be approved by their peers at a higher rate (78.6%) than code written by men (74.6%). But, that wasn't all. There was a twist, for this was only the case so long as the women programmers didn't reveal their gender.

As soon as the researchers made their discovery, they sought to understand the disparity. They studied several different factors, including whether women were making smaller changes to code, outperforming men in certain kinds of code, or benefiting from a reverse bias. And it was here where they discovered that women programmers were being penalised. Whether conscious or not, a pre-existing bias against women existed, as they were more likely than men to have their code accepted, unless their gender was identifiable.

---

2. https://qz.com/631455/a-scientist-cacluated-the-cost-of-not-being -a-straight-man-and-she-wants-a-tax-cut/
3. http://stackoverflow.com/research/developer-survey-2015#profile
4. https://yangsu.github.io/pull-request-tutorial/

Stepping outside of gender norms

It reminds me of a case study which is taught at many business schools. It involves Howard Roizen, a venture capitalist, former entrepreneur, networker and power player in Silicon Valley. Howard co-founded a successful technology company, became a senior executive at Apple, and sits on boards of prestigious companies. He also hangs out with Bill Gates, and when Steve Jobs was alive, was close to him. When students are asked to assess him, he's rated as being highly competent and effective, plus he's well liked, and most of the students would like to employ or work with him.

However, Howard's real name isn't Howard. It's Heidi. When another set of students is given the identical case study to review, but with a female character, Heidi, they find her to be as competent and effective as Howard. However, they view her as selfish, and no longer like her, want to work with her or employ her.

What comes to light is that the archetypal leader in their minds is male. As Heidi doesn't conform to what they believe is normal, unknowingly, they can't consider her to be competent and likeable at the same time. What's celebrated as self-confidence, vision and leadership in a man is perceived as arrogance and self-promotion in a woman. Furthermore, this is consistent across both genders, as men and women behave in the same way towards those who step outside of the gender norms.

I can relate. A few months ago, I was prepping for a presentation on personal branding. I was delivering a keynote to just over 100 cybersecurity women in London. My remit was to inspire and motivate the women attending so they could forge stronger networks and benefit professionally. The job I had to do was important, as it's well known that women have weaker ties than men to colleagues and cohorts both at work and outside. In fact, according to a study by Lean.in org and McKinsey & Co., 10% of senior female executives admit to having four or more executives supporting them to advance their careers compared to 17% of men.[5] Additionally, over 50% of these senior women said they believed that higher-level sponsorship was essential for career development.

So, when I discussed the content of my presentation with the event sponsor, I spoke about what success could look like when you build a strong personal brand and become a prolific networker in cybersecurity. I spoke about how the power of influence comes from being visible, connected, credible and valuable on the inner circle, and how on the inner circle there are many good opportunities shared between a few people, whereas on the outer circle there are few opportunities shared between many people. I brought up the weight of influence too, and how individuals are now being externally measured by companies like Influencer50 and used by forward thinking companies, ranging from emerging start-ups to global giants like IBM, Microsoft, Walmart and Michelin.[6] Furthermore, how these companies are using influencers strategically to grow their businesses and gain a competitive advantage.

Influencers are people whom the market is listening to, and there are online, offline and social influencers. Whichever category an influencer falls into, they affect sales, and some will provide new leads and new routes to market. When I communicated this to the event sponsor and how I'd been identified as a top fifty influencer in cybersecurity in the UK, he commented, 'Jane, this comes across as very arrogant.'

I was speechless for a few seconds as he'd taken me by surprise. It was not my intention to come across as boastful, let alone arrogant. Instead, I wanted to show why being an influencer is relevant, what's possible, and obviously to help others. However, I appreciated his remark as it drew light on to this issue and is utterly relevant to what I'm writing about right now.

---

5. http://womenintheworkplace.com/
6. http://influencer50.com/

Having been an entrepreneur for most of my career, I've been fortunate to face little gender bias. I built Corsaire, my penetration-testing consultancy, as a meritocracy without even considering diversity, let alone gender equality. The only thing that mattered was getting a good job done, and as that required pure thinking ability, gender had no part to play in this. As it happened I ended up with an extremely diverse team, and at times they'd comment that we were like the United Nations, for we had a company filled with men and women from Nigeria, Greece, Ireland, South Africa, Finland, Sweden, Germany, Spain, Bulgaria, and of course the UK.

So, when I think about the times I've experienced gender bias, aside from getting a client meeting because I'm a woman, or being remembered at conferences because I stood out for being different as I was the only woman present, there have literally only been a couple of examples.

The first was when a supplier came in for a meeting and focused on pitching to my male colleague. The supplier thought he had the buying power and had somehow failed to notice that I owned the company and would be making the buying decision. I was in my late twenties and it amused rather than riled me.

The second was when I was partnering with a company for a bid and was pitching to a room full of men. The male salesperson, whom I'd invited, stated that it was a good thing that he was there, as he was sure that I'd have felt intimidated without him. I ignored his comment, having managed large male teams for decades. He couldn't have been further from the truth.

The trade-off women face

Having spoken to thousands of women, I realise my experiences have been minor and atypical. I also appreciate that as bias can be subtle, it's highly likely that I didn't recognise instances when they occurred. By and large, women in cybersecurity continually face discrimination in the workplace daily, and they can't win either.

They're judged all the time, and face a trade-off between being liked and respected. If they conform to the feminine stereotype of being nurturing and caring, they run the risk of being regarded as likeable, but not competent. This is standard for male dominated professions, and even with a great many male supporters and sponsors, women in cybersecurity face criticism when being hired, developed, compensated and promoted. It's grossly unfair. Yet, repeatedly because of the biases that each of us hold, people tend to respond to successful, confident women much like they do to immoral men – they don't like them, and don't want to work with them.

Psychologists have spent years researching gender perceptions of occupational fit, and believe that the reason why people judge those who step outside of the norms in this way is because of their perceptions of what they believe is necessary to perform a typical male or female job. If women like Heidi, or me for that matter, show characteristics that are more associated with men and demonstrate that they can do a 'man's job' then they violate norms. As people are genetically programmed to stay together for survival reasons, as soon as women display the traits that are considered male, they unknowingly signal that they pose a threat to the stability of the status quo, and are immediately cast as outsiders and squashed, sidestepped or punished for being deviants. Women pay a price.[7]

Again and again patterns emerge of women in cybersecurity being treated unfairly at the interview stage or being bypassed for jobs or promotion just because they're outside of the status quo. Men tend to be judged on their potential, women on their performance.[8] Women are still seen as being a little more risky than men, too.

I spoke to a young female penetration tester recently who told

---

7. http://link.springer.com/article/10.1007%2FBF00055564
8. http://genius.com/Joanna-barsh-unlocking-the-full-potential-of-women-in-the-us-economy-annotated

me how she'd been interviewed for a position and deliberately been given a test that was harder to complete than the one given to the men who were applying. When she passed the test, the assessor appeared to delight in letting her know what he'd done. He justified his actions by saying that it was because he wanted to be sure that she was 'really capable of doing the job'. It's alarming, unjust and damaging. But, without formal, standardised methods of recruitment, and with so many small cybersecurity firms springing up, biased practices such as this prevail.

Jivika Govil's experience is different. Based in the USA, she's a Senior Risk Management Analyst at a bank holding company headquartered in Salt Lake City, Utah. She holds a master's degree in Information System Management from Carnegie Mellon University, a degree in Information Technology Engineering from Maharishi Dayanand University, and has written over thirty research papers on data intelligence, telecom networking and cybersecurity domain which have been published and presented by IEEE and ACM. Based on her experience, she told me that she'd noticed a pattern of bias whenever Human Resources (HR) were involved in the recruitment process. She believes that HR aren't tending to select female candidates because they're assuming that women in cybersecurity aren't open to travel, which is a requirement, and that they won't give more than eight hours to the job. They assume that women will be in a hurry to rush home after 5pm to collect children from school, cook food and so on.

Jivika explained, 'There was an instance where a job description matched my profile but I was not shortlisted to the phone interview round. When I called the HR Manager to follow-up, he informed me that I was not shortlisted because the job required 75% travel. He told me that because I was a woman, he'd assumed that I wouldn't be open to a job that required domestic and international travel.'

Another thing that happens is that women's ideas can be stolen. Time and time again, I heard from women in the industry about how they'd bring up an idea, yet they'd be ignored or overlooked. Then, when a man brought up the same idea a few minutes or months later, suddenly it was brilliant. But, no credit was given to the woman. It was as if she were invisible.

The relevance of System 1 and System 2 thinking

Unconscious bias is a huge problem in any industry, but it's one that's not really been confronted in cybersecurity. To understand what's going on in the brain when unconscious bias happens, you can refer to the book *Thinking, Fast and Slow* by Daniel Kahneman, a psychologist and 2002 Nobel Laureate in Economics. In his book, Kahneman discusses how our brain uses two modes of thinking, System 1 and System 2. System 1 is fast, in the moment, and uses a process Kahneman calls WYSIATI (What You See Is All There Is). It runs automatically, assesses information quickly and doesn't require the expansion of much effort. It uses heuristics, otherwise known as rules of thumb, to make sense of the world. It also relies on categorisation, and characterisation. It's what we all do instinctively when judging others. As it needs consistency and verification of previously held beliefs, it struggles with updating new information, particularly if that information contradicts its core beliefs.

System 2, on the other hand, is slow, controlled and based on conscious thinking. It requires much effort but is capable of abstract analysis, logic and rule-based thinking. Everyone naturally defaults to their System 1 thinking to draw upon stereotypes, economise their cognitive effort and make sense of the world. And, depressingly, unlearning is impossible. Once the brain has made a categorisation, it processes new information in a biased way.

The easiest way to demonstrate System 1 and 2 thinking is with the Stroop Color and Word Test. Originally described in 1935 by psychologist John Ridley Stroop as a way to differentiate between individuals who were non-brain damaged and brain damaged, the test is based on the observation that individuals can read words much faster than they can identify and name colours.[9]

If you try it out, which I'd encourage you to do, what you'll notice is how much longer it takes you to read the words out loud when they don't correlate to the actual colour they're written in. The brain has to work much harder, and sometimes as a result it trips over itself. When the colour matches the word, the brain uses System 1 thinking, but when it doesn't match, it uses System 2 thinking.

This is what it's like for our brains when we come across people who defy the gender norms. It takes longer for us to process the information, as it's not in accordance with the beliefs and stereotypes we hold. If we don't see women in cybersecurity, then it's more likely that we'll form beliefs that women aren't supposed to be in cybersecurity. This belief will go into our System 1 thinking. Then, when we do come across women in cybersecurity, even though we know that they're perfectly capable of performing the job, our brains will have to use System 2 thinking, and something may instinctively appear wrong or feel uncomfortable. Typically, they'll be asked to prove themselves much more often on their technical expertise.

Building on this test, the IAT (Implicit Association Test) https://implicit.harvard.edu/, which psychologist Anthony Greenwald created in 1994, can assess the degree of an individual's unconscious bias. Like the Stroop Color and Word Test, the IAT is fast, simple and insightful. It asks you to make connections between words of different categories, and is measured by how quickly you make associations. For example, do you quickly connect a man with reading and writing, and a woman with mathematics, or are they the other way around?

Whatever happens, it's important to understand that everyone

---

9. http://home.cbstrials.com/stroop-test/?test=Stroop%20Test&gclid=CjwKEAiAqozEBRDJrPemofPKtXoSJAD5sAyHlpp-hBwU_T6syyZwe-O9t9gkcrs83gHkSxxiox05W-xoCuoDw_wcB

suffers from unconscious bias, and also that people who make more gender-stereotypical associations in the test are less able to consider data on individual performance. That second point is crucial, for when hiring managers in cybersecurity can't easily measure quality in an individual, which is difficult when they're reviewing CVs rather than standardised tests, they revert to the norms and fill in the blanks with stereotypes. They also revert to maintaining the status quo, and unconsciously hire employees just like them, typically under the disguise of 'culture fit'.

For cybersecurity, this status quo bias may explain why 90% of the industry's employees are over thirty years old and predominantly white men. Yet repeatedly recruitment agencies inform the industry that women in cybersecurity just aren't in the talent pool, and hiring managers relay that if women were applying for the jobs, they'd most likely hire them.

Three studies that examine gender bias

Devoid of firm data, I can't disagree with this, although I remain sceptical. Drawing on an experiment by Stefanie K. Johnson, David R. Hekman and Elsa T. Chan, I'll tell you why.[10]

Three studies were conducted to examine what happens when the status quo is changed amongst finalists for a job position. The first study used an experimental setting and involved 144 undergraduate students reviewing the qualifications of three finalist job applicants. Each finalist possessed exactly the same qualifications, but they were of different ethnicity. Names were altered so they sounded stereotypically black (Dion Smith and Darnell Jones) or white (Connor van Wagoner and David Jones), and the job of Athletic Director had some ambiguity regarding the racial status quo.

Half of the undergraduates were told to assess a finalist pool that

---

10. https://hbr.org/2016/04/if-theres-only-one-woman-in-your-candidate -pool-theres-statistically-no-chance-shell-be-hired

had two white candidates and one black candidate, and the other half had to evaluate a finalist pool that had two black candidates and one white candidate. The undergraduates then had to reveal the extent to which they agreed that each candidate was most suitable for the job.

The researchers found that when a majority of the finalists were white, the undergraduates chose to maintain the status quo, and advocated to hire a white candidate. But, when the majority of finalists were black, the black job applicant became the preferred choice.

The second study focused on gender and involved 200 undergraduate students, and the researchers found a similar result to the previous study. They altered the names of the male and female job applicants, and the job that they were applying for was that of Nurse Manager. Convinced that the status quo would be to hire women, they included two men in the job application finalist pool. They found that when two of the three finalists were men, the undergraduates selected the man to hire, and when two of the three finalists were women, their recommendation was to hire a woman.

The third study involved the researchers examining a university's decisions to hire white and non-white women and men for academic positions. They reviewed 598 job finalists, 174 of whom received job offers over a three-year period, and the finalist pools ranged from three to eleven candidates. Once again, the researchers were keen to establish the likelihood of the university hiring a candidate outside of the status quo (women or ethnic minorities) beyond the expected increase due to probability.

Their findings were consistent with the other two studies. When there were two female finalists, the odds of the university hiring a woman were 79.14 times greater, and when there were two ethnic minority finalists, the odds of it hiring a minority were 193.72 times greater. The results remained consistent no matter what the size of the finalist pool was.

Furthermore, they demonstrated a tipping point for hiring when applicants didn't represent the status quo. When there's only one woman in a pool of job applicant finalists, the chances of her being hired are statistically zero, but when there are at least two women, that changes radically. Interestingly, the chances of a woman or ethnic minority being hired don't increase proportionally when more women or ethnic minorities are added to the job applicant finalist pool.

The study demonstrates unconscious bias, how important maintaining the status quo is for cybersecurity hiring managers, and highlights the consequences of deviating from the norm. It suggests that through manipulation – by adding at least two female candidates to a finalist pool of job applicants – the status quo bias can be changed, and women in cybersecurity have a fighting chance of being hired. But the question is: do we want to strategically do this in cybersecurity? Or, can we find another way for women in cybersecurity to be judged on their pure ability without gender coming into play?

How men and women are judged

Much has been written about how men are judged on their potential and women on their achievements. Additionally, how women have to provide more evidence of competence than men in order to be considered as competent. However, there's another obstacle for women in cybersecurity to overcome – themselves. Women are most likely to be unknowingly holding themselves back, and conforming to self-stereotyping.

The Emergence of Male Leadership in Competitive Environment illustrates this.[11] The experiment was run in 2006 and 2008 and involved 134 MBA students (100 men and 34 women) at the University of Chicago Booth School of Business. In an environment where MBA students behaved in accordance to their gender

11. http://ftp.iza.org/dp5300.pdf

stereotypes – males were overtly confident and women were less so, the experiment discovered that as a result male MBA students were more regularly selected as leaders.

Before the students selected their leaders, the researchers assigned a mathematics test. Students were told how well they performed and that they'd be paid in accordance with their test result. Fifteen months after the test, students were reminded of the mathematics test and had to recall the number of additions they answered correctly. They were then assigned to a group of two to four with at least one woman present and had to appoint a leader. That leader would then complete another mathematics test like the one they'd performed in 2006 and the group would be paid upon their performance. The assignment was also competitive within the MBA group.

Prior to the test, the MBA students had five minutes to consult one another and document how well each of them thought they'd perform. Interestingly, when the results were examined, male MBA students believed they'd do better in the test than their female peers. Their optimism on their future performance was on account of an inflated recall of their past performance – by about 30%. Women were also optimistic, but in contrast only misremembered by about 14%.

The study concluded that groups select highly skilled women to perform in competitive environments less often than they should because they're conforming to what's expected of their gender.

The additional major bind women face

These results aren't surprising. I remember a CISO bringing this up with me, along with a final hurdle that may happen when women do compete, get the opportunity, and defy the gender norms.

He said, 'Jane, all this work that you're doing is great and I'm hugely supportive, but women face a major bind. Obviously women are a minority in cybersecurity and stand out. However, do you realise that when women make a mistake it's noticed more, remembered for longer, and sometimes their success is attributed to anything other than their merit?'

Regrettably, he has a point. Shortly after having this conversation, I met another CISO who passed a flippant comment about how he'd recently employed a female cybersecurity analyst and she hadn't worked out. He talked openly about how that had put him off employing another female.

Although he was in the wrong, it was an entirely predictable connection for the human brain is wired to remember bad events over good. From our earliest beginnings, being aware of and avoiding danger has been a critical survival skill. Psychologists often refer to this as the negativity bias and the Prospect Theory, which advances the idea that people are more likely to choose things based on their need to avoid negative experiences rather than their desire to get positive experiences.[12]

And, here lies the paradox. Thousands of studies by psychologists and economists have reported on how women are more naturally risk averse and reluctant to compete than men.[13][14] Many have written about how women want to protect themselves from being disliked, singled-out or from failure. As a result, women have kept a low profile online and offline, downplayed their achievements, haven't spoken up during meetings, gone for promotions, or negotiated

12. https://www.psychologytoday.com/blog/wired-success/201406/are -we-hardwired-be-positive-or-negative

13. For summaries on gender differences in risk aversion in the experimental economics literature, see Eckel & Grossman (2008) and Croson & Gneezy (2009), who conclude that women exhibit greater risk aversion; Byrnes et al. (1999) present a meta-analysis of 150 psychology studies and show that although women are in some situations significantly more averse to risk, many studies find no gender differences.

14. http://web.stanford.edu/~niederle/NV.AnnualReview.Print.pdf

for better salaries. Some have even chosen not to enter a profession, such as cybersecurity, as it's overtly male.

Given that we know the reasons women have avoided taking risks such as these are the social and cultural rules surrounding their gender, unconscious bias, and the fact that their genes haven't been historically rewarded for doing so (epigenetics),[15] it begs the question: isn't it time to change our workplace culture's discomfort with women who step outside of the status quo and create an environment where women feel safe – a true meritocracy in the workplace – where women are rewarded alongside men?

The Golden Rules

- Everyone has social bias. Understand the extent of yours via the IAT, https://implicit.harvard.edu/
- Perform the Stroop Test to learn about System 1 and 2 thinking
- Recognise that by adding at least two female candidates to a finalist pool of job applicants, the status quo bias can be changed, and women in cybersecurity can have a fighting chance of being hired
- If you've hired a woman and it didn't work out, don't be discouraged from hiring more women, as this is not a gender issue. Instead, ask yourself what you could have done better.

---

15. https://www.livescience.com/37135-dna-epigenetics-disease-research.html

3. Mind The Gap

- The cost of the skills shortage
- Four stories
- Cybersecurity's operational issues
- Understanding generation cohorts
- Ways into cybersecurity
- Global setbacks: India's problem
- Global progress: Israel, the UAE and the Eastern Bloc

It's a regular day and my LinkedIn box is full of messages, as is my email. Three types stand out. The first type is typically from female graduates with degrees or masters. They tell me that they've worked several internships, and are asking about how they can find jobs and whether there are any training courses that could improve their chances. The second type is from hiring managers or senior cybersecurity leaders who are asking why their job postings aren't delivering the required calibre of cybersecurity professionals, including women, that they're after. The third type is from recruiters asking how they can get in front of hiring managers or CISOs as they've got candidates to place.

The cost of the skills shortage

Again and again we're told that cybersecurity has a skills shortage problem. It's hardly surprising. Cybersecurity is a buoyant business for both cyber criminals and cybersecurity companies. With an increase in awareness of attacks, global spending on cybersecurity is expected to rise to $1 trillion (US) from 2017 to 2021, and the cost of cybercrime to global businesses, annually, is estimated to be between $2 and $3 trillion.[1] However, although I don't dispute these facts, I do question whether cybersecurity really has got a genuine supply and demand issue. Here's why.

Facts first. Evidently cybersecurity job postings are growing three-and-a-half times faster than IT jobs; there are 1 million vacant cybersecurity jobs globally, and this is set to rise to 6 million by 2020. In 2015, (ISC)[2] detailed the deficit, and in a report entitled 'The *Global Information Security Workforce Study*' (GISWS) it predicted that by 2020 the industry will need an extra 1.5 million cybersecurity professionals in order to plug the skills shortage gap.[2] It claimed that the workforce shortfall was widening, and the reasons for this were not about money, as more organisations were making budgets available to hire more personnel. Rather, it was an insufficient pool of suitable candidates that was causing the shortfall. The report also stated that the top five positions most required, listed in order of priority, were Security Analyst, Security Auditor, Security Architect, Forensic Analyst and Incident Handler.

In 2016, Intel Security and CSIS also reported on the current cybersecurity talent crisis.[3] In a survey of cybersecurity profession-

---

1. http://cybersecurityventures.com/cybersecurity-market-report/

2. https://www.isc2cares.org/uploadedFiles/wwwisc2caresorg/Content/GISWS/FrostSullivan-(ISC)%C2%B2-Global-Information-Security-Workforce-Study-2015.pdf

3. http://www.mcafee.com/us/resources/reports/rp-hacking-skills-shortage.pdf

als in the UK, Australia, France, Germany, Israel, Japan, Mexico, and the USA, 82% of the respondents agreed that there was a large shortage of skills in their own organisation as well as their country. The highest shortfalls were attributed to Mexico and Australia, where highly technical skills were apparently most in demand. Instead of listing job titles, however, they listed skillsets and concluded that intrusion detection, secure software development, and attack mitigation were most needed. Contrary to $(isc)^2$, Intel found that those skills were in greater demand than softer skills, such as the ability to collaborate, manage a team, or communicate effectively. Both were in agreement that scarcity was driving up the value of personnel and salaries.

Intel's report also stated that half of the companies surveyed preferred a bachelor's degree in a relevant technical subject as the minimum credential required for entering the field. However, the respondents believed that the usefulness of a degree was more of a market signal than an effective method for developing skills. Rather, they ranked hands-on experience and professional certifications as better ways to acquire cybersecurity skills than a degree.

Interestingly too, most respondents saw an increasing reliance on cybersecurity technology as a way to compensate for skill shortages, with more than half believing that, in five years' time, cybersecurity solutions would be able to meet the majority of their organisation's needs. They also said that in-house talent shortages could be solved through outsourcing – especially services like threat detection. Finally, more than three out of four thought that their governments could do more by increasing expenditure on education and building cybersecurity talent programmes, plus improving cybersecurity legislation and regulation.

Facts aside, here are four stories that breathe life into these statistics.

Four stories

It was Adrian who first introduced me to Dana. As soon as Adrian and I met, we discovered similarities. Firstly, we'd both started our careers working for the same company, Hays. Secondly, we had a passion for helping people, and thirdly, we wanted to increase the numbers of women working in cybersecurity. Whilst I'd left Hays a year after joining to start my own information security consultancy, he'd remained, and over the course of twenty-four years had successfully worked his way up to a board position. I found him to be sharp and extremely humble, and I was impressed.

After a productive meeting, he mentioned a young woman he'd recently met called Dana, who was qualified in cybersecurity but struggling to find work. He asked me to contact her and help. Naturally, I agreed.

Let me introduce you to her. She's an American in her mid-twenties, and is living in the UK. A highly ambitious and hardworking Intelligence and International Security Masters graduate from King's College London, she has undertaken several internships with leading security and threat management entities, including Crisis Solutions and the US Department of State's Diplomatic Security Service. These placements, in addition to her strong academic background and analytical skills, have enabled her to develop specific security industry experience and the ability to analyse a vast amount of data and communicate findings in a clear and concise way.

People like Dana, who can analyse and communicate cybersecurity in writing and verbally, are sought after – or at least that's what we're consistently being told by the media. However, although Dana has been actively seeking an analytical or research position in cybersecurity to which she can bring immediate and strategic value whilst developing her current skill set further, she's been working as an Office Manager for the last nine months.

When we talked, she said she was ready to give up on cybersecurity. She'd applied for job after job, and aside from a low paid job offer in a prison, which wasn't what she wanted, nothing had materialised.

Jada is in her early thirties. She's a multi-skilled IT professional with over ten years' experience working in the finance, retail and education sectors. She's worked with people at different levels, including partners, senior managers, clients, and third party suppliers, and prides herself on being a team player who's adaptable and effective at improving efficiency of operations and systems. She has a 'can-do' attitude and her strengths lie in analysis, troubleshooting, creative thinking, organising, project coordination and training. Balancing her technical and soft skills, she's passionate about applying technology to meet needs, adding value by solving important problems, and making a difference in people's lives.

Jada graduated with a BSc in Computing in 2005 and gained an MSc in Computer Systems Auditing in 2007. However, after graduating, being unable to find a job in cybersecurity because companies were unwilling to recruit someone without experience, she resorted to working in IT, excelling in various roles. With her passion for security never waning, when she left her role in 2016 she was keen to try to get into the field she originally qualified in almost a decade ago. Now, twelve years later, she has finally landed a role in cybersecurity..

Unlike Dana or Jada, Trudi is in her forties. She's got three young children, and has a background in auditing. When I first met Trudi, she told me how she'd given up her career to become a full-time stay-at-home mum. However, when her husband was made redundant they both agreed that together they should look for work. Trudi re-entered the marketplace ahead of her husband, and secured a position with a major multinational entertainment conglomerate. Despite not having a background in cybersecurity, she was made a Head of Internal Audit and Risk Management, which included a remit for cybersecurity. Her husband took over the full-time care of their children for several months until he too found a job.

Smeeta is in her early fifties. She was educated in India and the UK, speaks five languages fluently and had a prominent technology career, specialising in telecommunications, which surpassed her husband's. She travelled the world, moving from one high profile assignment to another, and achieved promotion after promotion until her eldest child was five. After taking a sabbatical to study for her MBA, like Trudi, she decided to take a career break so she could care for her children full-time. She's not worked since, aside from voluntary charity work, but is now ready to step back into the workforce. However, she's fearful that her skills may be considered obsolete and be rejected when she applies, as it's been almost twelve years since she's worked full-time.

Whilst the women in these stories are unique, their situations aren't. They're common. I could write hundreds more. To think that the industry is suffering from a lack of cybersecurity professionals, diversity of gender, and that not enough people are entering the field with the required skills and remaining would be erroneous. The talent is there. What's more accurate, in my opinion, is that cybersecurity has operational issues – around recruitment and retention.

Cybersecurity's operational issues

The other day I was with Angela. She's a senior cybersecurity leader working for a large global technology company, and we were discussing the skills shortage. Like everyone, she had it on her agenda. She talked openly about diversity as she's leading a campaign, what the company's commitment was for increasing the numbers of women in the global workforce, and its plan for Europe. It looked impressive.

She showed me the data that she'd analysed and drilled down to give me more information. Then, she presented the figures for cybersecurity. Whilst the figures were nearing the company's target of 30% for gender diversity across its workforce, the numbers of women in HR and Marketing skewed them and they were falling short in cybersecurity. Consistent with those reported by $(isc)^2$ and a little above the average, they wavered at around 12%.

I asked Angela if the company was doing exit interviews, so it could establish why employees were leaving: if there was a particular demographic that was leaving, for example graduates; what rate accounted for churn and expansion; what the costs were to recruit; where the company was reaching out to recruit; what its recruitment campaigns looked like; and what the recruitment process was.

She didn't have all of that information to hand, and wasn't sure if it was all being captured or measured, but she said she'd investigate and compile the data. This would enable her to have more insight, and be able to build a business case to address the problem. I recommended collaborating with HR and Marketing too. Operationally, once the cost of the problem could be established alongside the cost to fix it, an informed decision could be made on what to do next.

There was a lot going on, and from our conversation I already knew that the organisation faced the usual retention challenges, particularly with graduates. After about six months of being in a client-facing role, many wanted to be back behind the scenes, which was mostly out of the question. Whether they were male or female made little difference, as the churn rate was roughly about the same. Angela conveyed her disappointment at the situation, for this year the company had had 43% female applicants, its highest intake ever. She was also concerned that the graduates were being treated with 'kid gloves', unlike the apprentices, who were succeeding and just being left to get on with things.

Understanding generation cohorts

Angela's comment was one I've heard 1,000 times. The graduates are Gen-Ys. Culturally, they have a very different outlook to their Team Leaders, Managers and Directors who tend to be mostly Gen-X or

Baby Boomers. Born between 1980 and 2000, Gen-Ys have grown up in times of technological change, and as a result have different priorities, expectations and worldviews. For example, many are not purchasing homes, cars, holidays, entertainment or luxury goods in the same way that their parents or grandparents did. Instead, they're sharing, collaborating, and becoming much better at resourcing. They're after access not ownership, convenience at the lowest cost, and are driving a shared economy. Technology is their friend and aid. Through it they're modernising the way the world communicates and consumes data, both personally and with one another.

They're social creatures, good networkers, and are visible online with a voice that's regularly heard by hundreds, thousands or sometimes millions. They're much more trusting than Gen-Xs, and speed is undeniably the currency of new business for this generation. Instant access, on demand, price comparisons, product information and reviews that are increasingly weighted by influence (both social and brand) are the new norms.

Defined by their sense of entitlement and lack of attachment, Gen-Ys make for a demanding workforce. Being the largest, most educated and culturally diverse generation to-date, they change jobs more often than any other generation, and many employers are finding them increasingly difficult to please.

Gen-Ys to many who manage them are hard work, but by 2020 they'll make up 50% of the global workforce.[4] They matter, and with 90% of the cybersecurity industry being over thirty years old, they form a vital demographic that it needs to understand better.

What's key is that Gen-Ys need to feel wanted and valued as employees in the cybersecurity workforce. According to Gallup, the questions that this generation asks their employers most are,

---

4. https://www.pwc.com/gx/en/managing-tomorrows-people/future-of-work/assets/reshaping-the-workplace.pdf

'Do you value my strengths and contributions?' and 'Will you allow me to do what I do best every day, and will you help me improve?'

For Gen-Ys, a job is no longer 'just a job'. They want it to have meaning, and both genders within this demographic are demanding to work in a different way. They want lifestyle, balance, and care about their health. They want to be around to see their children grow up, and not be absent parents, like many of their parents have been, or still are. These things are important to Gen-Ys, and I can see them being instrumental in changing the way we work for the better.

For example, as most employees are being asked to work longer hours because everyone is competing in a global marketplace and working remotely, or in transit, or from home, Gen-Ys need managers who understand these things and can offer flexibility as well as coach, mentor and develop them.[5] They want their strengths to be understood, and to have them nurtured. They need constant feedback and conversations, just as they've been having on social media and via their phones as texts.

As for trying to command and control them, forget it. Unlike previous generations who'd have stuck a job out for at least a couple of years before moving on for fear of a blip on their CV which would affect their career prospects, this generation won't just suck it up. Every day matters to them and they know they've got options, even if it means going back home to their parents. Working for a pay cheque won't do. They need more. They want environment, but I'm not talking about pool or ping-pong tables, free pizza, drinks or even cool sleeping pads, like many in our industry regularly suggest in order to retain them. Seducing them with material possessions is short sighted. Passion, purpose and care turn this generation on, bring out performance, and induce loyalty.

The generation that follows Gen-Y is Gen-Z, and right now this

---

5. http://www.mediapost.com/publications/article/170109/turning-on-the-no-collar-workforce.html#axzz2igqK3wts

is the generation that's enrolling on apprenticeships. Born after 2000, they have both similarities with and clear differences to Gen-Y. In fact, some argue that they're extreme opposites.

Starting with the differences, Gen-Zs are far more pragmatic. The turbulent times that they've grown up in – global depression, war, terrorism – have turned them into cautious realists, and they know that opportunities aren't limitless. If they're to succeed in the workplace, they need to master new skills and differentiate themselves.

Unlike Gen-Ys who want freedom and flexibility, this generation is more money conscious, and wants security and stability. Being more technology dependent, Gen-Zs are true digital natives, and have developed a much higher instinctual relationship with technology. As a result, they're more global in their thinking and interactions, which enables them to relate better with their global peers, and for diversity to become an expectation.

The downside of their technology reliance, though, is their focus. A world of constant change and perpetual updates has given them low attention spans. Being used to split-tasking, they shift from work and play, real and virtual in short concentrated bursts, and no doubt will redefine the way we work with this type of workflow.

Gen-Zs are less formally educated than Gen-Ys too, as many are choosing not to study for a college degree.[6] Being money cautious, they see no sense in making a major financial investment when alternatives are available. Starting when they're sixteen years old, many will opt for apprenticeships, internships, or online studies, and forego traditional higher education routes. Some may even choose to become entrepreneurs, as they're disruptive, valuing individuality and independent work environments. Growing up

---

6. http://www.businessinsider.com/generation-z-spending-habits-2014 –6?IR=T

with a digital footprint, they seek out uniqueness in the brands that they do business with, future employers, and their leaders.

The most important factors for Gen-Zs include opportunities for career advancement, followed by more money and meaningful work. Lowest on the list is having a good boss and working for a fast-growing company.

In terms of their similarities, both Gen-Ys and Gen-Zs seek career development mentorship, and don't expect to remain in a job for more than three years.[7] [8] [9] In fact, both generations are fairly sceptical of companies having witnessed their parents being made redundant after years of loyal service, the 2008 financial crisis, and WikiLeaks. Both believe in building effective personal brands and gaining transferable skills, which they can take to any job or leverage to become an entrepreneur. They're also both difference makers, and consider making an impact on the world to be more important than professional recognition.

Understanding generation cohorts – people born roughly at the same time, with similar attitudes and expectations – is essential when looking at the talent gap for women in cybersecurity. Often people will say, 'Just offer them more money, and they'll come, or stay,' but it's not as simple as this. And when it comes to women, they want more. By understanding the generation cohorts better, and where we're falling down when it comes to the demographics, we can then strategically market to women, and increase our odds of attracting them into our workforce and retaining them.

The other generations that are of importance are Gen-X and the Baby Boomers, as they're the generations that are mostly managing the other two.

---

7. http://mashable.com/2014/12/15/future-workforce/#1z8uknT7raqo
8. http://fortune.com/2015/05/22/generation-z-in-the-workplace/
9. http://www.forbes.com/sites/jeannemeister/2012/10/05/millennialmindse/

Baby Boomers are those who were born between 1946 and 1965. They can be characterised as having a strong work ethic, being independent and self-assured, competitive, goal-centric, team-orientated, mentally disciplined and resourceful. These are the men and women who, despite growing up in the aftermath of the Second World War, rebelled, got stoned, and made love not war. More of them went to university than any previous generation, thanks to free tuition and student grants. Some were idealists and campaigned for gender, racial and sexual equality – and other issues they believed in. Many also bought into capitalism and material goods, like houses and cars. This generation was the first to popularise holidays abroad, second homes and retirement.

Gen X typically has family issues such as children and/or ageing parents to contend with. This is the generation that usually leaves our workforce and rarely returns. Born between 1965 and 1980, Gen-X grew up in an era of emerging technology and political and institutional incompetence. They spent less time with their parents as most parents worked. Labelled latchkey kids and often having to act as young carers for their siblings, they also had divorce to contend with. As a result, according to psychologists, most grew up without being emotionally indulged, and with independence and self-reliance, rather than respect for authority. They experienced single-parenting and blended families, which helped this generation to become resilient, more accepting and embracing of diversity.

As Gen-X entered the workforce, the economic decline at the end of the 1980s struck. The jobs they expected after college and graduation didn't materialise, and the workforce was competitive and crowded. As they experienced this alongside their parents being made redundant, they redefined job loyalty. As jobs were no longer for life, they made commitments to their work, their teams and their bosses, rather than to their companies. Accordingly, Gen-X takes employment seriously, but instead of seeing it as a career ladder, they see a career framework where they can move laterally, or stop and start their career, or pivot. They also don't waste their time complaining. Instead, they're pragmatic, look for work elsewhere, and accept the best offer at another organisation.

Being a Gen-X, Angela found her route into cybersecurity was very different to that of her graduates, the Gen-Ys, but it was similar to her apprentices, the Gen-Zs. She didn't enrol on a Graduate Training Programme as she didn't have a degree. When she began, she had limited expectations, and worked her way up gradually. She had years of on-the-job and formal training in good technical and operational practices. Her roles, as she described them, 'were often to act as an interpreter between the techies and the business', which inevitably helped to build her knowledge and expertise.

Ways into cybersecurity

Angela's progression is typical for many who've been in cybersecurity for over a decade. Entering the field without a degree or industry specific qualifications was standard for most of today's senior cybersecurity professionals. Most worked their way up from secondary qualifications that they gained at school, having been given a chance in IT. Years later, with a good grounding in networking and hands-on experience in information security, they gathered a few certifications, sometimes just to prove to themselves or to others that they knew their field.

Ways in like this demonstrate that cybersecurity has never been a stand-alone discipline. It was born from IT, is a specialism within IT, and treating it otherwise may prove to be a costly mistake for our industry. However, the industry remains divided on this, for there are those who want to professionalise it, like accounting, law, medicine, and engineering, with charters, regulatory bodies, and formal education programmes. Others want it to remain vocational.

Those who prefer a more vocational route point out a couple of things. The first is that those from the Armed Forces and Police, who make up a large percentage of our workforce, haven't come from an IT background. However, they've taken the basic principles of physical security or intelligence and applied them to cyber with success. The second is that cybersecurity should be seen as a career for those in IT to aspire to, and not a profession with entry-level positions. They maintain that all positions in cybersecurity should be earned with significant experience in IT, and that a degree that's specific to cybersecurity isn't required. Rather, hiring managers need to become great talent spotters, looking first within their organisations for skilled professionals who, despite having no stated experience in cybersecurity, can quickly adapt to cybersecurity roles. Professionals could, therefore, be within IT or outside of it, such as HR, legal, customer services, personal assistants, or even sales, PR or marketing. Competent professionals who are capable of making the transition exist, as I've spoken to hundreds of hiring managers who've recruited them into their department this way, and have success stories.

Robert Duncan did just this. He's an American and is working as the CISO for a British insurance company that's listed on the stock market index. When he had a vacancy for a penetration testing coordinator within his team, he advertised the role internally, and found his candidate quickly. As she'd worked in numerous roles within the company, she had enormous insight and understanding of what was required for the job – something that a degree or cybersecurity certification would not have brought. Training her up proved straightforward and according to Robert, she's now learning about penetration testing and firewalls on her own, and is turning out to be one of their best hires.

Rachel Higham a Managing Director at a British multinational telecommunication company advocates a similar approach. Rachel shared her experiences with me recently.

A few months ago, she was recruiting for a cybersecurity position, and she felt sure that someone she'd worked with previously would be suitable. However, the female professional, who knew about the position being advertised, had not applied. When Rachel suggested she put herself forward for the role, she was hesitant. She didn't believe she had all the requirements to do the job, so didn't want to waste her time. Rachel knew she had and encouraged her. She subsequently applied for the role, and got it.

Unfortunately, this type of scenario is common. I'm discovering that many women, some of whom already work in cybersecurity, and others who could transition into it, need to be convinced that they can do the job prior to applying. They also seek assurance that their application is going to be successful.

This was true for Rachel's candidate. Due to the way the job advertisement had been written, the female applicant, who was in a sales role, didn't believe that she could do the job, let alone be considered for it. Yet, she had well-rounded experience in the organisation, knowledge of the product sets, plus sales, project management, and communication skills, and a willingness to expand her skillset. For this particular role, Rachel knew that she could actually make the transition faster than anyone with a degree in Computer Science, or even a few years' experience in cybersecurity from outside the company. She was open to finding someone who wasn't a perfect match in terms of cybersecurity qualifications and certifications, but who had the right attitude and the competence to do the job with a little bit of training and support.

Thankfully Rachel and her applicant have a positive story to recount. However, not all end this way, and much of the problem boils down to inept recruitment practices, which I'll discuss in more detail in Chapters 7 and 11. Arno Brok, the former CEO of AISA, agreed. He told me about what he witnessed in Australia, one of two countries that Intel Security and CSIS highlighted as apparently having the highest shortfall of skills.

'Take a taxi in Melbourne and you'll find that eight out of ten cab drivers will have experience in IT and degrees in Computer Science. They're driving cabs because they can't get work.'

To think that we're missing talent like this that could so easily be transitioned into cybersecurity is totally unacceptable.

Global setbacks: India's problem

Looking to India, Rachel, with a global remit, spoke about another setback that's taking place for women in cybersecurity: the retention problem. There, she'd noticed women leaving the workforce prematurely whenever they got married or had children. Effectively, she said, 'Their career is over as soon as they start a family.' This is hugely disappointing, as India does so well at producing women with STEM skills and attracting women into cybersecurity.

Jivika, whom I wrote about before, is from India. She explains, 'India is a world leader in software development with a large reservoir of technically skilled professionals, and 40% of the country's GDP comes from technology. Women are taught about IT from a very early age, and all children are asked to focus on STEM subjects. Parents brag in the playgrounds about how well their daughters are doing. By the time they get to high school, they're encouraged to take more IT related courses such as C++, Java, etc., and are exposed to cybersecurity as a professional career. As they have a large number of job openings, high awareness about various cybersecurity career options, or family members who are in cybersecurity, it's easy for girls to find female role models who instil confidence, normality, and encourage other women to pursue it.'

However, when it came to working mothers, she told me how India lacks flexible working hours and childcare provisions, such as au pairs, nannies, nurseries, crèches, and after-school clubs. Furthermore, there's the huge part that culture plays for women in India. As a patrifocal society, India sees women's work as secondary to men's, and mothers traditionally raise the children. They have huge pressure not to work, too, and instead conform to society's expectations. Even when their family will support them by helping out with childcare, women are made to feel guilty, or not accepted in the workplace, or viewed as the weakest link in the team. If they do return to work after having a baby, they're often given less responsibility and unimportant projects as they can't stay for long hours.

A report, which surveyed 1,000 women who were working in the capital, Delhi, and its neighbouring areas, found that only 18–34% of married women continued working after having a child.[10] And, according to analysis by Mercer International Inc., women in technology account for 40% of young recruits, then fall to 20% for middle management, and 10% for leadership positions. In 2013 the World Bank Study found that only 27% of the female population aged over fifteen was working in India, the lowest rate of women's participation in any workforce amongst the BRICS (Brazil, Russia, India, China and South Africa) countries, with the highest being in China at 64%.[11]

India has a unique problem to solve when it comes to women in cybersecurity. With qualified male professionals who can fulfil the requirements, the pressure to change things for women in the cybersecurity industry in India is slow. However, India's government is taking action, and preparing to extend mandatory paid maternity leave to six-and-a-half months. Some multinationals and tech firms are also implementing changes, as they recognise that keeping more women in the workforce is key to faster and sounder economic growth. According to the OECD (Organization for Economic Cooperation and Development) it's as much as 2% higher, and McKinsey & Co. have even speculated that if gender

---

10. http://www.bbc.co.uk/news/world-asia-india-32377275
11. https://data.worldbank.org/indicator/SL.TLF.CACT.FE.ZS

parity in the workforce could be achieved in India by 2025 it would add an extra 60% to GDP.[12] [13]

Without a doubt, more initiatives need to be implemented so that India can retain talented female cybersecurity professionals through the peaks of their careers. Ready-made, experienced and highly certified women in cybersecurity exist in India, and they want to work. The current wastage of talent from this pool alone is ludicrous.

However, if India is to address this, it has an enormous task at hand, as it faces culture changes in both society and the workplace, and it will take time.

Getting buy-in from mothers-in-law can help, for they play a central role in the family. Many have been known to pressurise women to stay at home to look after their husbands and children. Some companies, like General Electric Co. which makes medical and diagnostic equipment, are using this strategically, for they've started successful programmes that allow mothers-in-law to come into the office to see what their engineer daughters-in-law do all day. Other companies are contemplating flexible work programmes and remote access, so that their employees can work from home, around their family commitments. The latter could revolutionise the talent pool shortage, and help to reverse the declining numbers of women working in cybersecurity, but only so long as it's inclusive to both genders. If it's only offered to women, it will create division and resentment in the workforce.

Highlighting maternity leave without addressing the issue of parenthood will only exacerbate the problem, and regrettably the

12. http://www.oecd-ilibrary.org/economics/raising-the-economic-par ticipation-of-women-in-india_5js6g5kvpd6j-en;jsessionid=7je9fbmlvqu ap.x-oecd-live-03

13. http://www.mckinsey.com/global-themes/employment-and-growth /the-power-of-parity-advancing-womens-equality-in-india

proposed changes in the law ignore the highly tilted gender distribution of unpaid domestic and care-giving work in India. Without a legal framework, the government has left the problem to individual companies to sort out. In most cases, this means that if paternity leave is granted, it's restricted to one to two weeks. Unless other companies set a precedent, like Facebook has done by extending its four-month paid paternity leave to all its employees across the globe, nothing will change.

Global progress: Israel, the United Arab Emirates (UAE), and the Eastern Bloc

Finally, I want to mention Israel, the UAE, and the Eastern Bloc, as they're making marked progress when it comes to women in cybersecurity.

I'll start with Israel, for it's the only country that I've come across that has a gender diverse pool of cybersecurity talent, and no apparent shortage. With historical, political, and societal factors to contend with, Israel is quickly becoming an epicentre of cybersecurity innovation, now ranking just behind Silicon Valley. Israel's Prime Minister, Benjamin Netanyahu, has taken a strategic approach in order to fill the gap between the available talent of today and what will be needed to secure the future.[14] He's placed his governmental headquarters in and near universities in order to help educate the next generation of cybersecurity professionals and nurture innovation. He's also sponsored effective cybersecurity talent pipeline programmes.[15],[16]

Magshimim is one such programme. Beginning in 2011, it was originally founded by The Rashi Foundation, a philanthropic organ-

14. http://fortune.com/2015/09/01/why-israel-dominates-in-cyber-security/
15. http://www.rashi.org.il/magshimim-cyber-program
16. http://gvahim.org.il/

isation that's focused on supporting underprivileged Israeli youth. However, since 2013 it's been co-sponsored by the Israeli Ministry of Defense, and whilst more than 530 students have successfully graduated, it's now scaling things up so 4,800 participants can over the course of the next five years.

Principally serving as a feeder system, it's main objective is to nurture the cybersecurity talents of the country's youth in the periphery, i.e. those outside the well-populated and wealthier cities in Israel. Beginning in the ninth grade, teenagers are screened for the afterschool cybersecurity programme, which places a particular emphasis on recruiting girls. The programme accepts about 30% of the students who apply, and targets those who show strong academic and computer aptitude potential, as well as sociability, commitment and self-discipline.

After a rigorous screening process, the students begin a stimulating and fun three-year programme with two afternoon sessions a week. They'll study computing theory, architecture and computer network design, and work on coding projects, implementing cryptographic protocols, reverse-engineering malware, alongside motivational activities and visits to high-tech companies and Intelligence Corps units.

Once the students graduate, they've compulsory military service, and many join the Israeli Defense Force's (IDF) elite cyber branches, in particular Unit 8200, which is renowned for its world-class intelligence and cybersecurity alumni, many of whom enter the private sector and launch successful cybersecurity or tech companies.

Looking at the UAE, although the 2017 *Global Information Security Workforce Study: Women in Cybersecurity,* reported on the Middle East as having the lowest percentage of women in cybersecurity, having visited this region and spoken to male and female cybersecurity professionals it looks like they're making headway. The reputation of UAE women in cybersecurity is outstanding and according to Ahmed Qurram Baig, Co-founder of CISOCONNECT™, they reach out to more than twenty-five female senior cybersecurity executives in their region.

When I visited Dubai in 2017 and spoke at MESCON and MESA I wanted to understand more. I knew that the World Economic Forum's 2014 Global Gender Gap report ranked the UAE as a leader in gender equality in the region. However, what became apparent was their fundamental belief that women and men are equal partners in society. The UAE guarantees equal rights for both men and women in regards to employment, health and family welfare facilities. Under the Constitution, women enjoy the same legal status, claim to titles, access to education, the right to practice professions, and the right to inherit property as men.

Repeatedly, I was told how more women than men complete secondary education and enrol in university and post-graduate institutions; additionally, how women seek financial independence, professional success, and families are keen to see them achieve this. As a result, through many public and private sector initiatives, women are encouraged to play an increasingly stronger role in business, military and government. Today, women occupy two-thirds of all public-sector posts, and 30% of senior and decision-making positions.

The Eastern Bloc is also noted for consistently producing remarkable women in cybersecurity, and there may be several reasons for this. Firstly, girls are expected to take up technology from an early age in schools, and perform well. There's no stigma associated with studying technology either. Rather than approaching it playfully, girls there are focused, knowing that it will likely lead to a future career. When I interviewed women from these countries about why they excelled in cybersecurity and had such a foothold in technology they told me that they thought it was because of the Soviet era, when the advancement was made a national priority. Then, everyone was able to participate, parents understood the value it could bring their daughters, and women were especially encouraged to pursue careers in technology. They also attributed it to their national psyche. Culturally, women in the Eastern Bloc countries are characterised as having a forthright nature and this means they're more inclined to speak up for themselves, and be hardy to rejection, which is typically needed in a male-dominated environment.

The Golden Rules

- Recognise and accept the cultural differences between the generation cohorts
- Talent exists, so become good at spotting competent professionals
- Be open minded about recruiting from within your organisation
- Recognise that cybersecurity is all about challenging how the world around us works, so look for talent that can think well
- Offer training programmes and mentoring to increase your talent pool's security expertise. Use the right words to attract the widest group of applicants.

4. Qualifications Don't Make a Hacker

- Penetration tester profile
- Entering cybersecurity without formal qualifications
- Apprenticeships as an alternative way in
- Transitioning into cybersecurity
- Scholarships for women
- Using qualifications to bolster your career
- Confidence versus competence
- Hackers don't rely on qualifications

Just over a year ago, my eldest son, Tom, was home for the holidays and we were talking about his career. He'd graduated with a first class honours degree in Philosophy from a Russell Group University that summer.[1] He'd also just taken a MENSA test, and with an IQ test score of 158 had been invited to join.[2]

However, he was in a conundrum. He was working for one of the world's largest international business process outsourcing and

---

1. http://russellgroup.ac.uk/
2. www.mensa.org.uk/

professional services companies as an Efficiency Analyst. Whilst he was excited about getting the job, he was intellectually unfulfilled, working seventy hours per week, and perplexed because he'd just discovered that career development opportunities didn't exist for him within the organisation. Although he'd studied and sat countless exams and interviews in order to get into select schools, colleges, universities, and employment since he was nine years old, nothing had prepared him for that bombshell – some companies don't develop top talent.

We talked for hours about the workplace, how work was changing, what he wanted from his life and career, what success looked like for him, and what he would do. He was like most young men of his age. In life, he wanted to get married, have a family, a good work-life balance, and play an active part in his children's lives as they grew up. From his career, he wanted to be in an environment with like-minded individuals, use his brain and feel valued. Working seventy hours didn't bother him, but what did was not having an investment made in him and the opportunity for career development.

Having heard what he said, I brought up cybersecurity. I knew he had a good brain, could think strategically, solve complex problems, and communicate with ease. The industry needs professionals just like him. With growing cyberattacks and a huge shortage of qualified cybersecurity talent, the message from companies and government agencies, who are aggressively trying to fill their cybersecurity openings, is loud and clear: 'If you don't have a Computer Science degree, don't write off a career in cybersecurity. If you're lacking qualifications but have a passion for cybersecurity, then you can still get a job.'

His reply was terse: 'I don't have a Tech degree, Mum.'

Mine was similar: 'That's not an issue. Qualifications don't make a hacker.'

He then began to ask more pertinent questions, like how could he get into and progress in cybersecurity? Having been in information security since 1997, specialising in penetration testing, I'm ashamed to say he had me stumped. All I knew was that a career as a penetration tester wouldn't suit him. He didn't fit the profile.

Penetration tester profile

Penetration testers, sometimes known as ethical hackers, are those who probe for and exploit security vulnerabilities in web-based applications, networks and systems. They're typically introverts, extremely technical, live and breathe security, and mix mostly with their own kind – other penetration testers. As focused, highly intelligent individuals, some of whom are on the spectrum, they like solving problems, challenges and puzzles, and are creative, curious, strategic, unconventional, and at times elitist.

Importantly, though, penetration testers are self-starters. Many gain their knowledge from tinkering at an early age, reading books and blogs on the subject, watching online videos, learning code, attending conferences, hanging out with other penetration testers whom they may have met on Twitter or online forums, and setting up penetration testing labs at home. They often don't hold specialised degrees, and as penetration testing is more about skills than qualifications, they prefer to get work experience as soon as they can.

Entering cybersecurity without formal qualifications

Keren Elazari fits this profile, and if you don't know her, let me introduce her. She's an Israeli-born cybersecurity analyst, and senior researcher at the Tel Aviv University Interdisciplinary Cyber Research Center. Since 2000, she's worked with leading Israeli security firms, public organisations, the Big Four, and Fortune 500 companies. Her TED Talk, 'Hackers: the Internet's Immune System', has been viewed by over 2 million people online, translated into thirty languages, and was selected for TED's list of 'Most Powerful Ideas in 2014' and Inc.com's list of 'Top TED Talks for Entrepreneurs.'[3]

I first met Keren on Twitter, and discovered there were a couple of catalysts for her route into cybersecurity. Her story was featured in a book, which she co-authored with Tarah Wheeler, called *Women in Tech: Take Your Career to the Next Level with Practical Advice and Inspiring Stories,* an Amazon best-seller with eight amazing women.[4]

In the book, Keren disclosed that her primary catalyst was the 1995 cult film, *Hackers,* 'Which,' she said, 'blew my mind.' Not only did it feature a group of gifted high school kids who hacked systems and rollerbladed, but it also starred a cool girl, Acid Burn. Played by Angelina Jolie, she was the first female character on set to defy both female and hacker typecasts.

When storylines so often involved a damsel in distress being rescued by her prince, what Keren witnessed in Acid Burn was a defiant, intimidating young woman being a complete match for her male peers, in terms of both her technical and social skills. Keren related and was hooked.

She immediately signed up for a Computer Science class, started looking for hackers in her community, found a summer job at a local computer store, and continued to learn everything she could until she joined the Israeli Defense Forces (IDF), like most Israelis do, at eighteen. There, after basic training, she managed to get a job that involved network security, which fuelled her passion even further.

After Officer School, she decided to leave the military, and supplement her learning by enrolling on a Computer Science degree whilst working four night shifts per week at her local ISP's network

---

3. https://www.ted.com/talks/keren_elazari_hackers_the_internet_s_im
mune_system?language=en
4. https://www.amazon.com/Women-Tech-Practical-Inspiring-Stories
/dp/1632170663

operations centre. After a few months, she discovered what, sadly, many other Computer Science graduates discover – that the programming languages, technologies, and methodologies she was learning in class were obsolete; her professors were out of touch with reality; and her mathematics lessons had little to do with real-world security problems. Furthermore, she was actually acquiring more knowledge about computers and security on her night shifts than on her degree.

So she quit, and obtained a cybersecurity job at a consulting firm which was looking for fresh talent and open to those without academic degrees. Since then, Keren has performed a variety of roles from Risk Management Junior Associate to Information Security Architect, Operational Security Expert, Industry Analyst, and Researcher.

Although most of her learning has been on the job, and she didn't rely on qualifications to enter the field, over the years she's gained a BA in History and Philosophy of Science, an MA in Security Studies, and is certified as a CISSP professional.

Karolina Oseckyte's story is different. Born in Lithuania, and entering the UK when she was eleven years old, she began her journey into cybersecurity after college. At eighteen she knew that she wasn't ready for university. Like most young people, she didn't know what she wanted to do. However, she was adamant that she was going to leave a mark on the world from a very young age, do a job that had meaning, and inspire big changes. So when KPMG came into her college to present on apprenticeships, she attended to learn more.

As Karolina says, 'They promoted it as a scheme whereby you'd gain work experience across different departments on a rotational basis, and after a while they'd sponsor you to go to university. To be able to work for a prestigious firm, whilst being paid, and earning a degree of my choice made total sense.'

However, Karolina had one problem. When she first moved to

the UK, she struggled with her studies. 'I remember being frustrated by the language barrier, and was easily distracted, which led to me receiving bad GCSE grades. I thought having poor grades meant the end to good opportunities, especially like the one being presented by KPMG. So, when I was listening to the presentation, I dared to raise my hand and ask whether they'd consider taking someone with poor GCSE grades, but who'd performed well at college, and was determined.'

Thankfully for Karolina, the KPMG representative told her that they'd consider all cases on an individual basis, and when she applied she received an offer. Having worked at KPMG for five years on a range of diverse projects, moved to the USA and completed her Information Security degree, Karolina says that had she not dared to raise her hand in that presentation and speak up, she wouldn't be where she is today.

Keren and Karolina's stories highlight that it's entirely possible – and common – to get into cybersecurity without having a Computer Science degree or cybersecurity qualifications. Furthermore, as CISOs regularly complain about how ill prepared and out-of-date Computer Science students are with current technology and practices – sometimes by up to ten years or more, it's often a better route in.

Natalie Blackbourne, who's based in the USA and is Co-founder and President of Blackbourne Worldwide, a cybersecurity consultancy that uses artificial intelligence and specialises in threat analysis, social intelligence, research and development, agrees.

'I haven't found very many universities that teach the skills we need – penetration testers with CEHs that don't know how to hack, social engineers who only know theory, and so on. As a result, we've resorted to teaching skills in-house instead of relying on taking those with a university education.'

She told me how she'd just hired someone who chose Blackbourne's three-month internship over pursuing a master's degree because he needed to be assured that he'd get the best training for the job he wanted – penetration testing. That said, she did say how impressed she'd been with MIT (Massachusetts Institute of Technology), but only in so far as its graduates' knowledge base went, rather than practical experience.

To learn that many universities are failing their students and industry in this way is both shameful and unacceptable. Students waste years and accumulate debt – typically around £35,000 to £40,000 for a student on a three-year course outside of London in the UK. Obviously, the education system has to improve, but is there another way in?

Apprenticeships as an alternative way in

Apprenticeships can really kick start a career in cybersecurity. This is a chance for a school or college leaver who's interested in cybersecurity to take on a job that counts, with real responsibility from day one, and to earn as they learn, with support and development opportunities tailored to match their interests. What's more, apprentices are able to see that the work they're doing is making a real difference, and there's career progression in the form of a job straight after. Apprenticeships are hugely beneficial, and often companies will sponsor the apprentice through university or other qualifications if they so desire.

However, for someone who has a non-technical degree, like my son, the best route into cybersecurity would be on a two-year graduate training scheme. These are offered by some of the tech giants, like Fujitsu, IBM, BAE Systems, Capgemini, or the Big Four accounting firms, or banks like Lloyds Banking Group, which in 2015 launched a formal graduate programme to develop digital banking skills such as digital proposition development, e-commerce, fraud, and cybersecurity.

For most graduate scheme vacancies, any degree discipline is acceptable, so long as the graduate has achieved adequate grades, as training is tailored to the graduate's needs. Most have similar application processes. For example, completing an application form; taking an online assessment that could include aptitude, logical reasoning, processing, verbal reasoning, and numerical tests; attending an assessment day for more logical problem solving, group activities and presentations; and concluding with a final interview.

Once a graduate is accepted, they're then allocated managers who can oversee their day-to-day working activities, and others who can help with a range of training opportunities, from formal mentoring programmes and career development to peer support and professional development. Typically, cybersecurity graduates receive comprehensive training and development, which includes self-study and certification with organisations like (ISC)², ISACA, CompTIA, EC Council, ISSP, GIAC, SANS, CREST, and ISO. Just like the apprenticeship schemes, graduates have a job with the firm straight after.

Aside from offering programmes such as these, it's also essential for a company to demonstrate that it takes diversity and inclusion seriously if it wants to attract top female talent. Female graduates are in demand in any business, and with a severe shortage of women in cybersecurity, right now, according to recruiters, women at this stage of their careers typically receive more job offers at the application stage than men. As a result, women have a growing interest in corporate and social responsibility, and proof that a company is actually doing something about it rather than just talking about it.

This was certainly the case when I spoke to a young female cybersecurity professional from one of the world's central banks. She told me how much it mattered. 'If a recruitment consultant contacted me about a job I immediately assessed the potential employer. I looked for proof of gender diversity within the organisation, along with gender mobility, and leadership. I knew that if I didn't see this I'd be wasting my time applying and theirs.'

Lloyds Banking Group provides a good example of what a company can do in order to attract, develop, fully utilise, and retain top female talent. Recognising that companies with gender diverse senior management teams perform better, it has made a commitment to be a leader in gender diversity. Its goals are ambitious but realistic.

I met with French born Claire Calmejane, Director of Innovation & Digital Centre of Excellence and London Digital Ambassador, and she told me how in 2014 Lloyds Banking Group made a bold public commitment on gender equality in its Helping Britain Prosper plan. It's going to increase the proportion of senior management roles held by women to 40% by 2020. Moreover, by the end of 2015, with 31% of its senior management roles being filled by women, it was on track to meet its commitment.

Claire accredits the Bank's success – recognised in the Times Top 50 Employers for Women, Top 10 Employers for Working Families, Working Mum's Best Employer for Dads – to several initiatives. These include its Sponsoring Leadership programme, which continues to identify high potential women, and provide them with senior sponsors and its Returners programmes for agile working or job-sharing in senior positions. She told me how women in middle management roles completed this programme in 2015, and how the Lloyds Group works closely with its resourcing partners to ensure that it's able to attract the best female talent and have mandatory diverse shortlists for senior appointments. It also has an award-winning women's network of 15,000 members and 4,000 mentors, which held over fifty events in 2015, and it sponsors the Women of the Future Ambassadors Programme, which connects female mentors with 1,000 sixth formers from thirty schools. The network is inclusive of both genders.

Transitioning in to cybersecurity

These schemes and programmes are commendable. However, there's one big problem – they're mostly age dependent, and apprenticeships (if available at all) are usually capped when an individual reaches twenty-four years old. As statistics have repeatedly shown that women typically enter cybersecurity beyond the age of thirty, I've been keen to understand what can be done to alleviate the problem, especially when many within that demographic have far more financial commitments to meet than youngsters.

This was a question that was asked by Alisha, a twenty-four-year-old British Canadian whom I met on Twitter. She'd read one of my blogs and reached out to me. Being passionate about cybersecurity, she told me that had she known about it when she was at school, she'd have pursued it as a career. When I looked at her profile on LinkedIn, I noticed that she had first class honours in Law, her A Levels included Mathematics, and she was working as a cybersecurity recruitment consultant – in other words, sales.

When I asked her if she'd still like to work in cybersecurity if she could be given a chance, she told me, 'When you asked me that, you threw me, as I thought I'd missed the boat and given up on my dream.'

People like Alisha are out there and are much needed. They've transferable skills, and their value can be maximised. Making a career change from law to cybersecurity is relatively easy. Typically cybersecurity is the first department that's involved when there's a breach, so its people understand legislation, including data protection, and are used to reviewing documents, writing policies, and negotiating. Furthermore, their communication skills tend to be strong. Throw in a skill like selling, and their competence is looking pretty comprehensive.

Companies like BAE Systems, which has opened the National Security (NS) Academy, can provide a solution for women like Alisha, as they're open to those who may have been working in IT for a number of years, or who have a STEM degree or simply an interest for Computer Science. Employing over 4,000 people across eighteen countries in America, APAC (Asia-Pacific), the UK, and EMEA (Europe, the Middle East and Africa), BAE Systems helps nations, governments, and businesses around the world to defend against cybercrime, reduce their risk in the connected world, comply with regulations, and transform their operations. Encouragingly, BAE Systems is insisting that previous experience in software development isn't required, as its programme provides people with the technical knowledge and interpersonal skills to work with confidence in a wide variety of challenging business environments. Importantly too, it offers security clearance, which is an asset that's often hard to come by, especially for young cyber-security professionals.

CyberWayFinder in Belgium may provide another option. Although just starting out, and only localised in this region, their objective is to target mid-career professional women with other life and problem-solving skills and to divert them into cybersecurity. When I spoke to Co-Founders Patrick Wheeler and Rosanna Kurrer, they told me that their three-year programme offers training, including certification, a professional network, mentoring and on the job experience, whilst being paid.

SecureSet Academy, a cybersecurity boot camp based in Denver and Colorado Springs, USA, offers another way in. It's been set up to help recruit talent from non-technical backgrounds. Founded by Bret Fund, and with a mission to build an end-to-end community focused on fulfilling the promise of cybersecurity, SecureSet offers two programmes, plus professional development and workshops.

The first programme is CORE Technical and it's an intensive, 800-hour immersive curriculum that includes twelve foundational courses, extensive hands-on skill building, and guided product training. Students amass a wealth of knowledge in as little as twenty weeks, on either full-time or evening schedules. The transition takes general IT professionals ten years, yet via CORE, it's fast-tracked. Upon graduation, CORE students are then placed in employment as tier 1+ security engineers, analysts, pen testers and consultants.

The second programme is Hunt Analysis and it's equally intensive. It targets people who are good at mathematics, social science, business and problem solving. It offers a 480-hour immersive curriculum, includes eight foundational courses, extensive hands-on skill building and guided product training. The full-time programme was set up to train tier 1+ security analysts, threat analysts and hunt analysts. As with CORE, the evolution from general IT to cybersecurity analyst is fast tracked. What usually takes seven years, HUNT students can graduate for immediate employment in as little as twelve weeks.

With a 100% track record for placing graduates into employment after graduating, women appear to be particularly interested. At its cybersecurity meetups, women make up about 30% of the people gathered and the expectation is that HUNT Analysts programme students will make up 40 to 50% of the intake.[5]

It's crystal clear that if we're going to increase the numbers of women in cybersecurity, we need to break down the barriers to entry whilst building programmes, ideally in the workplace, that can give real-world training in both soft and hard skills. This is particularly relevant as trends indicate that people are changing careers more often and career reinvention will increase. Although we're becoming more specialised in what we do, we're also moving into other niches as technology rapidly develops.

What's therefore required more than anything else right now is an ability to acquire knowledge fast, as high-value cybersecurity work will require the mastery of deep-skills and being able to pivot or slide into other areas of mastery. As a result, this is where we really need to address the conversion and access aspect in cybersecurity. Only by recruiting from other industries will we be able to plug the cybersecurity gender diversity and skills gap in the timescales we require. The talent is there, and often within our own cybersecurity

---

5. https://secureset.com/

ecosystem or organisation, but we must look hard, and become better at attracting it, particularly when it comes to women.

With a growing need for skilled cybersecurity professionals, one company that's doing this is BT. In more than 180 countries worldwide and already employing more than 2,500 cybersecurity professionals at multiple security operations centres, BT has teamed up with (ISC)² and announced an agreement to offer training for CISSP and SSCP certifications within the BT Security Academy. The agreement enables BT's security employees, new recruits and key suppliers to pursue acclaimed professional certifications.

We can also learn from other professions that have solved similar challenges. Take accounting in the USA. In 1951 it recognised its talent shortage and gender diversity shortfall. Being predominantly male, with only 500 female certified public accountants in the country, it took action. It paired leaders across the accounting field with industry associations and academic institutions. Together they drove awareness campaigns and hiring initiatives. Today there are over 800,000 female certified public accountants in the USA.

Returnships

Returnships offer another solution for women who've had a career break. To entice them back to the workplace, the Society of Women Engineers (SWE), in partnership with iRelaunch, a pioneering company in the career re-entry space, are promoting employment opportunities within the STEM Re-entry Task Force initiative to cybersecurity professionals in the USA who are interested in getting back to their technical careers. Seven companies from SWE's Corporate Partnership Council are participating, and Booz Allen Hamilton is currently offering a 12-week, paid cybersecurity returnship programme aimed at helping stay-at-home mothers in the USA with a STEM background to assess whether they want to return to work and if so how.[6]

Scholarships for women

(ISC)[2] is particularly active when it comes to offering women in information security an opportunity. Through a scholarship, which is open to citizens of any country and administered by the Center for Cyber Safefy and Education, scholarships of up to US$40,000 can be awarded. Eligible applicants have to meet certain criteria: for example, they must be pursuing, or plan to pursue, a degree with a focus on cybersecurity or information assurance, be a senior in high school, an undergraduate student, graduate or a post graduate student and be attending full-time or part-time.[7]

The SANS Institute also offers another opportunity. However, like many others, for example The Raytheon Women's Cybersecurity Scholarship[8], the SWSIS programme[9] and ESET[10], it is only provided for women in the USA or permanent legal residents currently living in the US. Through the SANS 2017 Immersion Academy for Women, which is an accelerated training and certification programme, women applicants can complete up to three of SANS' world-class cybersecurity training courses and earn the associated GIAC certifications. The Immersion Academy is 100% scholarship-based, intensive and accelerated. It's been designed for completion in approximately six months, depending upon the programme selected, Customised or Open. Customised Immersion Academies allow employers or sponsors to choose the curriculum

---

6. http://reentry.swe.org/

7. https://iamcybersafe.org/scholarships/womens-scholarships/

8. In conjunction with the (ISC)[2] Women's Cybersecurity Scholarship Program

9. http://cra.org/cra-w/scholarships-and-awards/scholarships/swsis/

10. https://www.eset.com/us/about/newsroom/corporate-blog/eset-women-in-cybersecurity-scholarship-now-accepting-applications/

that best suits the needs of their organisation. Those applying must have a degree in information technology, security or audit, or three to five years of work experience in those domains.[11]

Using qualifications to bolster your career

When the female talent is there, is it worth them certifying in order to bolster their chances of being hired? This is a question I regularly get asked, particularly when a cybersecurity professional enters the market. My answer is always the same. Unfortunately, when starting out in cybersecurity, certification counts for little, as it can't get someone over the chicken and egg situation of needing experience to get experience. Certification also can't change how hiring managers or HR filter CVs.

Having viewed thousands of CVs over the last two decades, I've realised whenever they've arrived with certifications but without experience, all they've communicated is the applicant's deep desire to get into the industry, which is commendable, and that a particular certification can be achieved without gaining experience, which is not. Unfortunately, it does nothing to help that individual get hired, as when hiring for entry-level positions, CVs are usually filtered as follows:

- Disregard all who lack the required degree or certification
- Disregard all who lack experience specified on the job advertisement
- Disregard all who have experience but aren't certified
- If any have been disregarded but have been referred by a trusted source, add them back in

Although I'll discuss recruitment in Chapter 11, what this demonstrates is that without experience, possessing certification is futile. Furthermore, it's more beneficial for an applicant to work

---

11. https://www.sans.org/cybertalent/immersion-academy

on personal branding, forging relationships with the right connections, ideally within the organisation they're applying to join, and being sponsored in. With the cost of cybersecurity courses at an all-time high, averaging £2,000 for an entry-level course in the UK and $5,500 in the USA, and technology, exploits, and tools changing so fast, which affects the shelf-life of a course, hopefully more professionals will try a different tactic rather than signing up for a course in the hope of being hired, and getting into further debt. It will also benefit those hiring, as frequently I'm told that qualifications don't signal an individual's capability.

Cyril Haziza, the CISO for a French cosmetics company, has been in cybersecurity for over fifteen years and agrees.

'In France we tend not to rely on certifications so much. That said, I did become a CISSP professional recently. Although I have a master's degree in Computer Science and an Engineer diploma, I learnt mostly about security on the job. As someone who's self-studied, and learnt through experience by getting into technology in the 1990s, I wanted to assess my skillset. I was also curious to know if I could pass the examination without much effort, based on the experience I'd acquired throughout my time in security. The other reason I did it was because increasingly I've found that in order to do business globally, particularly with the USA, a certification, such as CISSP, is expected. You won't be taken seriously without it.'

But, what if the female talent is experienced? Is there merit in attaining cybersecurity qualifications? Whilst this isn't a question I get asked, it's something I see women succumbing to. Time and time again I've seen top female cybersecurity professionals managing teams, performing in complex environments, and succeeding. Yet, unlike many of their male peers, they've attained qualifications retrospectively in order to prove their worth to their male peers, and to advance their career.

Alex is one of these women. She's a Head of Information Security, holds an MBA, a BSc, and is ITIL and Prince2 certified. She's worked in multiple sectors, has specialised in complex strategic and service management delivery, and has proficiently managed globally dispersed teams across business and IT offshore divisions. With strong communication skills, she's also provided consultative services to core stakeholders, up to and including partner, C-suite, and board level. However, Alex is studying for her CISM. She feels she needs this qualification in order to be taken seriously within her job, to prove to her male peers that she is indeed competent, and to progress her career.

Confidence versus competence

This chapter couldn't be completed without bringing up the following statistic, which you've probably heard: men apply for a job when they meet only 60% of the required qualifications, but women apply only if they meet 100% of them. The finding comes from a Hewlett Packard internal report, and is often quoted in blogs online and books, including *Lean In* and *The Confidence Code*. It's usually raised as evidence that women need more confidence, and whilst I'm not going to dispute that, what many don't know is that there's no hard evidence regarding this. Stories are not studies.

It was Tara Sophia Mohr who decided to investigate this further. Being sceptical of the report, she surveyed 1,000 professionals, both men and women, and predominantly from America.

With a list of stock answers, she asked, 'If you decided not to apply for a job because you didn't meet all the qualifications, why didn't you apply?' Her findings confirmed what she'd suspected all along: there was little difference between genders. She discovered that the barrier to applying was not a lack of confidence. Instead, the most common reason for men and women not applying for a job was because they didn't think that they'd meet the qualifications, and didn't want to waste their time and energy applying.[12]

What became apparent from Tara's survey was that professionals were being held back on account of a mistaken perception about the hiring process. As Tara reports, the respondents thought that the qualifications were set, and that they needed the qualifications not to do the job well, but to be hired.

With this in mind, I wanted to test this view on cybersecurity professionals, and to establish whether the findings would be similar. I remained completely neutral, so in July 2016, I created a short survey of ten questions, and included a replication of Tara's question. The survey is still being analysed, but will be reported on shortly.

Whilst HP's internal report is slightly misleading, it shines a light on the problem around hiring, and a heavier reliance on qualifications by more women than men, which no one can deny. When women know that others are applying for jobs even if they don't meet the specified criteria, it highlights that not everyone is playing by the rules, and gives women permission to do the same.

Although qualifications have historically been a woman's way in to the workplace, and a way of demonstrating that she's worthy of a placement and can do the job just as well as any man, it's interesting to note that young women still see the workplace as orderly and meritocratic – something that it's not – and older women, who know that it's not, still comply with this regime in order to get on. Unfortunately, too, if women know that they need more qualifications in order to be hired, and experience gender bias in their workplaces, it further promotes the issue of confidence over competence and keeps women stuck in a self-doubt mode and from applying for jobs for which they don't meet the qualifications.

---

12. https://hbr.org/2014/08/why-women-dont-apply-for-jobs-unless -theyre-100-qualified

Hackers don't rely on qualifications

Finally, I want to leave you with this thought. When we look at one aspect of cybersecurity, hacking, we see it attracts a varied range of people and personality types. There is no blueprint. Trying to find a hacker is like trying to find Wally in the *Where's Wally* book, when nobody has told you what Wally looks like. With a variety of hacking means available, from accessing files behind a system to social engineering, where the ideal personality is often someone who blends in or is outgoing – often female – and who's able to trick people into performing tasks or divulging usernames or passwords, anything is possible.

Data supports this. According to research by the online payments company Jumio in 2013, 43% of hackers are aged between thirty-five and fifty years old, 8% are under eighteen years old, 24% are women, and almost half of all hacking traffic originates from APAC countries – the majority from Indonesia.[13] Furthermore, hackers are not isolated; they collaborate and give to gain rather than to lose. They work in teams and operate like well-run businesses, with executives, managers, workers, and support contracts for the systems and tools they use.

Learning from these successful hacking groups, we can ascertain that professional hackers are non-biased in how they recruit. They don't place limitations on how or whom they recruit and as cybercrime is now a $445 billion business, with the average company handling over 200,000 security events per day, perhaps it's time for us to learn from them. After all, success leaves clues.

The Golden Rules

Not all cybersecurity roles require formal qualifications, for example, penetration testing

---

13. http://venturebeat.com/2013/02/22/profile-of-a-cyber-criminal-infographic/

- Apprenticeships can offer a way into cybersecurity without professional qualifications or a Computer Science degree
- Graduate training schemes also open the doors to individuals who may have studied a degree outside of Computer Science
- Think about devising a scheme like BAE Systems, as this helps women who are beyond the apprenticeship age to transition in
- Corporate and social responsibility are attractive to new females hires
- Understand that women typically rely more on qualifications than men, as they help to demonstrate their worth. The GISWS 2017 reported that 51% of women compared to 45% of men hold graduate degrees, yet occupy significantly fewer positions in executive management, and furthermore that 24% hold non-technical degrees.

5. STEM Is A Red Herring

- The merits of right-brain and left-brain thinkers
- What is STEM?
- The chronic under representation of women in STEM
- The role of parents and teachers
- Are STEM subjects for males?
- The fear of the B-effect
- Self-fulfilling prophecies in the classroom
- Is STEM a problem for all countries?
- Turning STEM into STEAM

Steve Jobs said in his Stanford speech, 'You can't connect the dots looking forward; you can only connect them looking backwards. So you have to trust that the dots will somehow connect in your future. You have to trust in something – your gut, destiny, life, karma, whatever.'

I now believe as he did. Here's why.

Soon after I graduated in Art and Design, I started a new relationship. I'd just broken up with a long-term boyfriend whom I was engaged to, and I was on a rebound. After a summer of love, I discovered I was pregnant. Being frank, choosing to keep the baby was a hard decision. As a nominated Young British Designer, I'd

73

planned to work as a freelancer and travel the world. Whilst I liked children, they weren't in my schedule until I was in my thirties. I was only twenty-two years old and highly altruistic.

The boyfriend gave me a choice – him or the baby. My parents offered support and didn't want me to deny them the chance of having a grandchild. It was only my brother who laid off the pressure and offered good independent counsel.

My life changed considerably just before I gave birth to Tom. To set the scene, I was living in a tiny hamlet that lacked transportation, my car had packed in, and I was out of cash. My Bank Manager refused to lend me any more money so I was unable to fix my car and support myself and the ageing horse that I'd owned since I was fifteen. My parents offered me a roof over my head, and agreed to help, but there was a condition. I had to move back home with them, and be 200 miles apart from my boyfriend who was in his final year at university. I agreed. My choices were limited.

Life back home was challenging. I had no money, and no one would employ me as I was pregnant. The boyfriend announced he didn't feel ready to be a father. I wasn't sympathetic. My life was a mess. Six weeks after giving birth, I was under strict instructions to find a job, which I did. I borrowed jeans and a T-shirt from my brother, as the only clothes I had were tatty or smattered with paint from my time at Art College. I rolled up the legs of the jeans, tied back my hair and started work as a shop assistant in a retail store, The Gap. Reluctantly I handed over my new baby to my mother each day. I've never felt so tired or alone as I did then, but I got on with it.

About a year later, I managed to move out of my parents' home, and I rented an ex-council house. My mother cried. I celebrated. I had my freedom back and was able to design again in the evenings. I visited my agent every few weeks so they had my fresh designs when they left for international trade shows. I never knew if anything would sell, or how much money I'd make, but I kept going, living off a meagre income and believing in my ability.

Life continued like that for a few more years until I reached a point when I could no longer pay my bills and was negotiating terms of repayment with my utility suppliers. I remember someone saying to me, 'Jane, you've got a good brain. It's time to call it a day with your art. You've been doing it for seven years, you now need to get a proper job and make a life for you and your family.'

The words cut deep, and the wound remained unhealed for years.

Whilst I'm the first to declare myself a Luddite, technology has always been my saviour. It's also followed me everywhere. It all started in Brazil in the late 1970s. Living in Rio de Janeiro for a short while, I got hooked on computer games, playing Light Tennis (a Pong clone) with my brother when we were unable to go to the beach. When I was at school in the mid-1980s, I was one of only two girls in my year to take an interest in computing. Once again, it was games that drew me in.

When I was selecting my Art and Design degree course, the one that appealed most had great technology. When I retrained after leaving my art behind in order to get a 'proper' job, I enrolled on a 'High-Tech Secretarial' course, and learnt office skills including shorthand. I then got a temporary job with a tech company, where I met my next boyfriend and future business partner, a techie. One year later, after a year working as a recruitment consultant with Hays, which set me up for entrepreneurship, I was working in my own tech company selling information security solutions.

I've always viewed technology as being exciting, dynamic, fun, and creative. To me, it's a tool, and can be used much like a paintbrush. It's constantly changing, just like nature, and has attracted me like a moth to the lamp.

When I started my tech company, although I could have sold anything, the reason I chose to lead with security was really because of image. I viewed it as being intelligent, fun, and glamorous – a bit like James Bond – and it certainly beat selling networking kit or high availability servers. Having worked in cybersecurity since 1997, or information security as we called it then, and having watched it evolve, I know it to be incredibly creative. It requires out-of-the-box thinking, the ability to problem solve, and consistently attracts creative people. Most of the professionals I know within it, especially in penetration testing, are talented musicians or photographers.

The merits of right-brain and left-brain thinkers

Professionals who have creative abilities, in many people's opinions, are much needed in cybersecurity. These right-brain thinkers use more perceptual, creative, and instinctive thinking. They often ask, 'What if?' They see the bigger picture, and they think holistically. But they need to complement the other types of thinkers we possess in our field – those who regularly pick out subtle anomalies, are more detailed, analytical, and systematic. These skilled professionals are left-brain thinkers, and they learn facts, and deduce logical answers easily.

Obviously, people have both right-brain and left-brain capabilities, but typically most people find that one thinking side of their brain is more dominant and exercised, and preferred to the other. In cybersecurity we need right-brain thinkers working with left-brain thinkers, as any time we have uniformity of thought, we miss out on the most creative solutions or tactics that will help us to beat the threat actors.

We also need women, as they're biologically programmed to see risk in a different way to men. I'll discuss this in more detail in later chapters. Whilst some cybersecurity professionals – often women – reject this view, the existence of risk taking differences in regards to gender has been extensively researched by academics through questionnaires and experimental studies and cannot be ignored.

For example, a meta-analysis by Byrnes, Miller, and Schafer in 1999 reviewed over 150 papers on gender differences in risk perception and concluded that the literature 'clearly' indicated 'male participants are more likely to take risks than female participants'.[1]

Any global assessment of perceived risk combines elements of data with a belief – how likely is it that something bad will happen? – and a subjective valuation of that outcome – how bad would that be? By using people with diverse thinking abilities in cybersecurity, we can be sure that we're seeing all risks, and mapping out all the scenarios for attack. Having this kind of diversity within our profession makes us stronger, and better at our craft. It increases our chances of beating our adversaries. Without this we are blindsided.

However, cybersecurity is being held back from achieving this, which increases our risk exposure now and in the future. With an escalation and sophistication in cyberattacks, organisations, individuals, and governments are more susceptible than ever to being compromised – knowingly or unknowingly.

In order to rectify this, cybersecurity needs an overhaul. Right now it's being underserved and misrepresented, for it's viewed as nerdy, geeky, formulaic, dull, old, white, and male, rather than cool, dynamic, safe, future-proofed, and diverse. Regrettably, too, this problem is being further compounded whenever the topic of women is brought up, as many see it starting in schools with STEM.

What is STEM?

STEM is an acronym that refers to the academic disciplines of Science, Technology, Engineering, and Mathematics. Wiki describes STEM as being the term that's 'typically used when addressing education policy and curriculum choices in schools to improve competitiveness in Science and Technology development. It has implications for workforce development, national security concerns and immigration policy.'

STEM skills are critical to every economy, and often STEM is

---

1. http://journal.sjdm.org/jdm06016.pdf

discussed as a pathway to preparing students for the changing workforce and the jobs of tomorrow. STEM signals innovation, job creation, and economic prosperity. As a result, the demand for skilled workers in STEM is closely linked to a country's global competitiveness, and that's why many governments are embracing STEM and using it strategically.[2]

Although numerous STEM initiatives exist around the world, Brazil and their 'Science without Borders' programme serves as a good example. In 2014 Brazil's President, Dilma Rousseff, announced that 100,000 international scholarships would be given by her government to Brazilian students to study in other countries.[3] Her aim was to foster the training of students in the best education and foreign research institutions to promote the internationalisation of science and technology, stimulate the studies of Brazilian students abroad, and increase exchanges and mobility for students in their undergraduate and graduate years.

The chronic underrepresentation of women in STEM

Whilst governments have done a lot of fantastic work to encourage women and girls to embrace STEM, they're still chronically underrepresented. In the UK they make up just 14.4% of the STEM workforce; in Australia it's 16%; and in the USA they fill less than a quarter of all STEM jobs.[4] [5] When McKinsey & Co. surveyed 4,500 young people and 2,700 employers across 900 countries

---

2. http://reports.weforum.org/global-competitiveness-report-2015–2016 /competitiveness-rankings/

3. http://www.zdnet.com/article/brazilian-government-to-award-100000 -international-tech-scholarships/

4. https://www.wisecampaign.org.uk/resources/2015/09/women-in-the -stem-workforce

5. https://www.theguardian.com/australia-news/2016/mar/31/just-one -in-five-australians-working-in-stem-professions-are-women-and-theyre -paid-less

in 2012, they found that just 4% of women in the USA who were identified as high performers studied STEM subjects, compared to India which had 57%, Morocco which had 37%, and Turkey which had 25%. In fact, the USA performed the worst out of all the nine countries that were examined, and ranked behind Brazil, Germany, Mexico, Saudi Arabia, and the UK.[6]

This could explain why some organisations, particularly the American tech giants, are supporting education efforts in an attempt to improve the adoption of STEM disciplines, and the perception of them. Companies like Google, Hewlett Packard, Intel, Microsoft, Motorola, National Semiconductor, Texas Instruments, iRobot, IBM, Verizon Lockheed Martin, Raytheon, to name but a few, have created many initiatives and spent millions helping children learn, get access to technology, and prepare for college. Furthermore, some have directed their attention to girls-only programmes and initiatives.[7]

Take a look at Verizon's efforts and you'll find this to be the case. Its initiatives include a powerful commercial called Inspire her Mind that focuses on the language trusted parties and role models (typically parents) use when speaking to young girls (their daughters) and how it can impact the girls' later interest in STEM.[8]

GoldieBlox, a toy company, also used a commercial to positively promote the next generation of female engineers. Its viral campaign showed young girls watching other young girls who were dressed up as little princesses on a TV show. Having STEM skills, they decided to defy their gender norms with a complex creation that

---

6. http://www.mckinsey.com/industries/social-sector/our-insights/how-to-attract-us-women-to-the-sciences

7. http://www.adweek.com/news/advertising-branding/these-brands-want-girls-care-about-science-technology-engineering-and-math-158847

8. http://www.adweek.com/news/advertising-branding/ad-day-verizon-reminds-parents-girls-arent-just-pretty-pretty-brilliant-158269

ended up silencing the TV. It was fun to watch and reminded me of the game, Mousetrap.

And, then there's Google. In an attempt to get girls involved in coding, it's developed Made with Code and donated US $1 million to support Donor Choose, a non-profit that rewards teachers with money when they get four or more female students into a coding class.[9][10]

However commendable these efforts are, and whether right or wrong, STEM still leaves many young people, especially girls and young women, feeling cold and unexcited. When the UK Department for Business, Innovation and Skills reviewed the perceptions of STEM subjects amongst young people, it discovered a widespread sense that they were difficult, and choosing them could lead to failure.[11] When the British Science Association performed a review of Science, it too recognised the subject to be in a cultural silo, alienated from society and somewhat ghettoised.[12]

In the USA only 14% of teenage girls want to become a scientist, and when Accenture surveyed 4,000 girls, young women, parents and teachers in the UK and Ireland, it disturbingly found that STEM subjects and careers were perceived as being 'better suited to male personalities, hobbies and brains.' More than 60% of the twelve-year-old girls surveyed believed that STEM subjects were too difficult to learn, and 51% of the teachers and 43% of the parents said this perception helped to explain the low uptake of STEM subjects by girls.

When it came to the biggest influencers, the girls ranked their parents and teachers first. In terms of subject choices, more than 51%

9. https://www.madewithcode.com/

10. https://www.donorschoose.org/

11. Department for Business, Innovation and Skills (2014) *Project STEM: Book of Insights*

12. http://www.britishscienceassociation.org/Blog/a-new-vision-for-science

of them said they felt ill-informed on the benefits of STEM subjects. And, only 14% of their parents said they understood the different career opportunities that existed for their daughters.

The role of parents and teachers

These results don't surprise me. Last year my daughter Anja had to choose her GCSE subjects.[13] With a core base of subjects that were compulsory, she could only take three more subjects, and was in a quandary. She couldn't choose between Photography, Drama, History, Latin, and Computer Science. Although I know her to be technically competent as she's been coding since she was eight years old, and artistic as she'd received an art scholarship to her senior school, I didn't want to interfere with her decision. In the end, she whittled her choices down to Computer Science, History, and Photography. Her school then held a Parents' Evening to discuss these.

Now, I'm a huge fan of her school, and her Headmaster is certainly the best I've ever come across in all my twenty-six years of parenting. However, nothing could have prepared me for the reaction of the teachers when they discovered what subjects she'd opted for. Whenever they heard her say she'd chosen Computer Science, all but one pulled a disapproving face.

A member of the teaching team even leant forward and muttered to me, 'I can't understand why anyone would ever want to choose Computer Science.'

Rather shocked, I quietly replied, 'I'm really the wrong person to say that to. I work in technology, specifically cybersecurity, and this morning I was presenting to an audience on why we need more women in the industry.'

I then proceeded to tell her why. It only took me a few minutes, and at the end of it she said, 'Thank you for sharing this with me. I

---

13. https://en.wikipedia.org/wiki/General_Certificate_of_Secondary_Education

had no idea. Now I get it. Please will you come in to speak to the girls about this?'

Naturally, I agreed.

The only teacher who we spoke to who reacted positively to her choice of Computer Science was my daughter's Latin teacher. She's young, looks cool, and is one of my daughter's favourite teachers. As a role model, her opinion mattered, and thankfully her recommendation was, 'Anja, do what you love. Do something that inspires you to get you out of bed each morning. I think choosing technology is a smart decision. Technology is the future.'

I was relieved to finally witness a positive reaction and hear sage advice. The only thing I would have added is that technology is not just the future. It is the now.

The whole experience gave me much insight into why girls may not be pursuing STEM subjects as much as boys, particularly in the developed economic markets of the world. With only three out of forty-five girls choosing Computer Science at my daughter's all-girls school, where you could argue that the environment removed any social stigma attached to girls choosing subjects that could be considered more masculine than feminine, I questioned whether this was simply because males have more of a natural tendency to study STEM subjects than females.

Are STEM subjects for males?

Data drawn from the National Girls Collaboration Project (NGCP) in the USA suggests not. At K-12 Education, female students' achievement in Mathematics and Science was found to be on a par with their male peers'. Female students also participated in STEM courses at similar rates as their male peers, and Ivy League institutions like Stanford and Berkeley now report that about 50% of their introductory Computer Science students are women.[14][15]

McKinsey's survey indicates similar findings. In it, 55% of girls aged fifteen to eighteen years old said they found Engineering attractive, plus high school girls took almost half of the Advanced Placement tests in Mathematics and Science, and had higher than average grades in both subjects. The survey revealed that the crossroads for girls and STEM appeared to be at college, and by the time they'd reached twenty-three to twenty-five years old, the gender disparity was sizable. McKinsey found that the division wasn't being driven by a lack of ability. Instead, it was being driven by a belief that women would excel further in other fields.[16]

Often there's a tendency to think that girls don't pursue careers in STEM because of the reliance on mathematics. However, according to a report by the OCED in 2009, girls are just as competent in problem solving as boys. In fact in some countries like Sweden, Norway and Iceland, they outperform boys. Only in Macau do boys do better than girls. The problem is self-efficacy. Girls are just as capable as boys, they just think they aren't.

The fear of the B-effect

This perception of failure and risk aversion is extremely important for girls and women. Studies show that female students are more likely than male students to view their grades as an indicator of their ability in a subject. Rather than persevere with a subject, when they attain lower grades they lose self-esteem, and as a result are more likely than male students to drop courses.[17] In the USA, this

---

14. http://ngcproject.org/statistics
15. https://www.wired.com/2014/02/berkeley-women/
16. http://www.mckinsey.com/industries/social-sector/our-insights/how-to-attract-us-women-to-the-sciences
17. Shelly J. Correll 'Constraints into Preferences: Gender, Status and Emerging Career Aspirations'

Part One: The Assumptions

is sometimes referred to as the 'fear of the B-effect' and it's actually been identified as an important factor in explaining why women drop out of Science and Engineering majors.[18]

Parisa Tabriz, a Polish-Iranian-American who works for Google as a 'Security Princess', has blogged about this. Named as one of the 'Top 30 Under 30' to watch by *Forbes* magazine in 2012, she believes the lack of women in tech is because women put themselves down.

'There was a study done a few years ago which questioned people who had dropped out of their Computer Science course. Women who left tended to have a B-minus average and the most common reason they gave was that they were finding it too hard, whereas amongst the men the most common grade was a low C, but the reason they gave was that it wasn't interesting.'[19]

Carol Dweck, a Stanford University psychologist, has researched this phenomenon. She found that high-performing women who thought success in Mathematics and Science was down to having innate intelligence were less likely to persist when confronted with difficulty. However, when women believed that success was attributed to hard work, they embraced the challenge and performed at levels equal to or above those of their male counterparts.

Perhaps the biggest lesson for us with her work is in her conclusion. She suggested that if parents and teachers praised effort and persistence – 'You work so hard' – instead of results – 'You're so smart', girls and women could develop a more resilient mindset that would serve them better in the face of initial struggles.

Things are different in Asian cultures. There, there's more of a tendency to see struggle as an opportunity. Showing tenacity in overcoming hurdles, or something that you might not be naturally

---

18. Elaine Seymour and Nancy Hewitt, 'Talking about Leaving: Why Undergraduates Leave the Sciences'
19. http://www.telegraph.co.uk/technology/google/11140639/Googles
-top-secret-weapon-a-hacker-they-call-their-Security-Princess.html

good at, is treated as a chance to show that you've got what it takes to become successful. Teachers and parents support the next generations, knowing how important it is for them to learn about grit. They teach them how to embrace struggle, rather than shy away from it. By experiencing this, they learn a tactic, which builds confidence and prepares them for the real world.

Self-fulfilling prophecies in the classroom

Moving on from this research, I want to highlight something else that complicates the matter when it comes to performance for girls and women. Knowing how a female performs might affect how they're treated.

Research has found that top students and employees don't necessarily do better because of their natural ability. Rather it's because they get more attention, or receive better opportunities or working conditions. Malcolm Gladwell wrote extensively about this in his best-selling book *Outliers*, which examines the factors that contribute to high-level success.[20]

Robert Rosenthal, a Harvard psychologist, and Lenore Jacobson, the Principal of an elementary school in San Francisco, also studied this, specifically self-fulfilling prophecies in the classroom. They tested a range of children from kindergarten to the fifth grade across eighteen different classrooms and identified the top performers who had the potential for 'unusual intellectual gains'. Then they informed those children's teachers.

Although the students who had been identified as the ones with the most potential outperformed the other children for two years in a row, what the teachers were unaware of was the fact that the top 20% had in fact been chosen at random. The difference in performance 'was in the mind of the teacher'.

Worryingly too, from more studies, is the observation that

---

20. http://gladwell.com/outliers/

teachers' expectations of a gender group can affect the outcome of performance. Dubbed stereotype threat, this was studied by Claude Steele and colleagues in 1995 with a mathematics test. When women were told that they were going to find the mathematics test more difficult than men, they performed worse. However, when both genders were told that they'd find the test difficult, the gender disparity in performance disappeared.

As if the challenge couldn't be tougher, there's more bad news. Sociologist Dr Shelley Correll found that even when girls achieve similar grades to boys in mathematics, they rate their own abilities lower. They also set themselves a higher target, and are often held to a different standard.

Is STEM a problem for all countries?

According to a 2009 report by the Organisation for Economic Co-operation and Development (OECD), which has thirty-five member countries, there appears to be a greater chance of boys choosing to study science subjects in higher education and having more of a positive attitude towards science generally than girls. When women receive more than half of university degrees in the OECD area, they account for 30% of degrees in science and technology. And those receiving computing-related degrees varies across countries, for example, in Belgium, Switzerland and the Netherlands this is just under 10%, yet in Sweden and Finland it's 40%.[21]

Looking to the future, and at the uptake of STEM across the world, I can clearly see that not every country suffers the same challenges. For example, if STEM graduates continue to increase at the same pace, by 2030, China and India will create more than 60% of the OECD and G20 STEM graduates, and the BRIICS countries (Brazil, The Russian Federation, India, Indonesia, China and South

---

21. https://www.oecd.org/social/40881538.pdf

Africa) together will produce around three-quarters of the global STEM graduates.

However, Europe and the United States will fall behind with 8% and 4% of STEM graduates respectively. Obviously, this is a concern, so lagging countries are taking action to improve their position. For example, the USA aims to add another 1 million professionals with tertiary STEM qualifications by 2022. The European Union launched the 'Science with and for Society' programme in an attempt to make science more attractive, notably to young people, as well as open up further research and innovation activities in Europe. Additionally, it's looking at recent research that shows that a better way forward may be by developing higher education programmes with smart combinations of STEM subjects – those that bring in the Arts.[22]

Turning STEM into STEAM

Including the Arts in STEM would be a welcome change for cyber-security. Image matters, and if creativity, collaboration, communication, and critical thinking – all touted as the hallmark skills for 21st Century success – are to be cultivated in cybersecurity, we need to ensure that STEM subjects are drawn closer to the arts. This means we have to stop insisting on STEM disciplines for cybersecurity. It's an utter red herring – a logical fallacy that leads everyone to the wrong conclusions about our profession.

As cybersecurity evolves, we need STEM to evolve too, and that's why we need to start promoting STEAM. The additional letter (A) stands for Arts. Art based subjects incorporate things such as Humanities: History, Philosophy, or Law; Social Sciences such as Politics, Sociology, Gender Studies, or Media Studies; and the obvious subjects such as Art and Music. The Arts allow us to receive new ways to draw connections, and they help to stimulate

---

22. https://www.oecd.org/education/EDIF%2031%20(2015)--ENG--Final
.pdf

innovation in new cybersecurity products or services. By including the Arts, cybersecurity can open up its doors to a different kind of talent pool, and benefit from new ways of thinking.

Sir Ken Robinson, in his inspiring TED Talk, famously said, 'Creativity is as important as literacy.' In his book, *Out of Our Minds*, he asks us to look at creativity in a different way, and speculates that describing someone as creative 'suggests that they are actively producing something in a deliberate way. People are not creative in the abstract; they are creative in something: in mathematics, in engineering, in writing, in music, in business, in whatever. Creativity involves putting your imagination to work. In a sense, creativity is applied imagination.'

It's this concept that many believe we need to grasp in cybersecurity. Not all of our industry requires solitary professionals sitting in front of screens reviewing logs, code, or complex algorithms. A large portion of it needs professionals who know how to project manage, collaborate in teams, and communicate coherently, engagingly, and persuasively to different stakeholders. These types of people are often not found on Computer Science degree courses. Instead, many can be found working in other disciplines, in organisations, or on different degree courses.

In cybersecurity, we need variance – students and employees – men and women who are motivated and competent in their specialisms, and who can bring forth solutions to today's and tomorrow's problems. That's why we shouldn't focus exclusively on STEM. By adapting it to STEAM, and promoting this from early education and beyond, we marry the technology aspect with the creative, and become versatile, competitive, innovative, and ahead of our adversaries.

The Golden Rules

- Strategically recruit diverse teams of right- and left-brain thinkers
- Know that women have different risk appetites to men, and evaluate it differently
- Understand that the perception of failure and risk aversion are extremely important for girls and women
- Recognise cultural differences, and that STEM isn't a problem for all countries
- Talk about STEAM rather than STEM
- Look for creativity skills when you recruit, and develop these continuously
- Value attitude and aptitude and know that skills can be developed through training

6. Educate The Educators

- Education as a pipeline for talent
- The state of the education system
- New ways of teaching cybersecurity
- Learning through gamification
- The role of the teacher and lecturer
- Creating a new breed of educators
- Pairing technology with industry-led initiatives

When I was between six and eleven years old, my family lived in Scotland. Every summer my father would take some time off work and we'd drive down to Manchester, in the North of England, to see my grandparents, whom I adored.

I remember the scene as if it were yesterday. We'd set off in our car, with the family dog squeezed in between my mother's feet in the front car well. My brother and I would be squabbling in the back, arguing over territory, and who was encroaching on whose space. More shouting would soon follow from my mother, and my father would then threaten to turn back if we didn't pipe down. Frightened at that prospect, we'd quickly oblige, and then start creating things to do, like waving at other cars as we overtook them, or singing annoying songs that my grandmother had taught us.

Once we'd tired of those, my mother would hand out crosswords and puzzles to keep us busy for the five-hour journey. One of my favourites was a puzzle book called *Patterns and Puzzles*, and my grandfather had written it.

In those days, having a member of your family who'd written a book was quite rare, and I relished the opportunity to crack the codes he'd created for children to decipher. Being a headmaster at a British grammar school, he'd written the book to help students pass their Eleven Plus examination, and it contained a series of tests for verbal and non-verbal reasoning. There to support teachers too, these tests enabled them to assess a child's problem solving skills when working at speed, along with how effectively they could process information, think logically, and recognise patterns.

Although the book was difficult, I found cracking codes, solving problems, and looking for patterns fun. I also noticed that the more my brother and I worked through the exercises, the better we became, particularly when we could check our progress against the answers in the back. I remember my grandfather smiling and encouraging us to have a go, without cheating, and telling us, 'Practice makes perfect.'

Looking back, it's ironic to think that my love of patterns and puzzles lead me to creating patterns as a textile designer and then on to looking for patterns in cybersecurity. Yet, anyone who's ever worked in the industry will tell you how varied a field it is, and how it's one of the few professions that attracts and genuinely welcomes in as many conformists as it does free thinkers, rebels, rule breakers, and square pegs who don't fit into round holes. You can pretty much look any way you want – anything goes, from the cyber punks and youths in jeans and hoodies to those wearing the latest designer clothes and fashion accessories. You can speak any way that you want, too, so long as you can be understood, and your brain can operate in many different ways, as there are more people with Asperger's and autism in the cybersecurity community than any other industry.

All of these people I've just described are accepted, valued, and fit in, as they've gifted talents for being able to detect patterns and spot irregularities, or communicate threats to a range of stakeholders, and manage cyber risks. And some, like me, have even created their own products and services as entrepreneurs.

Education as a pipeline for talent

However, whenever I'm engaged to consult, or speak at conferences, or be interviewed by the press, or write for magazines about the state of the industry or women in cybersecurity, the first comments that typically arise don't refer to these degrees of diversity and tolerance. Instead, it's education – a topic that weighs heavily on our industry's mind.

People will say, 'Jane, if we're to effect change and get more women, or talent for that matter, into security, we need to get into schools earlier. We need to build the pipeline. And, when we do, we need to ensure it doesn't leak.'

They're right. A survey, 'Securing Our Future: Closing the Cyber Talent Gap', that's commissioned each year by Raytheon and the National Cybersecurity Alliance (NCSA) on the career interests and educational preparedness of millennials aged eighteen to twenty-six across twelve countries, reveals this.[1] Whilst the report is broken down for each country, Raytheon and the NCSA found that globally, 62% of men and 75% of women said no secondary or high school computer classes offered them the skills to help them pursue a career in cybersecurity. Furthermore, 52% of women, compared to 39% of men, said they felt no cybersecurity programmes or activities were available to them.

Education is, therefore, certainly a top priority, and one of the

1. http://www.raytheoncyber.com/news/feature/now_hiring.html

things that we need to be doing a better job of, particularly in some parts of the world.

Take the UK, for example. Renowned for the quality of its education, world-class research and innovation, surprisingly it's one such country. Despite increasing its entry numbers in computing at GCSE level, when students are aged between fourteen and sixteen years old, by 76.4%, from around 35,500 entrants in 2015 to around 62,500 in 2016, boys still study computing at four times the rate of girls.[2]

At A level, when students are aged between sixteen and nineteen years old, things have improved marginally in terms of the gender gap, as entries for girls have increased from 9% in 2015 to 9.8% in 2016. However, the total number of entries has fallen. In 2016, 8,700 students took the course, falling by 3,300 in five years, and Computing became one of the subjects with the worst results out of all that were entered for A Level examinations.[3]

By degree time, according to the latest figures from the Higher Education Statistics Agency, Computer Science accounted for 3.5% of all UK graduates. It was taught in 123 higher education institutions, and during 2013–14 there were 91,565 undergraduates (of all years) receiving tuition.

On the face of it, you could argue that at degree level, the UK has a positive story to tell in terms of those studying Computer Science. With a push on technology, and the dotcom boom since the 1990s, the number of annual graduates studying it has grown. In 1994–95 there were nearly 17,000 graduates, and in 2004–05 there were more than 37,000. Then, after the dotcom crash, numbers fell in 2013–14 to just under 27,000.

To put this into perspective for the most recent year for which

2. http://schoolsweek.co.uk/gcse-results-2016-trends-and-stats-from-the-national-data/

3. http://www.telegraph.co.uk/education/2016/08/18/a-level-results-2016-which-subjects-did-students-do-the-best-and/

figures are available (2011–12), Computer Science graduates in the USA accounted for 2.6% of all graduate cohorts, or nearly 50,000 students, and it constantly has a lower proportion of the total graduate cohort.[4]

Despite this progress, the UK has a significant challenge to overcome. Out of all the education subjects studied in the UK, those graduating in Computer Science face the highest rates of unemployment. Although the situation has improved, the levels are currently running at just over 10%. Wide regional variations occur too, plus there are differences associated with demographic background. For instance, some graduate cohorts report virtually no unemployment, whilst others have levels of around one in four.

And, then there are wider concerns. For example, the proportion of Computer Science undergraduates who progress into low-paid or non-graduate level employment; the volume of women accepting lower paid roles than their male counterparts; the reliance on international recruitment to fill Computer Science labs and postgraduate courses; and the skills, agility, and work-readiness of Computer Science graduates entering the workforce.

With something clearly amiss, most noticeably a mismatch between the cybersecurity capabilities of Computer Science graduates and industry requirements, the Council of Professors and Heads of Computing (CPHC) and (ISC)2, working with the British Computer Society (BCS) and other bodies, has created principles, concepts and learning objectives for the mandatory teaching of cybersecurity in accredited Computing Science degrees in the UK. Their aim is for 20,000 students per year to graduate with a firm understanding of security.

The Higher Education Funding Council for England also commissioned a major review, led by Sir Nigel Shadbolt, Professor of

---

4. https://www.timeshighereducation.com/features/what-should-we-be -teaching-the-next-generation-of-computer-scientists

Computer Science and Principal of Jesus College, Oxford, to chart a way forward. The ninety-one-page report, 'Shadbolt Review of Computer Sciences Degree Accreditation and Graduate Employability', assessed the shortcomings, and proposed actions to ensure students are introduced to materials and ways of thinking that will be immediately useful in employment, and a good foundation for future career development. The review recognised the speed at which Computer Science is changing, from cybersecurity to cloud computing, mobile applications to big data analytics, and the challenge to provide agile and relevant content whilst securing a common core of essential knowledge that's of value to the marketplace.[5]

Whilst comprehensive, what the review didn't report on was the dire shortage of educators with the necessary current skills in both teaching and the cybersecurity domains being taught – and at all levels within the education system. The reason this is crucial is because it's widely accepted that the single most important determinant of the educational outcomes for a child or student within a school or university is the capability of the teacher. If we're to improve the state of cybersecurity for men and women, plus girls and boys, we have to focus our attention on educating the educators. We have to insist that those who teach cybersecurity to children, teens or adults have an aptitude for teaching, know their topic, how it relates in the workplace, and are up-to-date.

The state of the education system

This emphasis on educating the educators became especially clear to me when my mother pointed out that children and adults learn differently, plus the education system is at the start of a reboot. She explained that just before it was last overhauled, more than 500 years

---

5. https://www.gov.uk/government/uploads/system/uploads/attachment _data/file/518575/ind-16-5-shadbolt-review-computer-science-graduate -employability.pdf

ago, the role of the educator, or lecturer (originating from the Latin word *lectura*, meaning to read), was clear.

With books scarce and literacy uncommon, educators taught others simply by reading from a book. Then, when the printing press was invented in the Holy Roman Empire by the German Johannes Gutenberg around 1440, the mechanics of education were radically transformed.[6] As books became more common and literacy improved, educators were no longer required to simply read. They had to do more, and their role involved disseminating a much broader set of information in a much more collaborative way.

My mother also explained how much religion has played a part in the education of girls, particularly from poor families. Before the 18th Century, girls from well off families were usually educated at home with a governess. However, during the 1800s, in the UK and USA, there was a wave of transformation, instigated by the British Empire under Queen Victoria, that would amend who was being educated and how. In 1833, the UK Government started to give grants to church-provided schools, and by 1880 education was made compulsory for all children aged between five and ten.

Certainly in places like Manchester, the first industrialised city in the world where my mother's family had moved from Ireland, the church saw that women were the cornerstones of the family. They knew that if girls were educated, they could bring a new moral and social standard to the family, and avoid sliding into the 'evils of industrialisation and urbanisation'. Her own girls' grammar school was founded by Roman Catholic nuns, who'd travelled from France to help improve the situation, and over 133 years grew from a tiny school with two classrooms to one that held over 700 girls.

Looking at education, and the way most boys and girls are taught, we can clearly see that it's remained static for all these years. Up till now, teachers and lecturers continue to teach a lesson to a class of

6. https://en.wikipedia.org/wiki/Printing_press

attentive students, give out and mark homework, and periodically test to see if the student has understood what they've heard or written down. No matter what your age is, it's the same. Schools are compliance based, and pupils are typically taught to memorise information, and then how to pass milestone examinations at various stages of their education. Many children, the world over, switch off, or drop out of school at these crucial stages, as they become bored of the repetition, unchallenged to engage their brain and to think.

At university, the same thing continues. Virtually all cybersecurity graduates will testify that they're being taught security topics in this manner – in classrooms, with the use of textbooks, whiteboards or blackboards, and slides. Their focus is on theory and case studies, and it's no surprise that students graduate ill-equipped to deal with real security challenges in the workplace.

In all but a few universities around the world, undergraduates aren't being taught that in cybersecurity you have to understand people, business, principles and concepts, as well as technology, or given methods to do so. Additionally, they're not being prepared for team working. However, they'll be required to liaise and collaborate with experts in many areas, like physical security, business, regulations, marketing, finance, and so on. And, many are, astonishingly, unaware that they'll have to stay current on advances on both the offensive and defensive sides, as they'll be expected to provide advice on which cybersecurity technologies will meet a particular business requirement, as well as understand how they fit into an organisation's overall cybersecurity posture.

Cybersecurity graduates are coming out of university book-smart but not work-ready, and many hiring managers are relaying their dissatisfaction with the current education system, and the implications in terms of increased susceptibility to cyberattack. As cybersecurity is a dynamic field, with new threats and defences appearing daily, they're right to complain, for there's a real need for a competent workforce with a sound knowledge of how to implement, coupled with experience and practical skills.

New ways of teaching cybersecurity

Consequently, many organisations and governments are looking towards technology as a way to radically improve how children and adult learners are acquiring their knowledge, including that of cybersecurity. Distance learning platforms, virtual learning environments (VLE), learning management systems (LMS) such as MOODLE, and massive online open courses (MOOCs) enable students of all ages to be educated on demand over the Internet, from anywhere in the world, in engaging multimedia fashions.[7] Students can watch video streams of classes or lectures whenever and wherever they happen to be, plus they can interact with other students and teachers through the platforms, download course work, upload completed assignments, access tools, and much more.

Companies like StormWind, which is aimed at adult learners outside of educational institutions, and those looking to up-skill in the workplace, or transfer from another field into cybersecurity, do just this.[8] Bringing a live Hollywood-HD quality experience to the world of e-learning, and using proprietary technology, StormWind is creating and delivering interactive online training for a number of areas in cybersecurity that are personal and engaging. It's also developing programmes for women-only, recognising that some women prefer studying together.

Secure Code Warrior is also using a technology approach to deliver its training.[9] Focusing on secure development, it has something to offer everyone – from entry-level professionals just beginning to develop their coding skills to seasoned experts. Users can

7. https://moodle.org/
8. https://www.stormwindstudios.com/
9. https://securecodewarrior.com/

improve their skills in familiar or unfamiliar areas, at a pace which is comfortable. Through a suite of hands-on interactive learning scenarios, Secure Code Warrior enables developers to master secure coding techniques in different development languages and frameworks. These go beyond the classic multiple-choice techniques, and offer hands-on challenges where software design and code need to be analysed for security weaknesses. Once these are identified, the developer can modify the code to remediate or mitigate the weaknesses.

By tapping into students' and developers' natural spirit of competition with game-based challenges designed to encourage teamwork, and making learning more enjoyable, Secure Code Warrior enables them to learn-by-doing through activities that focus on common application weaknesses in order to enhance the users' individual secure code development skills. Each developer can view their own scorecard showing their key strengths and weaknesses, and indicating areas where additional mastery is required. They can also benchmark their individual results against those of other developers within the same team, company, industry, or even university to help them gain a better understanding of how their skills measure up.

The ability to use technology in this way is useful, as it enables cybersecurity to be easily accessed and knowledge acquired on demand, in a controlled setting, and by a variety of learners anywhere in the world. It can also empower teachers and lecturers to further revise the way that they're teaching, for example, with flipped learning.[10] Rather than delivering a class and then setting homework, teachers and lecturers can make better use of their time by reversing this. They can set homework, with an instruction for the student to watch a pre-recorded video of the class, and then access any other resources that the teacher or lecturer wants to make

---

10. https://flippedlearning.org/

available through the VLE. The teacher or lecturer is then able to evaluate in class how well the students have understood the module, and can concentrate on interaction and individual attention, in person or online. With online analytical tools that the teacher or lecturer can access, a student can be fully supported. Technology also facilitates interaction and input from those working outside of the education system in industry, which can be particularly useful.

When I spoke to Jelena Mirkovic from the University of Southern California in the USA, she told me how she and her colleagues at the University have embraced this approach, and what they've done to ensure things change for adult cybersecurity learners. Having received funding from the National Science Foundation and the Department of Homeland Security, they've created publicly available and online education materials for active learning of cybersecurity concepts. Knowing that this type of learning increases engagement and motivation, and helps students to fully understand the concepts that they've learned in class, they've developed assignments that use a testbed in a safe but realistic network environment. With a team of cybersecurity educators, they've developed homework exercises on the DETERLab testbed,[11] hosted by USC/ISI and UC Berkeley, that demonstrate various attacks and defences.

Simulating real world examples, and granting user accounts with assorted permissions associated with different experiment groups, the DETERLab platform is proving popular. Since its launch in 2004, 9,012 users have used it in 148 classes and 100 institutions. Each group has its own pre-configured experimental environments running on Linux, BSD, Windows, or other operating systems. Users running DETERLab experiments can have full control of real hardware and networks running preconfigured software packages.

Additionally, students and lecturers can create and participate in

---

11. http://docs.deterlab.net/education/

Class Capture the Flag (CCTF) competitions. With their setup and scoring being automated, these competitions have been designed so that minimal support is required from the lecturer – at least at this stage. The exercises require minimal preparation time from students, too – roughly about two weeks, and they can be completed during a two-hour class.

Teams work on attack and defence scenarios, taking on both roles as this increases their understanding and enables them to acquire the adversarial thinking needed for a career in cybersecurity. During each CCTF, students focus on one security topic (e.g. cryptography, exploits, denial-of-service, etc.) so they can practise the skills they've learnt in class. Upon completion of the competition, the lecturer then dissects it with the students so they can identify what they did correctly, which further increases their learning to a deeper, more masterful level.

Jelena told me, 'In cybersecurity, our main challenges are not solely dictated by technological limitations, or the theoretical complexity of the underlying problems. Rather, cybersecurity advances are driven by a clash of minds – researchers create new defences and criminals adapt their attacks in response. This adversarial game is at the heart of each cybersecurity challenge, and as it's sadly absent from cybersecurity education, that's why we've created our platform with these online active learning education materials.'

As Jelena has just described, and we're repeatedly being told, success in cybersecurity comes from creativity of thought, an ability to make the right decisions quickly, to communicate effectively, and work in teams. As these skills are needed daily, the better equipped students are with them when they graduate, the more quickly and competently they can enter the workforce, and the more effective they can become at securing assets from increasingly harmful cyber threats. By using gamification, students can play out scenarios, learn from them, and the lessons can become more interesting and memorable.

Learning through gamification

For teens and children, gamification is certainly being heralded as the best way forward, and part of a broader hands-on learning approach that augments and expands upon more traditional classroom work. With a variety of games available already, from those that are role-based and interactive where children crack passwords, craft code, and defeat malicious hackers, to quizzes, the expectation is that these learning experiences will get children and teens more enthused about pursuing a career in cybersecurity and the quality of applicants will be uplifted.

Looking at CyPhinx, the brainchild of the Cybersecurity Challenge, which was modelled in part on World of Warcraft, we can see a learning tool that's being taken one stage further.[12] Designed for a wide age range, with users creating a character which they insert into a skyscraper in a virtual 3D world, the game serves as a portal to a number of other games that can be used to train and then test users in a variety of disciplines, including network defence, ethics, forensic analysis, and risk analysis. The games all vary in terms of complexity, styles, and levels of visual impact. For example, some are file downloads containing instructions, documents to decrypt, or fake websites to make safe from exploitable vulnerabilities, and others are richer and more visual.

However, what's unique and exciting about CyPhinx is that it offers more than just access to gameplay. Through a lobby area that's been designed as a virtual hub, cybersecurity talent and future employers have the opportunity to come together and provide learning experiences. Visitors can share ideas, consult each other on tips for games and competitions, be mentored, showcase their performance, and even meet and discuss employment opportunities. In time it's expected that CyPhinx will develop further and

12. https://cybersecuritychallenge.org.uk/cyphinx/

become a learning hub for all cyber talent in the UK, containing training and education opportunities, learning advice, and career enhancing opportunities such as lectures and walkthroughs for previous games.

What's fascinated me with these new online approaches to learning and development is the uptake in terms of women in security, and the gender division. At the beginning of 2016, I looked into how many women and girls played online games, as I was concerned gamification could appeal more to boys and men, thereby amplifying the gender disparity even more.

Having been introduced to technology through gaming when I was a child, I was relieved to find that this was not the case. In fact, studies show that adult women have taken over as the largest single demographic in gaming. Furthermore, according to a Pew survey, 'Teens, Technology and Friendship', with additional investigation by Kotaku, 60% of all teen girls play games – and a wide variety online, socially and by themselves.[13] [14] The reason more people aren't aware of this, and remain ignorant, is because most girls turn off their microphones when playing, largely to avoid abuse from male players. Only 9% of girls who play games online use voice chat.

Now I'm a huge fan of gamification and competitions, such as CCTF, as they're incredibly useful, but I have a caveat, especially when it comes to women in security. If we're to effect change and attract more women into cybersecurity, gamification needs to be used in a safe environment, such as the classroom, under expert guidance from a teacher or lecturer, and with clear and communicated objectives. The reason why is because of gender differences in attitudes to risk and competition.

---

13. http://www.pewinternet.org/2015/08/06/teens-technology-and-friendships/
14. http://kotaku.com/teenage-girls-are-playing-video-games-you-just-might-n-1724547085

Research suggests that women are often less likely to want to compete than men, and when they're used as a means to recruit, competitions can put many women off from entering. They can also affect their performance.

Evidence from neuroscience reveals that when people feel threatened or stressed, their reptilian brain (the limbic system), which sits in the centre of the brain, shuts down the prefrontal cortex, the part which learns, processes information, and makes executive decisions.[15] Attitudes to risk and competition is something that I'll discuss in more detail in Chapter 10, specifically in the context of women.

The role of the teacher and lecturer

Although technology has the power to transform education and student learning, it can only do so in certain environments. If the underlying belief is that learning will improve if students are only provided with direct access to learning and development technologies, the new teaching initiatives I've described in this chapter aren't going to work. Studies into MOOCs show that they're not delivering upon their objectives: course completion rates are typically fewer than 7%, often because of minimal contact with a lecturer or teacher, and the younger a learner is, the more guidance they require from a teacher.

Finland illustrates this perfectly. Coming out of an economically crippled agrarian society in the 1960s, and with a labour force that had stopped growing, the Finnish people knew that the future of their country in terms of economic growth depended on increasing knowledge skills and productivity. Furthermore, they couldn't leave any child behind if they were to prosper. So, they set about revising

---

15. http://www.patheos.com/blogs/camelswithhammers/2013/04/the-neuroscience-of-how-personal-attacks-shut-down-critical-thinking/

their whole education system, and started by consulting with the students and going into classrooms.

Although Finland is a small country with few immigrants, it has an incredible success story. It's consistently ranked highly for technical achievement by the UN and the World Economic Forum, and outperforms other countries in international tests, having been featured at the top of the Programme for International Student Assessment (PISA) administered by the Organisation for Economic Co-operation and Development (OECD) ever since it was first administered.[16] [17] The share of women gaining computer-related degrees is amongst the highest too, at 40%. Finland accredits its success primarily to investing in the quality of its teachers, along with some other bold approaches, which are in stark contrast to many other countries.[18]

Instead of using a compliance-based system, which unintentionally advocates what the minimum is that a student must do to get by, and how to memorise or repeat some basic knowledge or subject matter in order to excel in a test, in Finland it's more important to inspire students to want to learn, and to teach students how to think. Finland also believes in having a free education system, operating no single sexed schools, small class sizes, minimal homework, short school days, and long play-times. Creativity – Art, Drama, Dance and Music – is considered an essential and valuable part of a child's education. Additionally, children are not streamed, and there are no standardised tests until upper secondary when students have to demonstrate their knowledge on the country's matriculation exam in order to attend university or vocational training.

---

16. http://reports.weforum.org/global-information-technology-report-2016/report-highlights/

17. https://www.oecd.org/pisa/aboutpisa/

18. http://www.politico.com/story/2014/05/finland-school-system-107137#ixzz4LG9Ee8Do

Unlike much of the developed world that's now focusing on interactive, individualised learning experiences driven by new technology, teachers in Finland use a mixture of traditional and innovative teaching strategies in the classroom, but without a heavy reliance on technology. In fact, at some stages of the students' education, the reported use of technology by teachers in Finland has been the lowest in the European Union. Yet, this has no bearing on the uptake of those who go on to study Computer Science or producing students who are extremely competent technologists.

What does have a bearing is the ability to teach well. In many countries of the world, teaching is something you do if you can't get a job or want something to fit in with your family. There's often a stigma around teaching, and many of us know the saying, 'those who can, do; those who can't, teach.' In Finland, however, teachers are no longer considered mere assembly workers. They've become sought after knowledge workers who trust their students and work collaboratively with them for continuous innovation, ensuring all achieve at the very highest levels. Teaching is a revered and respected profession. It's highly paid, too, and only about 10% of those who apply to become teachers are accepted. Teacher training requires a master's degree and takes five years to complete. As a result, teacher training students are highly motivated and exceptionally well-educated.

In Finland, teachers understand what good looks like and are taught to be reflective enquiry teachers. The emphasis is on teaching students how to learn and think without imposing penalties for mistakes. The education system is built on the premise of equity and equality, as well as trust, which after three decades and hard work is now incorporated into Finland's culture. Students, parents, and the government, whom teachers work with hand-in-hand, and who have no bearing on assessing their performance in the classroom, trust them.

Being realistic, not all countries can operate education systems like Finland, as population density demands much larger classes and worse teacher-pupil ratios. So, going forward, when innovation, creativity, and independent thinking are increasingly crucial to the global economy, what exactly can we do to improve the situation?

One answer is obviously to induce our governments to revise the dominant model of education that's still fundamentally rooted in the Industrial Revolution that spawned it. Nowadays our requirements have totally changed. The system is obsolete as we value different metrics and no longer need to prepare students for the world of work in the same way we did before.

Right now, thanks to technology, we have no way of knowing what the jobs of the future will look like. That's why we need a new breed of educators, particularly for cybersecurity and technology, who are inspired by everything from the Internet to evolutionary psychology, neuroscience and artificial intelligence. We need teachers, particularly in primary schools, who can inspire, provide prompts without giving answers, and then step aside so students can discover the answer themselves or with one another. Essentially, we need to make learning fun, for if a student is interested, they'll learn. If we can teach them how to code, that's great, but we don't have to bombard them with vast amounts of technology in order to make progress.

Creating a new breed of educators

The work by Dr Sugata Mitra illustrates this, albeit radically. In 1999, he began an experiment which is known as 'The Hole in the Wall Project'.[19] Working as a Chief Scientist at NIIT in New Delhi, he wondered what would happen if he placed a freely accessible computer into a hole in the wall that separated his office from the adjoining slum in Kalkaji.

---

19. https://www.ted.com/talks/sugata_mitra_shows_how_kids_teach _themselves

Within a few hours, slum dwellers appeared, especially children. Having never seen a computer before, they quickly learnt to use it on their own. This prompted Dr Mitra to question whether 'the acquisition of basic computing skills by any set of children can be achieved through incidental learning provided the learners are given access to a suitable computing facility, with entertaining and motivating content and some minimal (human) guidance'.

Wanting more verification, but expecting a test result that disproved his theory, Dr Mitra took the project to another village 300 miles away. He tested whether Tamil speaking twelve-year-olds could learn the biotechnology of DNA replication in English (which they had no understanding of) by themselves in two months from a side street computer.

The results astonished him. Whilst the children believed that they'd not learnt anything despite visiting the computer every day, their test scores had risen from 0 to 30%. Fascinated, he wondered what would happen to their results if he introduced a teacher. However, he had one problem – there were none in the village. So, he asked a twenty-two-year-old accountant for her help.

She was worried, as she knew nothing about teaching or biotechnology, so he advised her to use 'the method of your grandmother – stand back and offer them praise'. After leaving her with the children for a few months, he returned to find out how they were getting on. To his bewilderment, when he tested them again, he found that their test scores had increased to 50% and were now exactly the same as children from the well-off Delhi schools.

Still unsatisfied, he repeated test after test with children aged between six and thirteen from remote villages in India, South Africa, and even the UK. He discovered that this age range could self-instruct in a connected environment but only if they were working together in groups. When he arrived in Newcastle in the UK, he asked for 200 grandmothers who would be prepared to volunteer 'over the cloud' for one hour per week. He called his experiment the Granny Cloud, and found that the recipe for successful learning outcomes was broadband mixed with collaboration and encouragement. Dr Mitra has defined this as a new way of learning: Minimally Invasive Education.

Technology, when used in the right context, has a powerful part to play in increasing learning objectives, which we can use in cybersecurity. Being increasingly affordable, and accessible to both individual learners and educators, it represents a solution that can be quicker and easier to deploy than recruiting proficient teachers with the necessary depth of knowledge in cybersecurity and Computer Science.

As the fiction writer, Arthur C. Clarke, once told Dr Mitra, 'A teacher who can be replaced by a machine, should be.' Technology can also offer a means to teach children, teens, and adults in areas around the world that are inaccessible, war ridden, or remote.

Whilst we must continue to develop technology as a learning tool, we mustn't lose sight of the importance of teacher education for technology and cybersecurity learners – those who've yet to qualify and those who are already in service. The prevailing priority for education policymakers still needs to be the teacher rather than simply rolling out technology solutions that could be seen as a universal shortcut to achieving higher school standards. Equally, the natural processes of child development and learning when a child is aged fourteen or younger are still seen to require a sound anchoring in human relationships and engagement with the world of people, ideas, and things. Technology cannot replace the teacher, who not only fulfils this role but also mediates the child's connection to the world of ideas and learning whilst factoring in their social environment.

From everything that I've seen and researched over the past year, I believe that we must continue to put pressure on our governments to improve the quality of our teachers, and to revise the education model so that it's better aligned to what we require. However, we mustn't wait for governments to take action. We need to take matters into our own hands by developing technology solutions for education, investing in them, and collaborating with partners. If we can pair technology with industry-led initiatives, we have a real chance of effecting change worldwide for cybersecurity learning.

Pairing technology with industry-led initiatives

The Raspberry Pi Foundation is doing just this, and has had enormous success. Its aim is to empower people all over the world, particularly children, so they're capable of understanding and shaping the digital world. It wants them to be able to solve the problems that matter to them, and equip them for jobs of the future.

The way it's doing this is by providing a series of low-cost, small single-board computers, and promoting the teaching of basic Computer Science in schools and developing countries. It provides outreach, free resources to help people learn about computers and coding, and trains educators who can then guide other people to learn. By September 2016, it had sold 10 million Raspberry Pis.

Companies like IBM, Cisco, Microsoft, and Symantec, which are at the forefront of cybersecurity skills training, are also developing initiatives. For example, in order to ensure that IBM gets the right staff, it's working (as an extension of its IBM Academic Initiative) with more than 200 educational institutions, and defining exactly what skills it wants to hone.

Cisco is spreading awareness about cybersecurity through its Cisco Networking Academy. Each year, it helps roughly 1 million people to develop technical skills and prepare for ICT careers. More than 9,000 institutions in more than 170 countries offer its curricula, which include courses on cybersecurity. It's also created cybersecurity groups that help build a network of mentorship and knowledge transfer, and it consistently reaches out to educational institutions to help with early education and awareness on cybersecurity issues. And, when it comes to women in cybersecurity, it sponsors the Women's Society of Cyberjutsu, which is helping to advance women and girls in the cybersecurity field.[20] [21]

Symantec Corporation also funded a girls' training initiative in the USA. In 2015, it invested in The American Association of University Women (AAUW), which had a remit to develop a cybersecurity core class for middle school girls interested in STEM. Through a successful week-long STEM summer camp programme they were able to expand the curriculum for the AAUW, which helped more than 1,600 girls at twenty one sites around the USA. They were also piloted at camps at Bowling Green State University in Ohio, Stanford University, and the University of California, Irvine.[22]

These companies are providing resources on scale, but there are many others that are also taking part and effecting change. The key thing to note is that it doesn't matter what size of organisation you are. What matters is that you play a part, and anything that you do will lead to transformation.

The Golden Rules

- Invest resources in educators to improve educational outcomes
- Teach students how to learn rather than what to learn
- Accept the limitations of technology in education
- Encourage educators to keep developing as fast as industry is changing, and be receptive to industry providing curriculum advice and support
- Lead the way for cybersecurity training rather than wait for governments to mandate curriculums or other solutions
- Ensure education is accessible for all, rather than just for privileged countries

---

20. http://womenscyberjutsu.org/
21. http://blogs.cisco.com/security/our-commitment-to-cybersecurity-education-and-training
22. http://www.aauw.org/article/symantec-cybersecurity/

7. HR Is Holding Us Back

- The problem cybersecurity has with HR
- The role of HR
- Understanding HR's turbulent history
- Measuring and tracking data
- Using data to inform decisions and reduce bias
- Learning to trust the data
- Quotas, targets, positive action, and positive affirmation

I never imagined myself in sales, let alone recruitment, but that's exactly what happened to me when I finally accepted that my art and design career was over almost two decades ago. With a degree in woven textile design, I knew that being able to work a loom, even if it was computerised, was not going to get me a job in an office. I therefore researched the market, looking for a course that could equip me with the necessary skills I'd need for an admin job.

A 'High Tech' secretarial course appealed, and over eleven weeks I learnt shorthand, typing, and word processing. After having a baby and working part-time in retail, I was happy to be engaging my brain again. I excelled in it, particularly at shorthand, and being rather competitive and a high achiever, I came top of my class, which was no surprise to those around me.

As I was unsure about what I wanted to do afterwards, I thought it sensible to temp for a while so I could determine the type of company I wanted to work for, and my way in. When a recruitment consultant from Hays came in to speak to my class about how to sign up for temp work, I paid attention. I was completely unaware that a few weeks later I'd be working with her as her protégé.

Nothing could have prepared me for the work that was to follow – the gruelling, long days, the daily 100 cold calls, the internal rather than external competition for placing candidates, the self-promotion for acknowledgement or career advancement, and the threat of losing my job for not meeting my sales target. It was all extremely uncomfortable for an introvert, but as the months went by, I learnt, adapted, survived, and then thrived. Supporting my son drove me. This practical need helped to focus my mind whenever things got tough.

I have much to thank Hays for. For a start, I had a good grounding in how to run a business, how to sell, negotiate, present, compete, form alliances, and push myself forward. Importantly, I was also taught how to hire, and this is one of the reasons why I'm particularly intolerant to shoddy recruitment practices amongst recruiters, HR practitioners, and hiring managers.

Here's a good example.

The problem cybersecurity has with HR

A few months ago, I was sitting with Mark, a senior cybersecurity leader from a financial services company, talking about gender diversity and one of the challenges we have – recruitment. He nodded his head knowingly, and then proceeded to tell me about what had happened when he'd recently recruited for a vacancy. He'd advertised the position internally, and after several interviews selected his candidate, who happened to be a woman.

She started, worked diligently, and he was over the moon at finding the right person for his team. However, when he noticed that she wasn't earning the salary that she should have been, he approached HR to correct this. HR refused. He was dismayed, thought this unfair, and told the HR people quite plainly that if they didn't increase her salary immediately, he'd have to report it as 'gender discrimination'. He argued that HR had taken advantage of this woman for years when she should have been on the same pay grade as her male peers, as they were all doing exactly the same job. As a result of his insistence, the HR people corrected her salary immediately. However, they didn't apologise for having taken advantage of her, or backdate her pay, and to this day she remains unaware.

The practice of paying women less than men in cybersecurity is persistent. Over the last year, it's become increasingly clear to me that when it comes to attracting and retaining the numbers of women in cybersecurity, one business function is holding us back – HR. Multiple stakeholders report issues, from hiring managers and employees to applicants and recruitment consultants. No one is happy.

HIRING MANAGERS, typically senior cybersecurity leaders or CISOs, have told me, 'Jane, I've got a three-month window of opportunity before HR gets involved. I'd like to recruit a more diverse team. Can you help?' Or, 'HR is driving me mad. It's taken me months to find the perfect candidate, but HR is refusing to let me pay them what they're worth. If I can't do that, I'm going to lose them, and then I'm back to square one.' Or, 'HR won't increase her pay grade more than 35%, but it'll increase his by 42%. If she finds out, we'll lose her.' Or, 'HR doesn't understand my requirements. It's doing keyword searches, and I found out recently that unless the candidate has the word "cybersecurity" on their CV, HR is rejecting them despite them having relevant security experience.' Or, 'HR is insisting that we only use its preferred agencies, but they don't specialise in security, have no idea what the job involves, and the candidates they're selecting are simply unsuitable. Yet, I've got to abide with its ridiculous process, which loses me time, before I can prove it's ineffective and instigate my own.'

FEMALE EMPLOYEES who've had an issue in their workplace, and have reported it to HR, have said, 'HR doesn't want to know. It's not interested in gender bias, or sexual discrimination. I've just reported what's gone on, and HR is not going to do anything about it. It's clear I've got a choice – to put up and shut up or move on. It's farcical, especially as HR says it's committed to gender diversity and has set targets that it's promoting.' Or, 'For months I've been taken advantage of by my manager. He's shirked work, passed it on to me, and then claimed credit for it. He's played truant, too, and I've been subjected to bullying tactics if I've objected to any of his unreasonable demands. When I thought it was time to report this, I found myself in front of HR, and my manager. I went through disciplinary proceedings, which ultimately ended up with me being asked to leave.'

WOMEN APPLYING FOR JOBS have said, 'I've applied, attended an interview, but I've not heard back from HR. I don't know what's going on, and HR won't return my calls or emails.' Or, 'HR people have just asked me about what provisions I have for my children, as the job requires travelling abroad and long hours. However, I know they didn't ask the fathers who applied, as we compared notes.' Or, 'I've just attended the most ridiculous interview, where I was made to complete a mathematics test. As a CISO, with twenty years' experience and certifications, I didn't expect that. I find this process nonsensical, as it's not required for the role.' Some female applicants have even discovered that the reason HR didn't shortlist them was because they were women, and HR presumed they wouldn't be interested in working late or the travelling.

RECRUITMENT CONSULTANTS are frustrated too. They've told me, 'It's a sellers' market, and candidates, especially female candidates, are in short supply and in demand. HR has a total lack of understanding of this, and the security market in general. It shows little proactivity in terms of understanding it, either.' Or, 'HR focuses far too much on certifications.' Or, 'HR is a reactive function of the business. It lacks vision, and strategic insight. It's mostly administrative, and if it does get involved, usually it's to block.' Or, 'HR adds no value, gives hiring managers no training on how to write job descriptions that are gender neutral, or on how to interview without bias. When candidates are put in front of these managers, this can be a mess.' Or, 'With the volume of jobs that are available, we're having to headhunt candidates, and coax them into considering a job. Many don't want to move, and getting them to an interview is hard work. Then, when we actually get them there, HR is jeopardising our hard work. Instead of selling candidates the opportunity when they're being interviewed, HR is behaving as if they've got multiple applicants and only focusing on getting the candidates to answer why they should be hired.' Or, 'It's no wonder thousands of jobs remain unfilled. If HR people, or the hiring managers for that matter, were open to training candidates, who may not have all of the skills that they're looking for right now, they'd find that they'd fill their jobs faster, achieve the required competency in a relatively short period, and at a fraction of the cost.'

The feedback is alarming, and when human capital and cybersecurity are both boardroom priorities, this ought to be investigated. However, some say there's a paradox. Being responsible for business performance, HR is the corporate function that consistently under delivers. Although HR complaints are often cyclical – for example, when hiring managers are struggling to find talent, it's seen as a valued business function, and when things are going smoothly, everyone wonders what HR actually does – the problem we have in cybersecurity right now is that this is not the case. We're struggling to identify and retain talent, and HR is not helping. In fact, it's holding the business back, and if we can't find talent to secure our business assets then you could argue that HR is a threat to the business, as it's exposing it to unnecessary risk.

HR should be helping by designing and developing strategic processes and procedures; running communication campaigns that attract the best talent from the job market; retaining talent with attractive compensation packages and working environments; heading off problems with regulations and staff turnover; building corporate culture; addressing morale problems; and nurturing talent that's left but could return – but most are not. Instead, most HR practitioners have alienated themselves from cybersecurity professionals to the brink of obsolescence. They're viewed as being competent administrators of pay, benefits, redundancy, and retirement, but little else. They're seen as working reactively, rather than proactively. And, by measuring vanity metrics they provide no insight, or actionable, relevant information for us. Clearly, something is broken, and over the past year, through my research, I've sought to understand exactly what's going on. Here's what I've discovered.

The role of HR

Let's start with what HR actually pursues – efficiency, and it's prioritised over value. The reason why is simple – it's easier to measure. HR can readily provide the numbers of people who join and leave, the percentage of performance appraisals completed, and the extent to which employees are satisfied or not with their benefits. However, HR rarely links any of these metrics to business performance. And, this is perplexing. Why not?

Equally perplexing is the misconception of whom it serves – the business. It doesn't work for the employees, and consequently there's tension. Responsible for protecting the business's people assets, HR has to ensure that the business complies with workforce legislation. As a result, HR says 'No' more often and pursues standardisation and uniformity in the face of a workforce that's heterogeneous and complex. In HR's view, exceptions expose the business to risk and charges of bias, plus they require more than rote solutions and are, therefore, time-consuming and expensive to manage.

In cybersecurity, we understand this, but change still needs to occur. The challenge needs to be resolved, as exceptions drive the business. Companies keep their best employees by acknowledging and rewarding remarkable performance, and not by treating everyone the same. But, HR continues to work in this manner – to benchmark salaries, function-by-function and job-by-job against industry standards, keeping pay, even that of its top performers, within a narrow band determined by competitors. It stands rigid on bonuses or pay increases when managers request them during performance appraisals, or when they've found sought-after talent that merits a different pay grade.

HR forfeits long-term value in favour of short-term cost efficiency, and whilst its behaviour is understandable, it shouldn't be beyond reproach. There's much room for improvement, especially as so little has been done in the past half century to examine the value of widely used HR practices.

Understanding HR's turbulent history

HR has always had a turbulent history with the business thanks to the economy, and it's worth understanding what's gone on, as this brings us insight and enables us to address what can be done now, and what to plan for in the future.

HR really started with the Industrial Revolution in Britain in the 18th Century. As large factories emerged, efficient production became a priority. Factories hired thousands of workers, who toiled in harsh conditions, and often up to sixteen hours a day. Women and children were used regularly, as they were cheap forms of labour and enabled higher profit margins.

Factories were unsafe and appalling places to work, but when factory owners discovered a correlation between their workforce's happiness and productivity, many began to modify their environments. Real progress was made when the government intervened and introduced some fundamental human rights and work safety legislation.

By the beginning of the 20th Century, most organisations had a personnel department that dealt with employee related issues, and ensured compliance to the newly introduced work safety laws. By the 1920s, when the world's economy was booming, and workers were crucial to business, personnel departments started to make their executives treat their employees well.

However, progress was set back with the Great Depression, as workers were forced to put up with anything to stay employed. Line managers took advantage of the situation, and complained that personnel departments were getting in the way of production. At that time, line managers had enormous influence over the business, and were able to push forward the 'drive system' – a method that involved threatening workers, or beating them if they failed to perform.

After World War II, with a pressure to build the economy, a new talent shortage, and an urgent need to develop and retain a workforce, companies brought in revolutionary practices such as coaching, developmental assignments, job rotation, 360-degree feedback, assessment centres, high-potential tracks, and succession plans. By the 1950s, huge transformation had occurred, and virtually all positions, including those in the top ranks, were filled from within. Large companies dedicated an entire department, HR, to planning for their workforce's needs.[1]

Since then things have changed considerably. Most of today's hires are external, and most large businesses use recruitment agencies to fill their vacancies. They also spend less time on developing

---

1. https://hbr.org/2015/07/why-we-love-to-hate-hr-and-what-hr-can-do -about-it

their internal talent pool and forecasting their future talent needs. The reason why is because a new mode of working set in during the economic slump of the 1970s. During that period, many businesses made redundancies, and as labour was readily accessible, most undid the post-war programmes that they'd previously designed to develop talent.

New companies, especially those in tech, like Apple and Microsoft, led the way for others and hired a ready-made workforce without having to make a training and development investment. The view many executives held was why should they train people when their competitors were willing to do it for them?

They had a point.

Then, during the recession of the 1980s, HR lost even more influence, and executives were given the tasks that HR had traditionally performed, like hiring, development, reviews, and compensation. But, being responsible for managing larger teams, they soon discovered that they had neither the training nor the time to do these tasks properly. When the economy picked up during the dotcom boom, around the late 1990s, and competition was rife for talent, HR was called upon again to help executives attract and retain it. Businesses valued HR's skill, as they needed to be seen as the 'employer of choice'. However, when the dotcom boom bubble burst a few years later, HR lost influence yet again, and thanks to the Great Recession of 2008, it's remained in this position until now.

With so much variance of HR's responsibilities whenever the economy has shrunk or expanded, and with it typically reporting to the Chief Financial Officer whose interest is in saving money and cost cutting, it's hardly surprising that so many employees and leaders feel suspicious of HR, or that it's meddling whenever it gets involved. Despite this, if we're going to transform the numbers of women in cybersecurity, and successfully protect the business assets, HR has to become a trusted partner. We must find a win-win solution, and build a bridge.

So, what's the best way forward?

Measuring and tracking data

The first thing we can do is to acknowledge the importance of meaningful data and metrics. If we don't determine what we need to measure and why, then all this signals is that it doesn't count or that it can't be fixed. We therefore have to apply a new rule, 'what gets measured improves', and base our decisions on data and evidence.

Like most things, showing works far better than telling, particularly when a financial value can be attributed to the consequences of not investing in gender equality. And, as businesses are always keen to maximise their financial performance, by capturing certain data, and correlating it to gender or other demographics, we can make things much easier for ourselves.

Unless you're Google, or a high tech business that's already using big data and analytics for HR, you may want to start by tracking what you're doing, why you're doing it a certain way, what will happen if you keep things as they are, and what to do in order to maximise good outcomes and prevent bad outcomes. You might, therefore, seek to obtain the following data:

- Where are you short on talent?
- What characteristics and skills (not certifications) do you really need in order to plug your talent gap?
- How will you measure if the plug is working?
- How are you attracting talent?
- Where do your new recruits come from?
- What demographics are you attracting, and are they the same at the onboarding stage?
- What's the cost to attract talent and onboard it?
- What's the timeframe for new recruits to become productive?
- What are your attrition levels?
- When do they occur and why?

- What's the financial impact?
- Why does one person outperform others?
- What impact do your training programmes have on your revenue?
- Why do certain employees succeed and others fail?
- How happy is your team?
- Is there a correlation between the team's happiness and performance or productivity?

Once you've captured this information, you can share it with HR, and work with them to compile even more meaningful data than that which they may already be capturing, typically from annual performance appraisals, leavers and joiners, etc. Furthermore, I'd encourage you to be aware of new technology advancements that will improve your people decisions. I'm referring to people analytics, one of the few tools that promises to revolutionise HR management, particularly in regards to gender equality.

Using data to inform decisions and reduce bias

People analytics, which is also known as talent analytics or HR analytics, is a method of analytics that helps managers and executives to make decisions about their employees. By collecting data from an individual at the beginning of their hiring process until their last day of employment, and using complex applications to measure relationships between variables and detect patterns and trends, it exists so you can find better applicants, make smarter hiring decisions, and increase employee performance and retention.

When it's predictive, it can advise you as to the real reasons why people apply for a job, at what point in the application process they reached their decisions, and the parts of your branding proposition that are resonating, or not. It can help you ascertain whether your boss was correct when he said that English Literature graduates with first class honours degrees from the top universities in your country make the best security analysts, or whether personnel from a military background highly correlate with performance in information security leadership. Unless you measure, you won't know. People analytics provides evidence, and helps you to check the intuitive associations you make.

With this information, identifying characteristics for high-performing consulting, delivery, and leadership teams, selecting suitable applicants, predicting compliance risks, and analysing flight risk, engagement, and culture becomes not only much easier, but much more diverse.

As you'd expect, giant tech companies are applying data analytics to staffing faster than any other sector, and the methods they're using will likely set new norms for the way we all work in the future. Companies such as Google, Microsoft, Apple and Netflix have literally ripped up the rulebook on HR, and are pioneering HR innovation. They're using people analytics, workforce analytics, and other methods largely because they have a dire need for specialised skills in a competitive talent market. They understand that human capital is their key differentiator, their major asset, and they don't just play lip service to this. They walk the talk.[2][3][4][5]

Take Google. Changing the name of its HR department to People Operations, or POPs for short, Google is famous for its pioneering HR approach, and use of data to support its people decisions. Running a bit like an 'employee science lab' under the direction of Lazlo Bock, Google constantly runs experiments and tracks data to optimise performance and procedures. Like most tech companies,

---

2. https://www.eremedia.com/tlnt/how-google-is-using-people-analytics
-to-completely-reinvent-hr/
3. https://www.microsoft.com/itshowcase/Article/Content/582/Moder
nizing-HR-at-Microsoft
4. https://hbr.org/2014/01/how-netflix-reinvented-hr
5. http://www.furstperson.com/blog/a-quick-overview-of-people-and
-workforce-analytics

men dominate in the gender of employees, yet executives continue to make concerted efforts to address the gender gap by attracting and retaining more women.

When the data told Google that twice as many women were leaving the company as men, and that they had a happiness problem, Google investigated further. Its reasoning was not on account of gender equity or unhappiness, but because this situation was affecting the company's bottom line. By analysing the data, it discovered that its issue was not with women but with new mothers.

At that time, Google offered new mothers an industry-standard maternity leave of twelve weeks, and seven weeks of paid leave for all new parents who worked in its California office. Armed with new data-driven insights, Bock changed the maternity plan so that new mothers would get five months off at full pay and full benefits. They were also allowed to split up that time so they could take some time off before giving birth if they wanted. Furthermore, he extended the seven weeks of paid leave to all new parents globally.

The changes were successful and resulted in a 50% reduction in the attrition rate for new mothers, which put them back in line with the average rate for the rest of the company. Importantly too, it was cost effective, for the new policies resulted in savings when recruitment fees, lost productivity, and unhappiness were factored in.

Google's approach is encouraging in lots of ways. Many companies would have just examined the data and determined that women of childbearing age were too expensive to employ. Google didn't, and you can bet that the reason why is because it understands the true value that women bring to its business. It's also because Google's HR management approach is driven by a thirsty ambition.

Prasad Setty, who leads Google's people analytics, says, 'What we try to do is bring the same level of rigour to people decisions that we do to engineering decisions. Our mission is to have all people decisions be informed by data.'

For a tech company, such as Google, it makes perfect sense

to work in this way – to implement sophisticated employee-data tracking technologies and then have the results analysed by a team of social and behavioural economic scientists and analysts. It can then make confident decisions that are based on firm evidence about every aspect of a Google employee's life.

And, Google delves deeper into its data than most. For example, it's not just tracking and analysing the ideal compensation plan, but it's also assessing criteria such as what constitutes the optimal productive environment? What's the length of the interview process? Which employees are most likely to become a retention problem? Which job applicants have the highest probability of succeeding once they're hired? What's the value of the top performers and the cost associated with the performance disparity? What's the best value of workplace design?

By using technology, Google is capturing what many would view as trivial, irrelevant data, such as the size and shape of the cafeteria tables or the length of employees' lunch lines, but whatever it captures, it makes relatable to the goals of the company.

Few companies will invest in data analytics for their people decisions as much as Google, but many will do it on smaller scales. Take Marketo, a marketing automation software company. When it used an organisational development tool from Glint Inc., it was able to retain more women employees. By sending out 'pulses', or short surveys, it discovered that women in one of its departments were ranking their work-life balance substantially lower than others. Upon investigation, it found a staffing shortage in that area, and took immediate action by increasing staff before significant attrition became problematic. The analytics not only helped Marketo link actions to outcomes, but also to translate the situation into meaningful data and communicate a story.

Black Hills Corp., an energy conglomerate, saw positive results when it too adopted data analytics to help its people decisions. When it doubled its workforce to about 2,000 employees after an acquisition, it encountered several challenges – an ageing work-force, a need for specialised skills, and a lengthy timeline for getting employees to full competence. With a significant talent risk looming that portrayed a future turnover disaster – within five years the company was on course to lose 8,063 years of experience from its workforce – it used workforce analytics to calculate how many employees would retire per year, the types of workers needed to replace them, and where its new hires were most likely to come from.

Another story from McKinsey & Co. is also of interest, and one that we can learn from. When it began developing its own approach to retention via technology, it was surprised by the results. It expected factors such as an individual's performance rating or compensation to be the top predictors of unwanted attrition. However, its analysis revealed that it was actually because of a lack of mentoring, coaching, and 'affiliation' with people who had similar interests that caused the attrition. Unsurprisingly, when it addressed this and successfully implemented programmes, its flight risk reduced by 20% to 40%.[6]

Data analytics is powerful. Not only can it help to uncover the real problem for attracting and retaining talent, but it can also banish bias. When Hays surveyed more than 1,000 hiring managers in Australia on the attributes and suitability of a candidate, it was unprepared for the results. Having created two identical CVs under the names Susan and Simon, it sent half of the hiring managers Simon's CV and the other half Susan's. It discovered that in large companies (over 500 employees), 62% of hiring managers said they'd interview Simon whilst only 56% said the same about Susan. Smaller companies revealed similar preferences.

With further probing, Hays found that hiring managers who recruited more than twenty people per year also favoured Simon

6. http://www.mckinsey.com/business-functions/organization/our -insights/power-to-the-new-people-analytics

over Susan (65% versus 51%). Moreover, the data showed that the hiring managers, no matter their gender, were recruiting in their own image. However, despite this, in the end they all selected to interview and hire Simon.[7]

As we know from Chapter 2, unconscious bias is a huge problem, and we all have it. Whether we're aware of these biases or not makes little difference. Biased decisions will always occur, and research shows that people who say they don't have unconscious beliefs actually make more biased decisions than those who acknowledge their unconscious beliefs. Furthermore, if we try to address it through training, it can lead to several issues.

The first is moral licensing, where people respond to having done something good by doing something bad, and this can make it worse. Whilst there have been countless studies into moral licensing, whenever I'm explaining it, I usually use a health and fitness analogy.

Whilst we may know fitness fanatics who frequent the gym and are toned and buff, most of us know more people who go in an effort to shed a few kilos, but either remain the same weight or gain more. The reason this happens is because of moral licensing. When people think that they're enjoying the benefits of exercising and doing something good, they grant themselves a moral licence to eat more.[8]

The second issue is that people routinely fall victim to the halo effect, a cognitive bias named by psychologist Edward Thorndike, in which an observer's overall impression of a person, company, brand, or product influences their feelings and thoughts about that person's character or thing's properties. Halo effects are widespread

---

7. http://www.news.com.au/finance/work/careers/the-same-resume-wi
th-different-names-nets-different-results/news-story/a2a182fb4570e948c2
7ce63139ee66b1
8. https://www.pickthebrain.com/blog/moral-licensing-how-being-good
-can-make-you-bad/

and, as I'll discuss later, have been proven to alter a person's views in a job interview.

Only by using data analytics and structured processes can we enable change. Whenever I'm speaking to senior cybersecurity leaders or HR about recruitment, I recommend focusing on the values and behavioural traits of the candidates they need in addition to, or at the exclusion of, core skills, depending on the job role. By determining what good looks like for an organisation, and then using assessments that involve complex algorithms to compile, process, and compare the fundamental values, behavioural compatibility, and diversity, we can predict the potential strength of the interpersonal relationship between those who apply for our jobs and those we hire, and bypass any initial bias in the hiring process. This is extremely useful.

Hopefully, you can now see how data analytics can be used positively and in a number of different areas – sales and recruitment, productivity, compliance and risk, and culture. However, although the potential of data analytics to help close the gender gap is huge, and that's what this book is all about, it also serves another purpose, which is particularly relevant for us in cybersecurity.

Data analytics can help us to mitigate our insider threat by identifying employees who are, or are more likely to become, 'toxic' (lie, cheat, break the rules, develop unethical behaviour, commit crimes, or go rogue), and this benefit can increase our justification for its implementation. Figuratively speaking, if we use it well, data analytics may give us the ability to kill two birds with one stone.

Learning to trust the data

This thought leaves me excited. However, not everyone's like me. Often there's an aversion to technology that uses algorithmic judgments, and many people remain sceptical. They'll question whether a machine can really be better than a human mind, and if it makes mistakes – even if they're only occasional – can it be trusted?

A group of researchers from Wharton School decided to find out, and to discover not only why people failed to use this type of technology, especially when they knew it consistently outperformed human forecasters, but also how their aversion to it could be overcome. What the researchers learnt was that during financially incentivised forecasting tasks, people were considerably more likely to choose to use an algorithm, and consequently perform better, but only when they could modify its forecasts, even if these modifications were severely restricted.

It turns out that giving people the freedom to do this is the key. It makes them feel more empowered, more tolerant of errors and satisfied with the forecasting process. And, as a result, they're more likely to believe that the algorithm is, in fact, superior to a human brain, and more likely to choose to use it to make subsequent forecasts.[9]

Finally, although I urge you to consider using people analytics if you can, for all its promise, it's not a silver bullet to solving our gender diversity issue in cybersecurity, or eliminating the problem we currently have with HR. There are still risks when it's implemented as data collection invades our privacy, and it can be tempting and sometimes inaccurate to make causal interpretations based on correlation. The methodology that's used is of paramount importance, as is the quality of the people assessing the data. And, no matter how much care you take in designing it, false positives may occur and need to be investigated.

When I spoke to one CIO, she concurred and told me, 'I had a leadership vacancy, and four internal candidates were encouraged to apply. Three were women, and as the senior leadership team had worked with all of the candidates, we knew their capabilities. However, we were all surprised by the results of the data analytics,

---

9. https://marketing.wharton.upenn.edu/mktg/assets/File/Dietvorst%20
-Overcoming%20Algorithm%20Aversion.pdf

and couldn't understand what had happened as the candidate who came top in the assessment was by far the weakest. Rather than modifying anything at that point, I promoted all four applicants, and got rid of some contract staff to offset the cost. I then worked with HR to revise the assessment.'

HR has a useful part to play in helping cybersecurity leaders move forward with more female talent, but only if we work in collaboration. As Christine Maxwell, Governance, Risk & Compliance Director at BP, says, 'They have to listen to the business, and feel the pain. If they don't understand our market, particularly the nuances surrounding pay grades and salaries, we're in trouble. Providing salary benchmarking as proof and selling it to HR can help them to be persuaded.'

Quotas, targets, positive action, and positive affirmation

Quotas and targets are typically used interchangeably whenever gender diversity is discussed, so it's important to know exactly what they are. A target is a specific, measurable objective, generally set by an organisation within a timeframe. A quota is like a target, but it's a mandated outcome that must be achieved. It's also usually imposed on an organisation by an external body with authority, and includes penalties for failing to meet it.

When it comes to meeting gender diversity targets or quotas, one of the challenges that arises is positive action or affirmation verses positive discrimination, and what's lawful. Positive discrimination is unlawful in the UK. It's where an employer recruits a person (in this case a woman) because she's a relevant protected characteristic rather than because she is the best candidate for the job. Positive action is lawful. It is a term that's used in the UK, and is permitted if it's enabling or encouraging people who share a protected characteristic to participate in an activity in which their participation is disproportionately low, for example women in cybersecurity.

Affirmative action is also lawful. It's a term that's typically used in the USA for the policy of favouring individuals who share characteristics, for example women, which currently, or historically, cause them to experience unequal treatment in employment-related decisions. Affirmative action enables organisations to proactively hire, promote, or increase in representation certain classes of people, and some federal laws mandate it.

The main differences between the UK and USA are that in the USA tough action can and, in some instances, must be taken to advance women, whereas in the UK (other than a few exceptions) this would be deemed unlawful. In the UK, hiring targets are not unlawful, but hiring quotas would give rise to the risk of unlawful positive discrimination claims. Obviously, all countries' (or in some cases states') laws are different, so it's essential to validate what's lawful and unlawful when taking action to recruit.

The message of this chapter is this: we can't give up on people if we're to eliminate gender discrimination in cybersecurity, but we can work in partnership with advanced technology to bridge the gap of inclusion. HR has an important part to play in helping us attract and retain more women in cybersecurity. Only by using their skilled services will we see an improvement. We cannot transform alone.

The Golden Rules for security leaders

- Meet with HR to find out what it's doing and whether it can help
- Take the lead and decide what data you're going to measure so you can understand patterns and trends
- Analysis is one of your key strengths, so analyse the data and tweak what you're measuring accordingly
- Make sure you have competent resource to support you, be that from HR, marketing, behavioural economics or risk

- Tell a better story with the data you've captured
- Ensure you share information with HR, and don't leave them out
- Talk to your team regularly so you understand their mindsets, challenges, and needs
- Don't rely purely on technology even if you have it for your people decisions
- Routinely review performance ratings and pay grades by gender to check for disparities that translate into differences in opportunities
- Call out poor HR practices such as inconsistencies with pay grades

The Golden Rules for HR

- Learn about cybersecurity by taking an introductory course – in the UK there's one specifically for HR, which takes seventy-five minutes and is free[10]
- Be proactive and reach out to the cybersecurity department to see if you can help it with its people decisions
- Seek to understand the immediate pressures that the cybersecurity department is facing, and work together to make a compelling evidence-based case for what matters
- Review what you're doing when it comes to attracting and retaining women in security
- Determine who's at risk of resigning
- Remember that you share some common objectives with cybersecurity, and may be able to share budgets in order to meet them

Thanks for reading Part One. Now you know more about the assumptions and how important a change agent you can be. If

---

10. https://www.gov.uk/government/collections/cyber-security-training -for-business

you've not taken our pledge yet go here: https://bit.ly/in-security-pledge.

PART TWO
The Challenges

Challenge One: Attraction

8. Hoot The Horn

- The merits of Corkscrew Thinking
- How the media has influenced women in cybersecurity
- How marketing has influenced women in cybersecurity
- Assessing buying needs and building personas
- Transitioning into cybersecurity
- How to build a pipeline
- Marketing to girls and their influencers
- Initiatives to get girls interested
- How to publicise our marketing efforts
- Repackaging and over correcting

My father is sighing. It's a regular occurrence whenever I mention his least favourite topic – gender diversity. It starts a heated debate.

I'm particularly interested in what he has to say, as his profession, civil engineering, like cybersecurity, is working hard to attract more female talent. I hear his views, and all about the work that civil engineering is doing to encourage more young women into the field, and I draw comparisons with what's going on in cybersecurity. I'm also paying attention as the two professions are essentially in competition.

Then my mother pipes up, 'You can't force women into a technical field if they're not interested.' I'm in agreement, but I also contend that we're not marketing cybersecurity effectively, and that women have played a significant role in it for decades. I refer to Ada Lovelace, who's often heralded as the first programmer. Then, to World War II, upon which point I take her back to that time.

It's cold, it's London, and it's January 1942. Britain is sixteen months into World War II and a string of letters have just landed on the editor's desk at *The Daily Telegraph*. Apparently, the paper's crosswords aren't difficult enough and can be solved in a matter of minutes.

The notion is quite frankly preposterous, so the Chairman of the Eccentric Club, a man called WAJ Gavin, suggests that the crosswords be put to a test. He offers a £100 reward, which is to be donated to charity, to anyone who can solve the crossword in fewer than twelve minutes. The competition is advertised and then held in the newsroom on Fleet Street. When five people beat the time, the story, along with the crossword, is printed in the next day's edition, so other readers can try their hand. Its purpose is merely to entertain, and had it not been for a certain prying eye, that's all it would have done.

However, unbeknown to anyone, the War Office is watching, and several of the winners are invited to see officials as a matter of 'national importance'. Shortly after being interviewed, many find themselves at Bletchley Park, working for the government, breaking German military codes.

The humble crossword served as a great recruiting tool for Bletchley Park, which during World War II was being run by the Government Code and Cypher School (GC&CS). By the end of the war, many of its 10,471 workers, 7,000 of whom were women, had either been recruited this way, or straight out of school or university because they were linguists, translators, mathematicians, or chess champions. Apparently crosswords, where the player has to make connections between letters and words, require the same sort of lateral thinking ability as ciphering code. With a need to get inside the mind of the opponent and think differently, the War Office found crossword experts particularly suitable for this task, especially for taking up a defence position in signalling and intelligence.

The merits of Corkscrew Thinking

During the war, the Allies found themselves in a situation of stalemate with the Germans. Both sides thought that they could outsmart one another by relying on their linear thinking and problemsolving skills. However, as they were both thinking in the same manner, all that happened was that the stalemate continued.

Winston Churchill soon realised that in order to win the war, the War Office had to think unconventionally, and in a way that the Germans wouldn't expect. He called this Corkscrew Thinking, which involved creative problem solving, and doing more with less. It became his secret weapon, and he recruited creative thinkers from a wide range of professions and backgrounds, from Alan Turing, who was gay and most likely autistic, to Ian Fleming, who was a writer and the author of the *James Bond* books, to top women code breakers like Mavis Batey, Margaret Rock and Joan Clarke to develop unconventional plans and solutions to defeat the Germans.

The environment at Bletchley Park was exceptional, especially for women as they were valued and suffered less discrimination. They undertook a multitude of roles, too, from the Y-Service, which intercepted enemy codes, to the code breakers, Bombe and Colossus operators, administrators, clerks, cooks, cleaners, maintenance workers, dispatch riders, and transportation staff. Some women worked alongside men, and others, like 'Dilly's Girls', didn't. Instead, they worked as an all-female unit at the request of Dillwyn 'Dilly' Knox, an Enigma machine cypher. He claimed that men were too easily distracted, and whether Dilly was on to something with that or not, his 'Girls' broke the Abwehr Enigma machine, which allowed Britain to control the German spy network and feed misinformation back to the Germans. According to historians, they shortened the war by two to three years, saving thousands of lives.[1] [2]

The women at Bletchley Park weren't alone in their computing and security efforts. At this time, too, women were programming the US Army's Electronic Numerical Integrator And Computer (ENIAC), which today is recognised as the first electronic general-purpose computer. Hedy Lamarr, a Hollywood actress and inventor, was developing a new torpedo guidance system for the U.S. Navy, which used spread spectrum and frequency hopping technology to counter signal jamming. Although not used until decades later, the principles of her work have been incorporated into modern Wi-Fi, CDMA and Bluetooth technology.

A few years later, in 1952, Grace Hopper came up with the first computer compiler, and established the programming language COBOL. Mary Keller helped develop BASIC, and Radia Perlman built some of the early Internet's protocols. In 1958, Elsie Shutt founded one of the first software businesses in the USA, Comp Inc., and a year later Dina St Johnston set up the first British software company, Vaughan Programming Services.

In 1962, Dame Steve Shirley followed suit and started another British software company, Freelance Programmers (later renamed Xansa), where 98% of the workforce was female, and working around family commitments. By the time the company was acquired by Steria in 2007, it had 8,500 employees, was valued at over $3 billion, and had made over seventy employees millionaires.[3] In 1967, working in computing was so attractive that *Cosmopolitan* magazine wrote an article called 'The Computer Girls'[4] which proclaimed:

1. http://www.huffingtonpost.co.uk/2015/01/25/bletchley-park-enigma
-female-codebreakers_n_6532856.html
2. https://www.google.com/culturalinstitute/beta/exhibit/QQZ2YSRa
3. https://en.wikipedia.org/wiki/Steve_Shirley
4. https://www.siliconrepublic.com/people/women-in-technology-the
-computer-girls-cosmopolitan

'Now have come the big, dazzling computers – and a whole new kind of work for women: programming'.

By the 1980s, numbers of women in technology were at an all-time high of 38%, and security was on a roll. Women like Becky Bace, known informally as the 'den mother of computer security', was directing research in information security for the US Department of Defense and teaching the first generations of cybersecurity professionals.

Pioneers like these women should have multiplied. However, they didn't, and since then, there's been a steady decline.[5] It's an absurd situation to be in, especially at a time when cybersecurity is well paid (often on a par with or higher than doctors', lawyers', engineers', and accountants' salaries), women in many parts of the world are outperforming men in higher education, attending university at twice the rate of their male peers, and governments are prioritising and subsidising STEM subjects. But whilst the situation is improving for some STEM subjects, it's not for Technology, which creates a pipeline of cybersecurity professionals. One reason could be because of the way it's being portrayed in the media and marketed.

How the media has influenced women in cybersecurity

Going back to the 1980s, when the numbers of women in technology started to decline, PCs were mass marketed as 'boys' toys'. Then movies like *Tron* in 1982, *War Games* in 1983, and *Weird Science* in 1985, featuring male computer hacker heroes, surfaced to enforce the male stereotypes. Since then, aside from Acid Burn in the film *Hackers*, perceptions of security have remained largely fixated on a geeky, hard-core tech, isolationist, and male image.

Dennis Nedry from *Jurassic Park* serves as a perfect example.

---

5. http://www.scmagazine.com/2014-women-in-it-security-becky-bace/article/360957/

He's easy to remember, as he's a sweaty, overweight, nerdy untrust-worthy, computer programmer, who disables security systems in order to traffic dinosaur embryos out of the park. Boris Grishenko, the Russian hacker from *GoldenEye*, serves as another example. He's a misogynistic narcissist, who's cowardly and conceited. Then there's Q from the *Bond* films, who's young, male and nerdy, and nothing like the real-life version from MI6, who's actually female.[6]

Elliot Alderson from *Mr. Robot*, the latest American drama-thriller television series, also conforms to the hacker stereotypes. He's young, male, anti-social, and whilst he's lovable, he's delusional, depressed, addicted to drugs, and tormented with a social anxiety disorder. Just when you thought the media could have portrayed an alternative hacker character, Lisbeth Salander from *The Girl with the Dragon Tattoo* is presented as highly introverted, awkward, anti-social, paranoid, friendless, obsessive and a psychotic who survives on junk food.

As a result, many women who don't identify with these personas have been left feeling uninspired, uninterested, and unwelcomed. We can't blame them for this, either, for cybersecurity has never been normalised as a profession. Research suggests that when women choose to study computer science, it's often because they want their work to affect the world. It's surprising that this hasn't been seized upon by marketing and used more prolifically in recruitment campaigns, for many professionals in cybersecurity are driven by a desire to protect people, information, and livelihoods. This is what keeps me in cybersecurity, as my core values are freedom, empowerment, and entrepreneurship, and all of my work ties back into them.

Sarah Clarke, blogger and owner of Infospectives, an independent privacy and security consultancy, agrees. She told me, 'Cyberse-

---

6. https://www.theguardian.com/uk-news/2017/jan/26/the-real-q-is -a-woman-boss-of-mi6-launches-drive-for-female-recruits

curity needs to be put into context for women. The "why" and the "so what" bring the practical technical context to life. In order to do this, we require creativity, and big picture thinking, which is so often missed when the focus is purely on Science or Technology. These things draw women in, as women like to solve real world problems.'

Whilst I agree with Sarah, and remain in cybersecurity because of my core values, I have to admit that I wasn't initially attracted to security for a noble reason. What enticed me was the image, and the perception of what I thought cybersecurity, or, as it was called in 1997, information security, was. To me, thanks to the *James Bond* movies, it appeared cool, and it sparked my curiosity. Although much of the work that goes on in security is nothing like *Bond*, I know I'm not alone with this view, as countless cybersecurity professionals have confessed to joining for similar reasons, and many new recruits are still being attracted because of its 'cool factor'.

Without a shadow of a doubt, role models on screen make a difference and influence the roles women occupy off-screen. The data confirms this. When Geena Davis, the Academy-Award® winning actor, noticed how under represented women were in the family films, cartoons, and primetime TV her daughter watched, she questioned whether unconscious bias was affecting the amount of screen time a female actor was given, and how often they spoke. Taking action on this, in 2007 she founded The Geena Davis Institute on Gender in Media and began collecting data to analyse.

Over the years, with support from organisations including Google, the Institute has discovered that on screen men are actually seen and heard almost twice as much as women, yet when women headline films, they do better at the box office, earning 16% more than male-led films. When it drilled down on the data, the Institute also found that the only genre of film where women are seen on screen more than men is horror. This shouldn't surprise anyone, for portraying women as evil killers or powerless victims reinforces gender stereotypes. Women are rarely depicted as heroines, and if they are, they still have to conform to their label by being egoless, generous, considerate, nurturing, and usually subservient.[7]

Hidden Figures, the film that tells the true story of three brilliant African-American women – Katherine G. Johnson, Dorothy Vaughan, and Mary Jackson – who worked as NASA's pool of 'human computers' during the 1960s, and served as the brains behind one of the greatest operations in US history – the launch of astronaut John Glenn into orbit – does a great job of this. Nonetheless, it's enjoyable, and commendable for becoming the top-grossing Best Picture Academy-Award® nominee of 2017, showing that films centred on women resonate with audiences.[8]

Films that show women at the helm or as leading figures, particularly in technology disciplines, are important. In 2014, Google commissioned a multiyear comprehensive research project in collaboration with Gallup to understand better how computer science was perceived amongst students, parents, teachers, principals, and superintendents in the USA, and found that only 15% of K-12 students remembered seeing women performing computer science tasks 'most of the time' in film or TV.[9]

Figures like these, and data from the Geena Davis Institute on Gender in Media, can influence filmmakers and bring about change. When the Institute presented statistics to filmmakers, it found that 68% reconfigured two or more of their projects after hearing the numbers, and 41% stated that the statistics had impacted four or more of their movies.

7. https://www.google.com/about/main/gender-equality-films/
8. https://www.theatlantic.com/entertainment/archive/2017/01/hidden-figures-review/512252/
9. https://services.google.com/fh/files/misc/images-of-computer-science-report.pdf

How marketing has influenced women in cybersecurity

The way we go to market and communicate what we do about attracting more female talent needs to be carefully managed, and it doesn't stop with film or TV. Online channels, including social media, represent new channels, and as IBM discovered with its #HackAHairdryer campaign, it's not a simple undertaking.

With a barrage of criticism, largely over Twitter, IBM was forced to pull its campaign and publically apologise to women. Unfortunately many, especially in cybersecurity, found it patronising and sexist, as it unintentionally implied that if you want women to be interested in cybersecurity, then all you need to do is make it all about 'girl stuff' and apply some corporate pink-washing.[10]

Obviously, this isn't the case, and it's not what IBM believes. Since Thomas Watson Senior's time, IBM has been committed to creating an equitable workforce where women, amongst other minorities, have been recognised and promoted. For example, in 1935, IBM pioneered women in the workforce by recruiting its first female hires – twenty-five college graduates – to work in systems service. Breaking more ground in 1943, it appointed Ruth Leach Amonette as its first female Vice President, and since 1995 it has grown the number of women executives by 562%.

Each year IBM's positive impact on the careers of women in the USA is recognised by the National Association of Female Executives (NAFE), and from 2012, 'Ginni' Rometty has been leading the company as its first female Chairwoman, President, and CEO.[11]

Cybersecurity has much to offer women, and career opportunities within it are vast. However, what's key to attracting more women is portraying the huge variety of offensive and defensive

10. http://www.huffingtonpost.com/entry/ibm-apology-hack-a-hair-dryer_5665a739e4b08e945ff004c9
11. http://www-03.ibm.com/ibm/history/ibm100/us/en/icons/equalworkforce/transform/

roles that are available. For example, if someone is more technically orientated, then they'll most likely want to consider specialising in security assessments, penetration testing, or secure development; fraud and security forensics; security architecture; endpoint security, threat intelligence, or encryption. But, if someone is more business or process orientated, then governance, risk, and compliance (GRC); security auditing; security strategy; security awareness; security operations and programme management may appeal more.

Equally important is depicting the types of company a person would want to work in, as this is so often overlooked. It surprises me, too, for when I consult with cybersecurity entrepreneurs, and train them or their business development teams, one of the first exercises we work on is the profile of their target buyer – the avatar. I inform my clients why they must know who their target buyer is in great detail if they're going to attract them, develop relationships with them, and ultimately win business. This means understanding their challenges, fears, and aspirations along with their demographics and buying habits.

In cybersecurity, if we're going to attract more women, we must adopt the same rigour, and compile avatars for the three main buyers, who I categorise as being CISOs, suppliers (software vendors, system integrators, and consultancies), and female candidates.

Assessing buying needs and building personas

CISOS are typically managing small teams of fewer than ten people, unless they're in the financial services sector, whereupon they could be managing hundreds, or even thousands. Their job requires a lot of outsourcing to suppliers who have deep cybersecurity expertise. They need strong stakeholder management skills, as they're not simply dictating broad security policies to the entire business. Rather, they're regularly collaborating with the individual business unit leaders so risks can be understood and managed. Consequentially, good communication skills, plus big picture and strategic thinking skills are essential for them and their team, as their stakeholders' knowledge of security and technology is often limited. These skills are also frequently preferred over deep technical skills.

As Lynn Terwoerds, Executive Director of the Executive Women's Forum, said, 'when I fill jobs for a CISO, they're asking me to find someone with strong business acumen and a strong leader who can articulate concepts and issues that the board can understand. None of those things are specific to having a technology degree. Gone are the days that cybersecurity is some geeky person wearing a hoodie and staring at a computer.'[12]

Discussing the challenge with CISOs, specifically in relation to women, I'm always keen to hear whether this actually matters to them, and if so, why.

Naveen Vasudeva, the Founder and CEO of CISO International Limited, explained his reasons. 'When I worked in banking the reason I wanted more women in my department was not just because they'd bring a different perspective and change the workplace culture so it was more balanced. It was actually because they could get business done faster. The bank I worked for was very alpha male. If I need to get buy-in from a stakeholder, sometimes there could be friction when two men were in a face-off. However, the behaviour changed when women were introduced. As they weren't seen as a threat, women could dispel tension, often communicate much better than their male peers, and buy-in to my projects happened in a more timely manner.'

SUPPLIERS are providing services and/or software to companies which need to manage their risk. They need a workforce that's trained, experienced, and billable as soon as possible, particularly

---

12. http://www.denverpost.com/2017/03/19/cybersecurity-industry-hopes-women-will-help-fill-1-million-jobs/

if they're small. Suppliers typically don't have time to train up new recruits, and usually have a heavy reliance on security qualifications so they can satisfy the companies, who'll use these to differentiate between suppliers if there's nothing else to go on. They're after excellence, brand loyalty, and employees who'll go the extra mile.

If they're larger suppliers then there's more that they can do. Carmina Lees, who's spearheading IBM's Security Business Unit for the UK and Ireland, sets a good example. She's storming ahead in the UK and Ireland, and using her innate business development and leadership ability to take market share and position IBM Security as a viable contender for robust, scalable cybersecurity solutions.

Having begun with fifty-three consultants in 2014, just after returning from maternity leave, and by her own admission knowing little about cybersecurity, she's grown her department to around 250 consultants. With higher targets to meet for next year, being driven, she knows that in order to exceed them, she's going to need a capable, diverse team of men and women who'll have strong technical skills, as well as business acumen and communication skills.

Carmina is savvy, as she understands that this non-technical element is becoming increasingly important in cybersecurity so a more balanced view can be achieved across a business. That's why she targets Arts graduates and veterans, as well as STEM candidates. She recognises that they see things differently, and when they're given an opportunity coupled with a training investment, they can bring a lot, particularly when they're women.

Being hugely committed to changing the perception of cyber-security, she's now working on a programme to attract a pipeline of more technical women, and is, therefore, reaching out to girls in schools earlier in their education. Additionally, she's stepping up to become a visible and approachable role model who practises what she preaches by employing a senior leadership team that in 2016 amounted to almost half being women.

CANDIDATES are made up of those who are ready now, and those who may come and join us later. Those who are ready now are working in a sellers' market, where their services are in short supply. They seek an employer who can offer good market rates plus workplace flexibility, and a culture that matches their own values.

Candidates who may join us later are our pipelines, and they can be split into two groups. The first group are adults, and they have similar needs to the candidates who are ready now, except they'll need training as they'll be transitioning from another career. The extent of their training will vary depending on where they've come from, and what their skillsets are.

Many women move into cybersecurity beyond the ages of thirty with Arts and Humanities degrees, or from other non-technical routes, such as military, law, and HR. Many have also been former PAs and some have even ranged as far as an astro physicist, nurse, hairdresser, florist, dry cleaner, singer, actor, artist, and builder. Although I always recommend staying vigilant and flexible, the best place I advise my clients to start targeting women is in technology, law, accounting, and marketing, as they share skillset commonalities, and the transition can be swift.

Whatever sector you go after, know that women will seek career stability if they're to pivot their career, and that they'll work really hard to get up to speed. Furthermore, they're a fairly easy group to target and sell to, as technology is disrupting so many professions by replacing staff, yet cybersecurity is growing and well-positioned for the future. That's attractive to them, and this excites me no end, for if we get our marketing messages right, cybersecurity, particularly GRC, could easily supersede career choices like accounting, a profession that has traditionally attracted many women, but is increasing becoming viewed as a dying career due to technology disruption. This information is particularly important for women, as they're generally more risk averse than men, and seek more security as a result.

Transitioning into cybersecurity

Dr Jessica Barker's story is one that I want to share. Originally, Jess was a sociologist with a PhD in Civic Design, but she fell into security, like so many women have done, shortly after graduating.

'My first degree was in sociology and politics. I then worked in urban regeneration for a few years before doing an MA and PhD in Civic Design. My PhD drew on sociology to explore governance, partnership working and the Internet economy. On completing it, I was headhunted by a cybersecurity start-up in London specialising in the defence sector. I did a lot of reading up on cybersecurity and thinking about how I could fit into the field, and realised that a lot of my knowledge base and previous work was more relevant than it might first appear.

'I took the job, which gave me a foundation of great experience in the industry. My role was developing a tool to measure cyber-security maturity in organisations, then using that tool to conduct and subsequently lead maturity assessments. I also developed and delivered awareness-raising training, primarily at the board level, covering roles and responsibilities for cybersecurity in an organisation, as well as general awareness-raising training of whole organisations.

'Four and a half years ago, I decided to strike out on my own and set up a company. I haven't looked back, and feel like my place in the industry has gone from strength-to-strength. Last year, I co-founded a new company, Redacted Firm, where we are bringing together the human, technical and physical elements of cybersecurity.

'When I started working in cybersecurity, the human aspects were very overlooked. Now it is widely accepted that human aspects are the biggest challenge. I work across a variety of sectors, for SMEs on my own, and as part of larger teams for global clients. My interests and specialisms are in attitudes, awareness and behaviours, culture, and language. My work spans consultancy, research, and training, and I increasingly do corporate speaking events and media work. I'm passionate about making cybersecurity a more accessible subject, both in terms of empowering people to become more secure online, and spreading the word about careers in the industry, and what a diverse and rewarding industry it is. This motivates me to engage with the media as much as possible, as well as supporting the Cybersecurity Challenge and TeenTech.

'I'm also keen to give back to the community as much as possible, and help make this industry the best it can be. As such, I speak at as many industry events as I can, including BSides, SteelCon, IRISSCON, EMF Camp and more.'

Helen Rabe is the interim Head of Information Security at a British multinational coffeehouse company, and an astute information security leader. Having worked on information security projects throughout her whole career, but exclusively since 2012, and with an MBA in Project and Programme Management, she tackles the transition into cybersecurity in a pragmatic way.

Every month she holds roundtable discussions on cybersecurity within her organisation. She advertises them internally, and makes it known that anyone can attend and find out about cybersecurity. Having run them for six months, she told me that she's never had an empty session. Importantly, too, she's been able to recruit fresh talent into her department, at least on a part-time basis.

The way she achieves this is by negotiating for time with people's managers. She usually obtains a 30:70 time ratio, sets the expectations for both parties, and removes the worry of the impact from their BAU (business as usual) job. Every week she reviews their progress, and feeds this back to them. By working in this way, she's able to enhance employees' skillsets as part of their personal development plan, retain them for longer within the organisation, thereby reducing human capital costs, and embed cybersecurity deeper within the organisation's workplace culture. Through her efforts, she's turning more of her organisation's employees into cybersecurity ambassadors and human shields who are better pre-pared to protect the organisation, plus she's developing a healthy pipeline of new cybersecurity professionals.

How to build a pipeline

The second group of pipeline candidates are younger, so this means getting into schools and talking to the girls. Looking at what's going on in schools, I find there's good and bad news. The bad news is that despite technology forming such an integral aspect of our working lives, and women having made huge progress in terms of equality, even in today's society, in most parts of the world, girls don't get as much opportunity to use computers in schools as boys.

Ariane Hegewisch, Study Director for the Institute for Women's Policy Research, says, 'They get fewer chances, in part because of a lack of encouragement, curricula that appeal more to boys than girls, and a negative stereotype about girls' technical abilities.'

Linda Ortenzo, Director of STEM Programs for the Carnegie Science Center in Pittsburgh, USA, makes a similar observation. 'Girls get very subtle messages early on ... that there are certain fields and certain endeavours that are "boy things".'[13]

And, as if that's not bad enough, we already know that many girls aren't getting advice on how to pursue a career in cybersecurity from their secondary or high school computer classes.[14] These challenges don't surprise me anymore, yet I remain optimistic about the future. It does depend on where a girl is studying, as these issues aren't necessarily universal.

Marketing to girls and their influencers

So how can we more effectively target this group? The answer lies

---

13. http://www.carnegiesciencecenter.org/
14. http://www.raytheon.co.uk/rtnwcm/groups/cyber/documents /content/rtn_278208.pdf

in marketing to not just the girls, but also to those who influence them – in other words, their teachers and parents.

Let's start with the girls. The sooner we can get into the schools, the better. When I was speaking to the Lean In group at BP recently, I encouraged them to take action. Christine Maxwell, the Governance, Risk & Compliance Director, led by example, and asked her local primary school if she could go in and present to the children.

She told me, 'You inspired me, and I suddenly began to imagine what could happen if every cybersecurity professional did this. If we all took a few hours out of our day, annually, how many more girls could we encourage to follow a cybersecurity path, and how many more young women could we attract?'

I agree, and know many dedicated cybersecurity professionals who do just this. Importantly, whenever they can, they're not just talking about their job role, or what the industry is like. Instead, they're taking software and tools into schools with them, and showing them. Or, as BP has been doing recently, they're making demonstrations interactive by doing tailored table top exercises that are based around scenarios using, for example, social media rather than business, so they resonate more with the girls, and become more fun and memorable.

This is what happened to my daughter recently. She came home from school and was extremely excited to tell me what she'd learnt when a cybersecurity professional had gone in to talk to the girls about identity management and privacy. It amused me no end, as even though I'd talked to her about the same things as he did, my words had washed over her head. But, teenage girls can be like that with their mothers. They tune in and out, whenever it suits them, and what matters most is that *someone* gets through.

It doesn't matter which gender inspires them, either. Although it's important for girls to have access to female role models, which I'll be discussing in the next chapter in much more detail, what matters most in this situation is passion and the ability to inspire another person.

I feel very strongly about this. Last summer, when GCHQ asked me to join a group of other women who'd be speaking to girls, I decided not to partake.[15] Although I helped them to find women who were prepared to speak, I fundamentally objected as they were segregating women from men, which I found discriminatory. Furthermore, research has found that feminine role models can actually reduce middle school girls' interest in STEM subjects and confidence in their own ability in mathematics compared to more gender-neutral role models. Women don't work in a homogenous workplace. Women work with men, and what's more, men can be incredibly inspiring to girls. Many men care deeply about encouraging girls in technology, and want to help.

When I was at Black Hat Europe in 2016, I met up with Sara Pérez Merino, who's the Lead Security Analyst and UK Senior Team Leader in charge of the penetration testing team at SensePost. We'd briefly worked together several years ago, and when we discussed this, she also agreed.

'When Daniel Cuthbert (SensePost's COO) went into a school recently, he talked to a bunch of teenage girls and they loved it.'

I smiled. Having known and worked with him for many years, I could imagine the scene. He's a good-looking guy, one of the best speakers on the circuit, passionate about his subject, slightly controversial, and very entertaining.

Initiatives to get girls interested

To complement these activities, there are other initiatives being implemented to encourage more girls to pursue careers in cybersecurity. Most of the largest technology players in global IT, and

---

15. https://www.gchq.gov.uk/

Big Four consultancies are taking an interest in cybersecurity and reaching out to get girls involved.

Smaller companies are helping too. When I interviewed Alisha Dattani, Cofounder of FMXA, a small integrated PR and marketing agency for technology firms, she explained how the company contributes.

'I've got two daughters, and every year I invite a handful of fifteen- to sixteen-year-old girls from their school to come in for a week. I then get them to create a cybersecurity awareness programme that can be used for the pupils, teachers, and parents. By the end of that week, the girls are inspired, more knowledgeable about cybersecurity, and so are their parents and teachers.'

Next Tech Girls, an initiative by Empiric, a recruitment firm, supports in another way. Having launched in 2016, it's committed to finding 5,000 British girls, aged between fourteen and fifteen, work experiences in technology and cybersecurity by 2020. Girls are reporting back that they're now at sixth form taking Computer Science courses and stating their tech work experience influenced their decision. Furthermore, organisations are reporting positive team cultural impacts, and in some cases they're adopting ideas suggested by the girls.[16]

Then there are clubs that are run after school or during the holidays all over the world, such as Code First: Girls, or Girls who Code, that are teaching programming and coding skills. The World Association of Girl Guides and Girl Scouts (WAGGGS) has a number of new achievement badges aimed at encouraging young women into STEM and, in conjunction with Palo Alto Networks, Girl Guides USA is to offer training from September 2018 on a variety of cybersecurity skills such as data privacy, identity theft, cyberbullying, coding, ethical hacking and creating firewalls. Girls

---

16. http://www.nexttechgirls.com/

from five-years- to twelve-years-old will be able to earn badges – up to eighteen of them – upon competence and completion.

Governments are also rolling out initiatives in a bid to recruit more female talent. I've already mentioned Israel and their Mag-shimim programme but girls in the USA, from grades 9 to 12 can attend a programme, known as GenCyber, that's being funded the National Security Agency (NSA) and the National Science Foundation (NSF). The curriculum includes core sessions like cybersecurity, programming, networking, and robotics as well as specialty electives, such as password cracking, web hacking, 3D printing, and multimedia forensics. The UK follows suit and now has a drive that's being organised by GCHQ's new National Cyber Security Centre (NCSC) whereby it will run 2,500 summer residential courses for teens, including a one-day event for eleven-year olds under the brand CyberFirst. It's also created a girls-only programme, CyberFirst Girls, and it held its first competition for schoolgirls aged thirteen to fifteen, which resulted in 2,000 teams, and over 8,000 participants entering.[17]

How to publicise our marketing efforts

To publicise our efforts requires us to get in front of our target buyers and hang out where they hang out. It involves us running appealing and compelling marketing campaigns that tell stories. These must be delivered in different communication mediums, such as text, video, and sound, and distributed to our target buyers via the communication channels that they use.

For example, if we're targeting teenage girls, then we might consider using Instagram, Snapchat, and YouTube as viable plat-forms as that's where we'll find them. If we're targeting women in their thirties, then we might use Facebook, or run an editorial in a

---

17. https://www.gchq.gov.uk/news-article/cyberfirst-girls-competition
-finds-worthy-winner

magazine such as *Cosmopolitan*, *Elle* or *Marie Claire*, or advertise on websites that they frequent.

The way we portray ourselves is vital, and as a picture paints a thousand words, we must be careful with the images we use. Photographs in particular are important as they guide our impressions, help form opinions, and seep into our consciousness. To help us with this, a number of initiatives, such as Sheryl Sandberg's Lean In Foundation, that's collaborated with Getty Images to change the way the world thinks about women in tech, and #WOCTechChat, will allow you to use their images for free so long as you abide by their terms.[18]

When I spoke to Yvette Lejins, the Head of Cybersecurity at an Australian low-cost airline, about the way we portray women in cybersecurity recently, she said, 'Companies need to stop posting event shots on Twitter and LinkedIn of all male events or with a token women. I recently saw a vendor photo posting on LinkedIn of a posh Sydney senior security lunch. It was a table shot with eighteen men, and not one female was present in the photo. So where were all the women? Plenty of women deserved a seat at that table, and there are plenty of senior women who work in security in Sydney, so why weren't they there?'

Repackaging and over-correcting

Her question is valid, and by demanding a change, we can ensure we make progress faster. However, we need to be conscious of repackaging cybersecurity to women, and not over correcting.

Currently, there are many websites, clubs, or organisations that are attempting to get girls and women interested in technology, and we can learn from them. Many have used a combination of words, like 'girls', 'geek', 'diva', 'nerd', or 'princess', to name themselves, and have used pink, purple, polka dots, or anything sparkly in their

---

18. https://www.flickr.com/photos/wocintechchat/

branding. They've handed out nail varnish, nail files, cosmetic mirrors, bracelets, or lip-balm at events in an attempt to attract more women.

One senior female cybersecurity professional told me, 'I was outraged when I attended 44Con, and found a Women in Security stand to be handing out nail varnish.'

Google has also tried to get girls interested in technology, and has come under fire. When it created Made with Code, it was criticised for its website, as the first item on a page of coding projects was a 3D-printed bracelet.[19]

Elizabeth Losh, a digital culture scholar at UC San Diego, said she found these 'ridiculous pink sparkly techno-princess land' projects insulting to women. She believed them to be highly gendered, and that they were perpetuating women as consumers and narcissists.

Whether she's being too hypersensitive or not, her opinion is useful to test. This is what Google's Megan Smith, who leads Made with Code, did and she defended its website page. She explained that the examples Google chose to highlight were simply the ones that scored highest in testing, and that they demonstrated the variety of what children could do with code.[20]

Testing is key, for we must ensure diversity within our profession, and not buckle to what others dictate or believe women in cybersecurity should conform to, otherwise we're still putting women into boxes, alienating our gender, and remaining a minority in the workforce.

Finally, we need to dispel some misconceptions about cybersecurity, for example, that it requires mathematical skills. Whilst mathematics has a part to play in several areas of cybersecurity – algo-

---

19. https://www.madewithcode.com/

20. http://www.sfgate.com/news/article/How-not-to-attract-women-to-coding-Make-tech-pink-5602104.php

rithms (in programming), statistics (in anomaly detection, traffic analysis and risk analysis), modular arithmetic and number theory (in cryptography) – there are many aspects of cybersecurity that require other skills. Cybersecurity actually calls for tremendous creativity and problem solving skills – Corkscrew Thinking – as solutions to problems are not always obvious. The abilities to spot anomalies, solve problems, think creatively and strategically, respond appropriately to requests, and communicate to project teams and executives outside of IT are drastically required. Only by strategically engineering diverse teams can we hope to beat our assailants.

Sympathetic sexism

This chapter couldn't end without cautioning you on sympathetic sexism. When we inform others through marketing campaigns, or in conversation that 'women can be scientists, engineers and mathematicians too' all we're doing is highlighting the fact that most of the time, scientists, engineers and mathematicians aren't women. When we're sympathetic, our sexism and prejudices are not only presented but reinforced.

Here's an example. Speaking on a panel recently about the cyber threat landscape and alongside other men who were experts on defence, risk, and geo-politics, the female moderator ended by saying, "I'd just like to thank the panel and also congratulate Jane for being the third most influential person in cybersecurity in the UK – and as a woman in a man's field.' I came away asking myself, did she really need to add that last bit? Why should it matter? The answer is it shouldn't.

Equally, when we emphasise that many women advance in non-technical cybersecurity roles, and may be more suited to them because women are typically better communicators than men, are we not guilty of benevolent sexism? Proposed in the 1990s, this term – for a non-hostile form of prejudice – enabled gender stereotypes to prevail and unjust systems easier to bear.

The Golden Rules

- Create avatars for each target buyer so you understand them in depth
- Look at targeting women from other sectors like technology, accounting, law, and marketing as there are many similarities between those sectors and cybersecurity
- Be careful of the language and colours you use in your campaigns so you don't over correct
- Don't exclude men when campaigning; they are valued and want to help
- Use data to influence stakeholders
- Watch out for sympathetic sexism.

A checklist for marketing to prospective female cybersecurity talent

✓ Set your recruitment campaign goals

✓ Decide upon your target buyers

✓ Compile avatars for your target buyer

✓ Review the competition

✓ Consider all sponsors (teachers, parents, spouses, etc.)

✓ Identify an offer

✓ Develop your go-to market strategy in accordance with your budgets

✓ Schedule your events and campaigns

✓ Create your message and ensure it's compelling, appealing, and the copy is gender neutral

- ✓ Depict an industry that's inclusive by using stock images from #WOCTechChat or Sheryl Sandberg's Lean In Foundation, or elsewhere
- ✓ Have your campaign reviewed
- ✓ Launch your campaign
- ✓ Test, measure, and revise your campaign, then repeat

9. Seeing Is Believing

- How to use female role models
- How we can use imagery more effectively to communicate

Marianne Williamson, in her book *A Return to Love*, says that our deepest fear is not that we are inadequate, but that we are powerful beyond measure.

I only came to realise the truth of this very recently. For a long time I ducked the limelight. Like most women, I just got on with the job, kept a low profile, and regularly suffered bouts of insecurity regarding my abilities. When I owned my penetration testing firm, I wasn't the spokesperson for our press, believing that no one would want to hear what I had to say. The press never pushed me on this, for being a woman in security wasn't as big a deal as it is now. Having evaded the press, I also avoided public speaking. As for most introverts, which people still find hard to believe about me, it was my greatest fear.

It was actually only a few years ago when I decided to step up, expand my comfort zone, and change things. Instead of letting fear paralyse me, I used it as fuel to propel me. Fear became courage, as my message had to be delivered. I understood that self-doubt kept you alive, and progressing.

I started by building a strong personal brand, which I'll come to in Chapter 14, and leveraging my achievements, once I realised they were rather special. According to a report by EY, only 2% of women-owned businesses break US $1million in revenue.[1] Having been one of those 2% of women-owned businesses in cybersecurity, I regret not pushing myself forward to claim the limelight. Hindsight is a wonderful thing, but had I known then how important it is to be a visible role model, I wouldn't have done that.

These days, I understand that many women need to see other women succeeding in things they want to do if they're going to believe they can also succeed. And that there's a caveat in regard to this. Female role models need to be used differently, and in accordance with certain variables.

How to use female role models

Let me start with a piece of work by Benjamin J. Drury, John Oliver Siy, and Sapna Cheryan from the Department of Psychology, University of Washington. These researchers looked at whether female role models benefitted women in STEM. They distinguished recruitment from retention, as they knew that female role models might be effective in the retention of women. However, they wanted to determine whether female and male role models could be equally as effective in recruitment efforts.[2]

LOOKING AT RETENTION, they understood from earlier research that female role models were helpful for women who were already in STEM fields. These women had to cope with negative stereotypes that were casting doubt on their abilities to perform well. As a result

---

1. http://www.ey.com/us/en/services/strategic-growth-markets/ey-3-adaptations-to-help-women-entrepreneurs-scale-big
2. https://depts.washington.edu/sibl/Publications/Drury%20Siy%20Cheryan%20Psych%20Inquiry%202011.pdf

of these stereotype threats, women were actually underperforming and feeling more alienated within their field.

However, the researchers found through interventions, such as deploying female role models, they could alter this. For example, when women who'd been identified as being competent in mathematics encountered a female role model who was also competent in mathematics, they performed better in mathematics tests than when they encountered a male role model who was competent.

Similarly, women were found to have more confidence and better attitudes to mathematics when they took a calculus course with a female professor. And, when women read about successful women who'd graduated from their university in the same major as them, they rated themselves more highly on success-related traits than when they read about a male equivalent.

LOOKING AT RECRUITMENT, the researchers knew that women weren't being attracted to STEM fields despite being just as capable as men, and that efforts to recruit more women typically relied upon the use of female role models. They cited the MIT Women's Initiative which sent female engineers to high schools, the National Academy of Engineering which publicised the careers of female scientists and engineers on its websites, and companies like Microsoft which ran camps specifically targeted at exposing girls to Computer Science and Engineering as examples. Apparently, the rationale for implementing these initiatives was based on the assumption that by showcasing successful women in these fields, they could have an immediate and long-lasting effect on girls' and women's aspirations.

Whilst this seems logical, unfortunately, empirical data suggests that when it comes to recruiting, this might not actually be best practice. Data compiled from several departments across three North American universities found there was no correlation between the high proportion of women in a faculty and the numbers of female students who'd majored in that field. Additionally, when women looked back on who'd influenced them to pursue STEM careers (traditionally a male-dominated profession), they reported that male role models were just as likely to have affected them as female role models. The same was true when more experiments were performed on Computer Science graduates – women were just as likely to choose to study Computer Science whether they'd interacted with a male or female Computer Science graduate previously.

In the spring of 2016, I met with a group of women in cybersecurity who'd served in the profession for over a decade. We discussed the state of gender diversity for cybersecurity, the many initiatives that were going on, and what we'd found to be successful. I was curious to know whether they'd needed female role models when they'd chosen cybersecurity as their career. They all said, as did I, the same thing.

'I didn't need to see a female role model in security in order to believe I could do it, or be successful in it. The lack of female role models in cybersecurity didn't prevent me from joining.'

The report by Benjamin J. Drury, John Oliver Siy, and Sapna Cheryan could provide an explanation for this. Their research suggested that the reason why female role models were more effective for women in STEM during the retention phase, and less so during the recruitment phase, was because the psychological threats were different for each phase. Negative stereotypes about a woman's ability to perform were less of a concern for women who hadn't joined STEM fields than they were for women who were already in them. Women who were yet to join STEM fields were actually more concerned about feeling like they belonged. Apparently, women perceived those in STEM fields to be unsociable, male, and overly preoccupied with technology, and as a result, they didn't feel as if they belonged, which deterred them from applying. Furthermore, communication not only played a huge part in their decision, but so did the environment, particularly when it felt non-welcoming, i.e. unsafe.

For example, in an experiment where women were exposed to a beginners' Computer Science classroom which contained objects that were stereotypical – *Star Trek* posters and video games – a higher proportion of women felt like they didn't belong, had lower interest in majoring in the field, and anticipated less success in Computer Science compared to women who were exposed to the same classroom with non-stereotypical objects – for example, nature posters and water bottles. This was regardless of whether they had a male or female professor in the classroom.

Similarly, when the women met Computer Science role models who expressed technical stereotypes through their clothing – for example, by wearing a T-shirt that said, 'I code, therefore I am' – and preferences – for example, by reading *Electronic Gaming Monthly*, their sense of belonging decreased, and they had a lower interest in majoring in the field and anticipated success when compared to women encountering a Computer Science role model who didn't personify those stereotypes.

When it came to what worked regarding role models for women in STEM, during both the recruitment and retention phases, the researchers found that it was a sense of perceived similarity, such as values, beliefs, and attitudes, to the role models, and that this was irrespective of gender. Furthermore, the greater the similarity was between the students' communal goals, for example to work with and help others, and STEM role models' daily activities, the higher the likelihood was that the students would gravitate towards the role models' career.[3]

In another experiment, known as My Fair Physicist, more light was shed on how female role models can be used more effectively, but this time with a focus on girls. University of Michigan psychology researchers Diana Betz and Denise Sekaquaptewa knew from

---

3. http://sciencewithart.ijs.si/pdf/How%20stereotypical%20cues%20impact%20gender%20participation%20in%20computer%20science.pdf

earlier research that if women were seen as being successful in STEM fields, they were disliked and labelled unattractive, incompetent, or unable to secure high salaries. Furthermore, these unfeminine perceptions of women in STEM negatively impacted the numbers of young girls who chose Science and Mathematics as academic and professional careers. They therefore conducted two studies about how middle school girls perceived female STEM role models.

The first study involved 144 eleven- to thirteen-year-old girls who completed surveys on computers. The researchers began by identifying those girls who had a preference for STEM. Then, the girls were given a magazine and asked to assess three prospective university student role models interviewed in it. Some had feminine characteristics, for example they liked wearing make-up, wore pink clothes, and liked fashion magazines, and others had more gender-neutral traits, for example they liked wearing dark-coloured clothes, wore glasses, and read extensively. They also displayed either STEM success or general school success. The girls then had to evaluate their mathematics skills, and complete a questionnaire about their future plans to continue studying it.

The researchers found that by showing the girls the feminine STEM role models, they decreased the girls' self-rated mathematics interest, ability, and short-term success expectations. Interestingly, they also negatively impacted the girls who didn't identify with STEM, which resulted in a decreased interest in studying Mathematics.

The second study involved forty-two participants. The researchers were keen to investigate why feminine STEM role models motivated girls who disliked mathematics and science less than the gender neutral role models. What they discovered was that girls who weren't interested in mathematics and science were more likely to view success in both domains as being unattainable. This implied that the lack of adoption was related to the perceived unlikelihood of combining femininity and STEM success. Subconsciously, this made them feel threatened rather than motivated, which turned them off the subject. The researchers proposed that role models who exhibited more than one competing stereotype could be less effective than role models who just encompassed one.

This confirms what I've always been led to believe. Women can be influenced if they either aspire to be like a role model, or can relate to them. Understanding these nuances is critical, and whilst I don't propose that attractive, glamorous, and successful women in cybersecurity are excluded from our recruitment efforts for girls, what I do suggest is that the risk is measured and managed. Additionally, other forms of representation need to be considered. For example, if we want to show that women belong in our profession during a recruitment phase, we could show how well represented they are by using images and illustrations rather than photographs.

How we can use imagery more effectively to communicate

This is what Iris Bohnet, a Behavioural Economist at Harvard University and author of a ground-breaking book on gender diversity, entitled *What Works*, did when she met with the UK Department of Business, Innovation and Skills, and was discussing the small number of female company directors. She recommended that instead of describing the small percentages of women who served on company boards, it focused its messages on the large percentage of companies with gender-diverse boards. She brought an image with her to make this easier for the Department to envisage.

Although the Department didn't implement her advice, the Secretary of State for Business, Innovation and Skills at that time, Dr Vince Cable, did alter the way he was reporting on the percentages. He said, 'Today, ninety-four of the FTSE 100 companies count women on their boards, as do over two-thirds of all FTSE 350 companies.'

This is a smarter way to deal with the challenge, and one that other companies can embrace as a strategy.

Take Fujitsu. It's committed to increasing the numbers of women in its workforce, and is working hard to achieve a gender diversity target of 30%. When the UK and Ireland team looked at how well the company was doing, they could immediately see that it was on track to meet its goals. However, they could also see that its target was greatly affected by the numbers of women in marketing and HR, traditionally female-orientated fields.

When the team looked at how well represented women were in technology, they soon discovered that the numbers of women, which were running at 15%, were lower than they would have liked. They therefore decided to compare women to women, and looked at the numbers of women who worked in Fujitsu's UK and Ireland team against the numbers of women who worked in its UK and Ireland technology team as a percentage. What they discovered was this figure became 45%, and immediately looked much better. Armed with this knowledge, Fujitsu could use it more positively and competitively when recruiting, whilst still working to increase the numbers of women in technology overall.

Presenting the numbers like this has a positive effect on attracting women into highly populated male industries and other cyber-security companies can follow Fujitsu's lead. For example, if they are shown to be doing well in terms of their targets, they can maximise the effectiveness of this by using social proof, a principle of persuasion that was created with five others (reciprocity, commitment/consistency, authority, liking, and scarcity) by Dr Robert B. Cialdini. Writing about it in his book *Influence: The Psychology of Persuasion*, Cialdini maintains that people are especially likely to perform certain actions if they can relate to the people who have performed the same actions before them. People are, therefore, more likely to accept a job offer when they know that others have done so in the past.

By using pictures and images to represent the numbers of women who work in cybersecurity in a letter to the candidate along with carefully crafted key messages, like the ones created recently by Capgemini – a day in the life of Jane, the CISO – companies could turn their described patterns of normality into prescribed reality. Perception can become reality when it's strategically engineered.[4]

The research detailed in this section brings us great news as it signals an inclusive approach to solving the gender diversity challenge in cybersecurity, and by doing so it makes it a people problem, rather than one of gender. It empowers all professionals in cybersecurity too, for together we can solve this issue and work to depict a diverse workplace without concentrating on our gender and further division.

The Golden Rules

- Role models need to be used differently depending on whether you're recruiting or retaining women in cybersecurity
- When targeting female teenagers, beware of using role models that portray more than one competing stereotype
- It's OK to use male role models with or without female role models when recruiting fresh talent so long as you concentrate on showcasing shared values and beliefs, and non-technical stereotypes
- Use female role models when retaining talent who are at each stage of a cybersecurity career, not just those at the height of their careers

Checklist for creating and using role models

✓ **Are you using the same type of role model for all your cam-**

4. https://www.uk.capgemini.com/resources/video/a-day-in-the-life-of-jane-the-ciso

paigns? You need different role models depending on whether you're looking to increase recruitment or retention and for different age groups, i.e. girls, teens and adults.

✓ **When you're devising a campaign to recruit women into your cybersecurity team are you ensuring you're conveying perceived similarity?** At this stage what matters most is the perceived similarity to values, beliefs and attitudes. Ambitious women will also want to be assured that your organisation will be able to offer them opportunities rather than discrimination, so that means presenting women like them achieving.

✓ **When you're recruiting women into your cybersecurity team, school, or college are you making them feel like they belong?** The easiest way to do this is by ensuring no stereotype threats exist in your office, or classroom or event space. Decorate walls with nature posters rather than *Star Wars/Trek* and know that technical stereotypes that are expressed through clothing, for example T-shirts, can be off-putting to women.

✓ **When you're focusing on retention, are you using role models like the women in your team or whom they aspire to be like?** Displaying similarities is important at this stage.

✓ **When you're targeting female teens or girls are you using role models that portray only one competing stereotype?** Using role models that display more than one completing stereotype, i.e. women who are attractive can decrease campaign effectiveness and interest. At this stage, it's good to use men as well as women as it presents a truer picture of the cybersecurity industry.

Challenge Two – Identification

10. Recruiting The X Factor

- The rising cost of cybersecurity salaries
- The recruitment process
- Using gender-neutral language
- Candidate selection
- The beauty premium
- The interview phase
- Blind auditions
- How to use structured interviews successfully
- How to use technology to support your recruitment efforts
- Using Axiology
- Boomerang hires and alumni management

We met in a hotel lobby at London Bridge. It was late morning, cold, rainy, and I'd just had back-to-back meetings. My first was with a client about future work, and the second was with one of my mentees, Luciana.

My next meeting was with Catherine, and I was looking forward to it immensely as I was interviewing her for the book. I'd been told, 'She's motivated, ambitious, and a results-driven leader of people, plus she's got great commercial awareness, and transfers understanding and passion to all levels. She's also got a strong and measurable track record for inspiring teams to deliver in fast-moving, multi-disciplined environments whilst creating motivational, enjoyable, and supportive team cultures. She's an A-list employee without a shadow of a doubt and I know you two will get on.' Taking my referrer's word, I couldn't wait.

Having looked at Catherine's profile on LinkedIn and seen that her background wasn't in technology, I was excited to hear her story, and understand how she got into cybersecurity and excelled within it. After exchanging niceties, she told me.

It turned out that a few years ago she worked for one of the world's largest gaming companies. As she'd succeeded in a commercial role there, she was encouraged to transfer into security and apply for a Head of Fraud, Risk and Security position that had become available. Unfortunately, the Security Department was failing. Like many other departments in many other companies, it was known as the 'department that liked to say no', and had severe morale problems, which resulted in poor performance and staff leaving. Although Catherine had lots of commercial experience, was familiar with turning around departments that were not performing, and was extremely well-regarded within the company as a leader, she faced one problem. She lacked security proficiency.

Unlike many women, when Catherine was approached about the role, she didn't question whether she'd be able to do it and if it would be the right career move for her. She felt confident in her abilities to perform in the role, and had the full support of HR, the Legal Director, and the CEO.

However, there was resistance higher up from the Group Security Director, who viewed her application as illogical as she'd not risen from a technical rank. When he came to interview her, he presented her with questions and scenarios, working hard to trip her up so she could be discounted. HR had not been informed and was not happy, but despite his attempts, she passed the recruitment test and was appointed.

Being responsible for all aspects of corporate security, including fraud, investigations, physical and information security, plus compliance, business continuity, and data disclosure, Catherine transformed the culture of the department in just under three years, raised commercial awareness, and beat the first year's fraud targets six times. Furthermore, she made a 176% year-on-year saving.

I was impressed, and found her story encouraging as it demonstrated that someone with good commercial sense and capability could perform well in a cybersecurity leadership position without having hard core technical skills or security qualifications. Catherine epitomises the argument for greater diversity of backgrounds, perspectives, and life experiences within cybersecurity, plus how HR can be a supportive and a highly functioning aid, rather than a road blocker. Her story illustrates how feasible it is for others, particularly women, to move into certain security roles from non-security or non-technical backgrounds, thereby identifying a new talent pool when the industry is in dire need.

The rising cost of cybersecurity salaries

The cybersecurity media regularly reports the challenges it has with identifying and recruiting talent, including diversity. As we know, cybersecurity job postings are growing at an alarming speed, and according to (ISC)[2] the average annual salary amongst the security professionals is rising. From 2017, they reported that 33% of security professionals in EMEA earnt over €95,000 per year and in North America the average was $100,000.[1]

Recruitment consultants from all over the world have also noted lucrative increasing salaries. SilverBull reported that the average median CISO salary in the USA is $204,000; Barclay Simpson, in

---

1. http://blog.isc2.org/isc2_blog/2015/04/isc-study-workforce-shortfall -due-to-hiring-difficulties-despite-rising-salaries-increased-budgets-a.html #sthash.LjTdB2Wa.dpuf

its 2017 salary guide, showed that a Head of Information Security in banking in the UK, with fewer than ten reports, could earn between £118,000 and £160,000[2]; and Greythorn in its 2014–15 salary guide depicted CISO salaries in Australia reaching up to AU $200,000.[3]

And it's not just the top jobs that are commanding high salaries. Those at entry-level are just as attractive. Yet, despite the number of roles available, lucrative salaries with a 9% premium over IT jobs overall, or men declaring that in order to increase our female talent, all we have to do is 'buy' it; many women still don't consider a career in cybersecurity, and if they do, they face being rejected during the recruitment process or held back for promotion. The figures validate this, too: 90% of the cybersecurity industry is male and over thirty years old, plus men are nine times more likely to be in management positions and four times more likely to be in executive management.[4]

The recruitment process

This is a worrying trend, and one I felt had to be investigated, so I'm going to start with the recruitment process, specifically the job description which plays a vital role in recruiting female cybersecurity talent and often provides the first impression of a company's culture.

The first thing I found was that job descriptions were largely inadequate. Often hiring managers just copied the last job role that they'd advertised rather than rewriting it. Few had thought about what they wanted their next team member to accomplish.

2. http://www.barclaysimpson.com/Security-Resilience-Market-Report-2017

3. http://www.greythorn.com.au/media/greythorn/greythorn%20market%20insights%20and%20salary%20guide%202014_2015%20australia%20pay%20rate.pdf

4. http://www.darkreading.com/careers-and-people/how-to-raise-your-salary-in-cybersecurity/d/d-id/1325068

Additionally, the descriptions were far too long and frequently contained numerous bullet points, sometimes up to forty-five, which detailed the key responsibilities. Then came qualifications, eligibility requirements, and desired characteristics – all very standard, just as long, and with most asking for between three and five years' worth of experience, either a CISSP or SSCP plus a Computer Science degree, and an ability to communicate effectively to business and technical teams.

As I described in Chapter 3, numerous requirements are off-putting for most women, as they'll discount themselves from the application for not meeting the bulk of the criteria. Remember, the most common answer women gave for not applying for a job was, 'I didn't think they'd hire me since I didn't meet the qualifications, and I didn't want to waste my time and energy.'

Workplace flexibility is also an important incentive when it comes to women, yet few companies were advertising this in their job descriptions or adopting it as part of their workplace culture. Could you imagine what would happen if flexible working arrangements were the default position until they were empirically proved to be untenable? And, how much female talent would become available in India where women have had to leave the workforce due to having children or being married?

Using gender-neutral language

The next thing I noticed was the language. Often unintentionally, it was gender-coded and played to a range of stereotypes, ideologies, and belief systems that were surreptitiously trying to justify the status quo. However, job descriptions that aren't checked for gender bias can put a lot of female talent off applying.

Even subtle word choices can have a strong impact and negative effect. For example, when Danielle Gaucher and Justin Friesen of the University of Waterloo and Aaron C. Kay of Duke University investigated whether institutional-level mechanisms existed that reinforced and perpetuated existing group-based inequalities, they found conclusive evidence to suggest that they did. Employing both archival and experimental analysis, their research demonstrated that when gendered wording was used in job recruitment materials it maintained gender inequality in traditionally male-dominated occupations. Results indicated that job advertisements for male-dominated areas that employed greater masculine wording, for example adjectives like superior, competitive, ambitious, driven, determined, leader, dominant, resulted in women perceiving that they would not belong in this work environment.[5]

Knowledge such as this must surely be a wake-up call for all companies hoping to recruit more women into their cybersecurity teams, and for practices deployed in the start-up community, particularly in Silicon Valley where job descriptions use 'brogrammer' language – ninja, work-hard play-hard, or cyber warrior – alongside free perks like pizza, Red Bull, beer, ping-pong or pool.

For companies struggling to attract female cybersecurity professionals, edited job descriptions have the potential to result in fast, tangible gains. The best place for hiring managers to start is by reviewing job descriptions for masculine terms and balancing these with feminine words, such as collaborative, committed, connected, cooperative, dependable, interpersonal, loyal, responsible, supportive, trust, and considerate, in order to convey a diverse workforce. Companies like Textio, an advanced machine-learning platform for writing better job postings, can make this much easier. Textio instantly predicts the hiring performance of your post by comparing it to more than 50 million others, along with providing clear guidance on how to improve it. Furthermore, it boasts that on average, hiring teams with a 90+ Textio score recruit a talent pool

<hr>

5. https://www.sussex.ac.uk/webteam/gateway/file.php?name=gendered-wording-in-job-adverts.pdf&site=7

that is 24% more qualified with 12% more diversity, and they do it 17% faster than those with a lower score.

This is exactly what the Security Department at Vodafone in the UK is doing. Led by a forward thinking and highly regarded CISO, Emma Smith, who has an ambitious goal to increase the numbers of women to 30% within her department, and working closely with a supportive and collaborate HR department along with some other best practices, it's now reviewing all its job descriptions for gender-coded language.[6]

Searches using recruitment agencies

Once I'd examined job descriptions, I then looked at whether recruitment agencies were being used, and if so what types of searches they applied. I knew from experience and from talking to other recruiters in the industry that there are three types:

1. Contingency
2. Retained
3. Engaged

A Contingency Search is typically the most popular, and it's when a hiring manager instructs multiple recruitment agencies. The reason they do this is because they think they'll maximise coverage, make recruiters work harder, and encourage more competition. With no fee to pay unless the recruiter is successful, the hiring manager feels confident this way will increase the likelihood of a hire.

What the hiring manager is often unaware of is that Contingency Searches actually reduce the chance of finding talent and the quality of the experience. The recruiter knows the risks that are involved with more agencies pursuing the prospective hire, and as a result they won't work as hard. If the recruitment agency is built on a Contingency Search model, the recruiters typically won't be able to

---

6. https://textio.com/

spend long taking the job specification. They also won't be trained and will lack knowledge of the industry. Without any investment, they'll perform keyword searches on their database for candidates who might fit the specification.

A Retained Search is when the hiring organisation pays a fee to retain a professional recruitment agency. Senior hires are usually recruited this way. Typically payments are staged and paid in thirds – the first is upfront, the second is when a shortlist of candidates is received, and the third at the time of placement. Retained Searches are usually more costly. However, they're extremely comprehensive, and an investment is made from the hiring manager and the recruitment agency. There may be multiple meetings onsite with all the stakeholders, so the hiring manager's workplace culture is understood, and potential candidates may be named prior to any search and then targeted. Both parties nurture a long-term relationship and often go into each search with an expectation that the job will take six months to fill.

The Engaged (or Contained) Search is a hybrid approach. It's less costly and more agile than a Retained Search, and gives the hiring manager more control and dedicated attention than a Contingency Search. With a small upfront fee that's paid as an advancement of the total recruitment fee, many believe this approach serves the hiring manager, candidate, and recruiter best and at the highest level.

Candidate selection

Moving on to the screening process, I discovered a variety of malpractices amongst recruitment consultants, HR practitioners, and hiring managers. For example, many were adopting a screening-in rather than out policy and simply filtering for keywords, degrees, or certifications. Few read the whole CV, including the covering letter, and as a result, details were often missed. Furthermore, smaller private companies regularly ignored any applicant who took the time to contact them to enquire about a position, despite the fact they'd advertised it on their website. And, some companies were even performing three rounds of interviews with senior business stakeholders before testing the job applicant's skills and capabilities.

The beauty premium

The subject of CVs leads me to the beauty premium – a phenomenon where attractive people are perceived (incorrectly) to be more honest, responsible, and intelligent than less attractive ones. As a consequence, they are regarded as more employable and are highly paid. Research performed by Bradley J. Ruffle from Wilfrid Laurier University and Ben-Gurion University, and Ze'ev Shtudiner from Ariel University, on whether good-looking people are more employable suggests that when a headshot is included on a CV, which for some countries, such as those in most of continental Europe and South America, Israel, Japan, Cambodia and China, is either obligatory or law, it can be influential in terms of selection during the recruitment process.

Let me tell you more. The researchers sent 5,312 carefully crafted and appealing CVs in pairs to 2,656 companies in Israel that were advertising jobs in ten different fields of employment: banking, budgeting, chartered accountancy, finance, accounts management, industrial engineering, computer programming, senior sales, junior sales, and customer service. To sidestep the issue of ethnic discrimination, they employed the two most common Israeli family names (Cohen and Levi) in all of their CVs. In each pair, one CV was without a picture, whilst the other, which was virtually identical, contained a picture of either an attractive male/female or a plain-looking male/female.

Upon analysis, they found that the numbers of employer call backs to attractive men were significantly higher than for men with either no picture or who were plain-looking, nearly doubling the latter group. However, strikingly attractive women didn't enjoy the same beauty premium. In fact, women without a picture had a significantly higher rate of call-backs than attractive or plain-looking women.

They also discovered that recruitment agencies and hiring managers at companies differed sharply in their responsiveness to beauty. Recruitment agencies strongly prioritised male candidates accordingly: attractive males followed by no-picture males followed by plain males. These same agencies favoured no-picture females whilst discriminating modestly against plain and attractive females. In sharp contrast, however, the companies that were hiring treated all same-sex beauty categories equally, with the exception of attractive females who were penalised relative to plain and no-picture women.

The result of this research is both alarming and empowering, depending on your demographic. For example, highly attractive males can be encouraged to attach a photograph to their CVs in cultures where the inclusion of a picture is left up to the applicant. Conversely, attractive and plain looking women would be advised (if possible) to omit their photographs from their CVs, for an inclusion actually decreases their chances of getting a call back by 20% to 30%, or more – up to 41% – for attractive women if the company at which the chosen candidate will be employed is also in charge of hiring.[7]

The interview phase

Once the initial screening process had been completed, some companies were performing phone interviews. Typically these were only being executed for entry-level positions where candidates were in good supply. If this was the case, few hiring managers sent the candidates a range of industry questions that they'd likely be asked, for example, 'What do you think the main threats facing a global [insert your sector] business would be?' However, those who did were able to test how resourceful and committed the candidate was to the position that was being advertised, which saved time. It separated

---

7. https://papers.ssrn.com/sol3/papers.cfm?abstract_id=1705244

out the candidates who were interested in a cybersecurity career from the ones who just wanted to get a position in the company and then transfer into a role that they were really after.

These hiring managers also asked their entry-level candidates questions like, 'Have you ever been in a situation where...?' or 'I realise that you haven't done much paid employment, but feel free to tell me about a time when...' These were better questions to ask than 'Tell me about how you solved or tackled...', as most entry-level candidates didn't have the experience. The questions also enabled the candidate to relax and open up so the hiring manager could find out more.

During the interview phase, I discovered huge issues, as many hiring managers were either using unstructured interview processes, or structured interviews that had been badly designed. Hiring managers seemed oblivious to the fact that they were inadvertently selecting talent in their own image. Repeatedly I heard them defend their informal approach, such as, 'We just go to a coffee shop/bar/pub and have a chat', claiming that cultural fit – the likelihood that a candidate will be able to conform and adapt to the core values and collective behaviours that make up the organisation, or the degree to which a candidate's background, hobbies, and self-presentation are similar to the organisation's existing employee base – was the reason why. Whilst I've reviewed multiple recruitment agency reports on how cultural fit is a top priority for companies recruiting, there are better and fairer ways to achieve this.

Thankfully, some leaders understand this and are implementing changes or creating radically different types of cybersecurity organisations. Dug Song and Jon Oberheide, the co-founders of Duo Security are such leaders, and they've looked at security through a fresh lens. Founding their organisation seven years ago, they set out to build a fundamentally different kind of company from those that were already in the market and driven purely by revenue. With a mission to build better security not more of it, the way they're accomplishing this is by focusing on people.

Both believe that security challenges are all about people. When a system is compromised, typically it's people who are targeted rather than technologies, so knowing how people use technology and understanding how consumerisation has changed the market really matters.

As a result, when they began hiring strategically for growth, they didn't look for employees with stellar security résumés. Instead, they hired for cultural contribution and looked for new recruits who could provide an outside-in point of view, and help them enhance their ability to service their customers. Essentially, they wanted people who reflected the broad backgrounds and needs of their customers. Only by being purposeful about diversity in their recruitment processes could they hope to deliver flowing creativity, continuous change, and a superior customer experience, which is where they are today.

Blind auditions

During the 1950s in the USA, many orchestras decided to modify their hiring practices in an attempt to overcome gender biased hiring. Until then, they'd relied on the conductor to handpick musicians. Convinced that they were not selecting musicians on account of their gender, some orchestras agreed to conceal the identity of the musicians auditioning by placing a screen in front of them so that those hiring could only hear the music they played, which was the criteria they'd established for selection.

During preliminary auditions, this increased the likelihood that a female musician would advance to the next round by 11%, and to selectionby 30%. In the years that followed, changes in the selection process meant the percentage of female musicians in the five highest-ranked orchestras in the nation increased from 6% in 1970 to 21% in 1993.[8]

Blind auditions enable greater levels of gender diversity and may provide a way forward. I say that with a warning, as they don't always work, and need to be tested in your company. However, on the basis that they will work for your company, they can get around the unconscious beliefs and biases that are so deeply engrained in the minds of hiring managers – that women aren't as good as men in technical professions, such as cybersecurity. They directly tackle both confirmation bias – the tendency to interpret new evidence as confirmation of one's existing beliefs or theories – and the halo effect – whereby commonalities, unintentional associations and rapport bind the candidate and hiring manager during the interview process and affect how subsequent information is assessed.

How to use structured interviews successfully

When I spoke to Vicki Gavin, Compliance Director and Head of Business Continuity and Information Security at an English-language weekly magazine-format newspaper, she agreed.

'As soon as the candidate arrives for the interview, they're met by my PA. Unbeknown to them, this will be their first interview. The aim here is to settle them and make them feel at ease. I then use structured interviews and multiple interviewers, at least five, including one female, rather than a panel.

'Prior to any interviews, we meet as a group and define what skills and competencies we're looking for in our next hire. We then compile the questions we're going to ask the candidates and circulate them amongst the group to check that the other interviewers are in agreement. Next, we devise our scoring matrices, which are

---

8. http://gap.hks.harvard.edu/orchestrating-impartiality-impact-%E2%80%9Cblind%E2%80%9D-auditions-female-musicians

typically on a scale of 1–5 for each interview question, and add their weights.

'During the interview, we talk to each candidate separately. We ask each one the same questions, and in the same order. We're careful of the language we're using, not to frame questions, and whether we're succumbing to any biases. Then we score candidates immediately after they've answered the question. At the end of the interviews, each interviewer compares each candidate's answers. We do this horizontally across candidates, and one question at a time. Then we submit our scores and meet as a group to discuss the results and go through any contentions, which so far we've rarely had.'

Vicki's approach works well as she collects multiple data points from at least five interviewers, which outdoes one data point from either one interviewer or one collective group, for example a panel. Additionally, by recording the score immediately after each question is asked to the candidate, she's able to ensure that the interviewer remembers accurately rather than misremembering, which is a real threat to an assessment because people are naturally wired to make decisions based on their most intense and recent experiences.

As you're probably gathering, performing structured interviews is much harder work than having an informal chat. But, when the top 1% of employees are twenty-five times more productive than the median employees, and given the importance of the jobs that we're performing, it makes sense to ensure you're recruiting in a manner that secures the best talent. There's good news, too, for technology can help.

How to use technology to support your recruitment efforts

The first tool I'm going to tell you about is GapJumpers. This asks each candidate to solve skills-based challenges anonymously to prove that they're qualified and capable of doing the job they're applying for.[9] The tool then removes each candidate's CV and personal identifiable information, such as their name, as it could reveal their gender, race, or ethnicity; their graduation year, as it could give away their age; their college, which could tell the hiring manager what type of school they went to; and their address, which could drive the hiring manager to make assumptions about their socio-economic background. Using algorithmic and human expertise, GapJumpers ranks the best applications for review by employers. It then allows the candidate and hiring manager to interact. The hiring manager is able to review anonymous work samples, which avoid CV bias, and to select the best diverse talent from a crowd.

In a similar fashion, Unitive actualises five hiring best practices across the entire hiring process in one easy-to-use solution to enable you to find the person who best fits each job from a broader, more qualified pool of candidates.[10] The first thing the tool asks you to do is to prioritise job skills by using its stackable drag and drop interface. It then leverages machine learning to write more effective job descriptions, checking for gender-coded language along the way. By removing the candidate's name, gender, and other personal identifiers, it ensures a blind audition, which helps hiring managers to focus on the most relevant criteria for the job. Once this is done, it preps for your interviews so you can focus on the best predictors of job success. At the end of the process, you'll be able to capture the right data to make predictive hiring decisions.

Applied is a more in-depth tool. It works from the premise that without structure, people make inconsistent and unexamined decisions, and that we're all unconsciously biased in any number of unexpected ways.[11] However, by structuring and blinding your applications process, it can help you to make the best hiring deci-

9. https://www.gapjumpers.me/
10. http://www.unitive.works/
11. https://www.beapplied.com/

sions for your organisation. As managers often shoulder the hiring burden alone, Applied puts your team to work, using their different experiences and perspectives to define roles and analyse applications. It also tracks and automatically responds to unsuccessful candidates to give them prompt replies and meaningful feedback. Its six-phase process is comprised of design, apply, review, interview, hire, and feedback.

It works like this:

DESIGN. Applied starts by designing the job description, as what you say changes whom you attract. Then it gets you to create predictive work tests, so you can test your candidates based on the job that they'll be doing. You can choose predictive tests from Applied's library (numerical reasoning, coding, analytical and situational judgement), edit these, or simply add your own.

APPLY. Once the design has been done, you'll have a live application for candidates to apply through. This can be linked to your social media or websites. Applied will then track and present your marketing performance, allowing you to optimise where you're marketing your roles. It will also tell you where you're finding your most diverse candidate pools, which ensures that your application is not going unseen. Furthermore, it lets you know how sticky your application is, and if candidates have failed to complete the application, it allows you to invite them back.

REVIEW. Without a name, gender, or age, Applied has found that candidates from more diverse groups get interviewed. By comparing candidates one question at a time, like Vicki does, it's able to ease the cognitive burden on reviewers by identifying the best responses. And, by getting three independent interviewers, it's able to harness the wisdom of the crowd.

Once the applications are in, Applied's results will give an order of merit and granular data on each candidate's performance. You can also see how the candidate demographics measure up.

INTERVIEW. With a data-driven approach and in-built calendar tool, Applied will automatically email the candidates whom you want to interview, saving much time. It will help with the structured interview process and advise you on the diversity characteristics of each candidate during each interview round. This enables you to measure and benchmark your gains as you create a more equitable and inclusive hiring process.

HIRE. Applied ensures you've made the right hiring choices, irrespective of candidates' background.

FEEDBACK. At the end of the process, Applied will email all the applicants and give them feedback on how well they did, including their strengths and weaknesses. Finally, as it's predictive, the tool learns from the whole process of each hiring round.

Using Axiology

There's one more practice that I'd like to mention for recruitment that could either complement the approaches I've written about so far or be used in preference to them, and it's based on the philosophical study of value. Traditionally there are three main ways in which people are recruited into a company – via academic qualifications, technical expertise, and psychometric profiling. However, what we're oblivious to is that all three could be flawed when it comes to recruiting for a career in cybersecurity, particularly one that's gender diverse.

Within security there are a significant number of professional qualifications, or certifications, that individuals can gain through experience or examination. Of these certifications, five are globally recognised and valued: Certified Information Security Professional (CISSP), Certified Information Systems Auditor (CISA), Certified

Information Security Manager (CISM), Systems Security Certified Practitioner (SSCP), and GIAC Security Essentials. Data from recruitment agencies, such as Burning Glass, show that over 35% of all cybersecurity jobs require at least one of these five globally recognised certifications.[12]

Whilst some hiring managers specifically require certain expertise, all jobs require far more than academic knowledge. Screening on academic qualifications or industry qualifications, either by subject name or grade, therefore, limits the talent pool from which you can draw. With fewer girls accessing Computer Science at a secondary or tertiary level, recruitment will continue to be limited to a small male-dominated group. Furthermore, there's evidence that the second most popular degree for recruiting cybersecurity professionals is English Language.

When it comes to recruiting using experience as the hiring criteria, many companies use competency-based interviews with questions based around 'Tell us of an example when.' However, this method is to some extent flawed because any examples the candidate gives will be based in the past. As our thinking is not fixed, and can and will change depending on our circumstances, there's no guarantee that because someone has been successful in the past, they'll be successful in the future.

Additionally, people are not honest, and it's easy to make up, embellish, or borrow examples of where they've demonstrated competencies. Research has also shown that men will tend to overplay their role in success, whereas women will tend to underplay theirs, so that the answers interviewers hear are not necessarily true representations of the candidates' strength in key competencies. And, there's no guarantee that competencies which a candidate has

---

12. http://www.darkreading.com/careers-and-people/how-to-raise-your-salary-in-cybersecurity/d/d-id/1325068

demonstrated can be accessed in an organisation's unique culture and working environment.

Recruiting using psychometric testing is not much better, as the tests rely on a degree of self-awareness and honesty, and whilst they claim to be objective, they're actually based on subjectivity. The outcomes can also be affected by cheating.

Recruiting using Axiology tools, which are what I use when consulting, is more reliable. Axiology tools measure the candidate's actual thinking process through their value thinking (i.e. how they make decisions), and the reports are based on direct analysis of this thinking process as they're one-step removed from the subject. By this I mean that the tool has no understanding of the candidate's thinking filters, focus, and biases. Each assessment is straightforward, takes fifteen minutes to complete, and asks candidates to rank items/objects/people/opinions in order of importance to determine their value structure.

Getting the right talent in requires an approach that is objective, future-focused, and non-discriminatory. Performance predictive methodologies, such as Axiology, when applied with a scientific benchmark defining desired current or future culture are even more relevant in an evolving industry such as cybersecurity where the skills and competencies needed are constantly changing as we try to 'out-fox' our adversaries.

Boomerang hires and alumni management

This chapter couldn't end without mentioning boomerang hires and alumni management, as they provide a way for an organisation to regain their human capital, and increase industry knowledge. Defined as an employee who leaves an organisation and re-joins at a later date, boomerang hires are growing in popularity. As jobs aren't for life anymore, and cybersecurity professionals may only stay with an organisation for a few years – three to five if you're lucky – keeping in contact with former employees who are known entities to the business makes sense.

From the dialogues I've had with women in the field, I know that the reasons they cite for moving jobs are misalignment to their organisation's culture, burn-out, unfair treatment, feeling bypassed for promotion, or on account of family. Furthermore, when they leave, most women in cybersecurity do so on good terms. Yet, at the time of exit, rarely, is the door clearly left open for them should they wish to return, and few remain in contact afterwards. Predictably, valuable, developed talent is lost.

One of the Big Four in the UK is certainly bucking this trend. When I met with a former employee of theirs, she told me how impressed she was with their alumni management system.

Looking at these models, most are built upon an organisation's existing HRIS platform, and they provide a fully customisable solution for helping organisations connect, stay in touch, and manage their alumni community. By maintaining a comprehensive profile of alumni, including their job role, employer and skills, the data that's captured can be integrated into internal recruitment or talent systems for boomerang hire opportunities. For an organisation's alumni, this means they can access a rich learning, sharing and networking resource, plus benefit from a range of perks, including referral fees for recommending new hires, as well as job offers.

The Golden Rules

- Assess your recruitment process to measure the demographics of the applicants
- Check your job descriptions and advertisements for gender-biased language and offer flexible work conditions if you can
- Ask recruitment consultants or HR practitioners to send you equal numbers of women applicants, but get them to remove

the candidate's name, graduation year, colleges and schools attended, address, and headshot

- Use a structured interview process with multiple interviewers, ensuring you include one female interviewer
- Be prepared to compromise on the detail of the job description, but not on the calibre of the candidate
- Measure your progress for diverse hiring at each level of management
- Keep in regular contact with your alumni

A checklist for identifying and recruiting female cybersecurity talent

Writing the job description:

- ✓ Approach the job description from a mindset of screen in rather than out
- ✓ Write your job descriptions from scratch
- ✓ Keep your key requirements/responsibilities to four or five bullet points
- ✓ Ensure the role is put into context
- ✓ Think about whether you want to include 'nice-to-haves', and if so be careful of how you phrase these
- ✓ Give your applicants clues as to what you're looking for
- ✓ Focus on what soft skills you're looking for, too
- ✓ Ensure the language you use is gender neutral

Screening candidates:

- ✓ Don't just look for keywords, degrees or certifications (check with your recruiter if they're performing this function)
- ✓ Read the whole CV, including the covering letter, as sometimes that's where you'll find the detail

197

✓ Assess everything

✓ Perform a phone interview if you need to filter, and send candidates a range of questions that they'll likely be asked so they can prepare

Before the interview:

✓ Decide what you're looking for in a candidate – skills and competencies

✓ Decide how many interviewers you'll use and their demographics

✓ Compile your questions and circulate with the other interviewers to ensure agreement

✓ Determine your scoring matrices on a scale of 1–5 for each interview question, then agree them with the other interviewers

✓ Send the candidates the types of questions they'll be asked.

During the interview:

✓ Interview each candidate separately

✓ Ask candidates the same questions and in the same order

✓ Consider the language you're using and whether you're succumbing to the halo effect

✓ Score candidates immediately after they've answered the question

After the interview:

✓ Compare each of the candidates' answers horizontally across candidates and one question at a time

✓ Submit your scores

✓ Meet as a group to discuss the results and any contentions

✓ Feedback to the candidates on their strengths and weaknesses and inform the successful candidate they're hired

Scoring process example

Score	Rating	Definition
0	No evidence	No evidence was provided.
1	Poor	Poor evidence was provided, along with few positive indicators and many negative indicators. Overall the candidate displayed strong limitations across most areas.
2	Some concern	Some evidence was provided and the candidate showed both positive indicators and negative indicators. Overall they displayed strong limitations in some areas.
3	Adequate	Adequate evidence was provided, which revealed a satisfactory level of positive indicators along with some negative indicators. Overall the candidate demonstrated strengths in many areas with some limitations.
4	Strong	Strong evidence was provided, and the candidate displayed many positive indicators and clear strengths in the majority of areas.

11. Enter The Dragon

- Hackathons, competitions, and challenges
- Are men more competitively inclined than women?
- The role environment plays
- How to attract girls and women to compete more

It was Sunday morning and, as usual, I'd received an email from Sunil Bali, an executive coach and speaker I'd been following for a while. This week he'd written about Sarah Blakely, the world's youngest self-made female billionaire to date. He wrote how she'd started an underwear company, Spanx, with only US $5,000 worth of savings, and every week on the agenda of her team meetings she has a line that reads, 'Oops, I did it again'.

This is something she says she learnt from her father whilst growing up. According to her, every week, he'd ask her and her brother to tell him what they'd failed at, and whenever she said that she'd tried out for something and was unsuccessful, her father would high five her and say, 'Congratulations! Way to go!' She said that by doing this, he helped her reframe her definition of failure and made her more resilient.

'Failure for me became not trying and not learning, rather than just a result.'

Sunil's email got me thinking. Few women have grown up in an environment like Sarah's, where risk and failure is celebrated and made acceptable. Fewer still, particularly in cybersecurity, where failure can be career suicide, work for an employer who values this. Many instead have been brought up from an early age to be compliant, and to perform. And, as I said in Chapter 3, they've also witnessed the harsh reality that if they want to get on in the workforce then they need to demonstrate their worth by obtaining qualifications, certifications, and degrees, and by being, to quote the women themselves, 'Twice as good as any man'. As a result, more women than men shy away from situations where they could be exposed to failure, poor performance, or rejection. And, as a consequence, lower numbers of women will readily put themselves forward to compete.

Hackathons, competitions, and challenges

Understanding this is particularly relevant for us in cybersecurity. Over the last few years, cybersecurity hackathons – events, typically lasting several days, in which a large number of people who are either working in, interested in, or studying cybersecurity meet at a venue or online to engage in collaborative ethical computer hacking competitions or to build new products or services – have become popular. The premise many of them are working from is that cybersecurity professionals, who are typically bound by insular organisational structures, can work better as large cooperative teams to develop countermeasures, and thereby outsmart attackers who are working collaboratively in disparate, more flexible collectives.

It's a sound principle, and governments and businesses from all over the world have seen hackathons as a means not only to solve problems or create new products or services, but to attract and recruit new talent. In many ways, they're working well.

In the UK, I recently came across this with the government's Department of Business, Innovation and Skills (BIS) when it partnered with The Accelerator Network to host a three-day hackathon. This saw fifty of the brightest cybersecurity students tackling the critical security issues facing those who supplied UK businesses and the national infrastructure. The event sourced talent from thirteen UK universities which had been identified as Academic Centres of Excellence in cybersecurity research.

Participants worked together on ideas designed to cover common and complex cybersecurity issues, and received tuition and expert advice from The Accelerator Network. They were also encouraged to develop commercial applications for real-life security problems. The hackathon then finished with a pitching competition, for which teams had to present their developments to an audience of partners, industry leaders, and investors.

Moving on from hackathons are initiatives like the Cybersecurity Challenge that occur in the UK, Europe, and Australia, and the Cyber Patriot Competition in the USA. Beginning around 2009, these initiatives focus on addressing the shortage of talent in cybersecurity, and each one provides a range of competitions, learning programmes, and networking that have been designed to identify, inspire, and enable more individuals to become cybersecurity professionals.

Teams consisting of professional bodies, government departments, private industry, and public sector organisations typically manage them, and although the teams operate locally to reflect their countries' priorities, they regularly collaborate with one another. Holding a series of competitions throughout the year, they're able to test a range of skills – for example, how to spot vulnerabilities, how to defend networks, and how to extract and analyse complex information.

When contestants win one of these competitions, they're then invited to join a grand final or master class, competing with other finalists from across the competitions. The winner is then crowned and awarded prizes worth tens of thousands of pounds, euros, or dollars along with educational and career development opportunities, such as bursaries, paid internships, private sector training courses, and mentorship, not to mention PR.

Although commendable for attracting some new talent, events like these have their own challenge to solve: attracting female talent. As a result, they're missing a pool of resource and aren't working as effectively as they could.

Josephine Wolff has a view on why, and she writes about it in 'Hackathons Have a Gender Problem'. She contends that hackathons are positioned for young, energised, anti-establishment males and are putting a lot of women off. Marie desJardins, Professor of Computer Science and Associate Dean at the University of Maryland, USA, describes what the vast majority of women think about these events.

'These hackathons are not very pleasant places to hang out. You're supposed to think, *I'm gonna wear the same clothes and stay up all night working on this thing because I'm so brilliant and so dedicated.* I think even the word hackathon is just a really unappealing word – it brings up a certain set of images which aren't usually very appealing to women.'

If you look at the photos on their websites or have ever attended a hackathon or competition, you may understand what she's referring to. Events like these can be intimidating to women, and that's probably why Deloitte Women in Technology ran a women-only hackathon late in 2015 in London. Although it wasn't purely focusing on cybersecurity, this event is worth mentioning, and the reason why will become clear shortly.

Being one of the first all-female hackathons, it brought together five teams of women for one day who were made up of representatives from Deloitte, its clients, and students. Their big task was to use their creative and programming skills to compete in designing and building prototype products that would encourage women and girls to pursue careers in technology. The hackathon then culminated in the teams presenting their products to an esteemed industry panel of judges, and being available for questions and answers.

Are men more competitively inclined than women?

Looking at the low uptake of women at hackathons, competitions and challenges, and having trawled through a multitude of research papers and spoken to gender equality experts, I now have a clearer understanding of why more women may not be participating in these events. Research suggests a few reasons.

The first is that women, due to their gender, have different attitudes to risk and competitions than men. So, could the reason more women do not compete in hackathons, the Cybersecurity Challenge and the Cyber Patriot Competition, be as simple as the fact that men are more competitively inclined than women? I wanted to find out.

In a field experiment on gender differences in job-entry decisions, Jeffrey A. Flory, Andreas Leibbrandt, and John List sought to look into the differences between men and women in accordance to competitiveness. Their reason for doing so was based on prior gender and competition laboratory experiments. Briefly, these experiments typically involved a researcher who recruited a group of students to participate. They introduced a task, for example, solving mazes, completing mathematical problems, tossing a ball in a bucket, and so on, and then asked each participant to choose their preferred compensation regime. The participants usually had a choice between either a piece rate or a tournament incentive scheme.

Under the former, the participant was paid $1 per successful attempt, and under the latter they were paid $3 per successful attempt if they out-performed an anonymous partner, and $0 otherwise. Unanimous conclusions emerged from these experiments: men tended to prefer the competitive environment to the non-competitive environment, whereas the opposite was true for women, even in tasks where women were more able.

To test whether men and women were indeed affected differently by reward structures characterised by competition and uncertainty, the three researchers conducted a natural field experiment on job-entry decisions in sixteen major cities in the USA. They investigated the extent to which alternative compensation methods affected the proportion of female applicants to actual jobs advertised in different labour markets by posting advertisements to an Internet job-board in cities with different market wages. The set of possible compensation regimes was identical in all cities, and job seekers were randomly offered either fixed-wage compensation, compensation depending mildly on individual relative performance, compensation depending heavily on individual relative performance, team relative performance, or elements of uncertainty. Thereafter, each job seeker decided whether to apply for the position formally.

In addition, the researchers advertised two different job types. One job advertisement presented a job task that was more male-orientated, whilst the other was more female-orientated. Comparing the application patterns for these two job advertisements would clarify the relevance of task-dependence and gender-task associations.

With nearly 7,000 interested job applicants replying to their advertisements, what they found was that whilst both genders disliked competitive environments, women disliked them more. Interestingly, they withdrew from competitive work settings disproportionately compared to men when the position's compensation was advertised as being extremely competitive.[1]

From these experiments and more, we could easily deduce that women have a higher aversion to risk, dislike competitions, and have lower self-confidence than men. However, women are complex and it's not quite as straightforward as this.

From further experiments, researchers have found that the

---

1. http://www.nber.org/papers/w16546

gender gap in competitive environments reverses when men and women compete in teams. Allowing women to choose the gender of their co-participant can also boost their self-confidence and increase their willingness to compete, but it can lower men's. As men become concerned about their team members' abilities, more withdraw from competitive environments, and this is more pronounced amongst high performing men when their compensation is determined by team performance. Furthermore, a higher predicted competitiveness of women induces more competition. [2] [3]

Another interesting twist arises out of sponsorship. A sponsor is often a person of influence within a company who, unlike a mentor, acts as an advocate for a protégé in what is ideally a transactional relationship. The expectation of a sponsor is that they'll use their knowledge, expertise, and connections to advance the career of their protégés, and in some companies their salary is dependent upon their protégés' performance.

Building on prior research, which suggests that sponsorship increases confidence, compensation, and willingness to compete within one's cohort, Nancy Baldiga and Katherine Baldiga Coffman performed a laboratory experiment in which they tested whether women's advancement could be improved using a sponsorship programme. Testing in a public accounting professional environment, they found that men were more willing to compete than women, and sponsorship increased this. Additionally, men were more confident in their ability to perform than women; they made significantly more money; and sponsorship benefitted low-performing men the most. But, they also found that women were more willing to com-

2. https://halshs.archives-ouvertes.fr/halshs-00661770
3. http://ftp.iza.org/dp2001.pdf

pete when their sponsor signalled they were doing well, particularly highly talented women.[4]

The role environment plays

Getting women to compete readily is difficult, but can it be easier if you provide conducive situations and environments? This was a question that Laura Gee of Tufts University wanted answered, specifically in regard to how job seekers online were responding to information on what other job seekers were doing. So, in 2012, she used data from LinkedIn and assessed the behaviour of about two million job seekers, most of whom had a degree, were from more than 200 countries, and were viewing about 100,000 jobs.

In the field experiment, the job seekers viewed a wide variety of jobs that had been posted by about 21,000 companies, mostly from high tech or finance sectors. Then Laura randomly split up the job seekers. One lot saw the number of job seekers who'd applied for a job online, the other lot didn't. When she analysed the data, what she found was that men weren't interested in knowing how many job seekers were applying for a job online, but women were.

Furthermore, knowing how competitive a job was didn't put women off applying; in fact, it increased the likelihood. It turns out that the desirability of a job mattered more than the tougher competition. Her intervention increased the probability of a person starting or finishing an application by 2–5%, representing a potential increase of thousands of applications per day.[5]

How to attract girls and women to compete more

So even armed with this knowledge, the question still begs: will we ever attract more women to cybersecurity hackathons or com-

---

4. http://gap.hks.harvard.edu/laboratory-evidence-effects-sponsorship -competitive-preferences-men-and-women
5. http://econpapers.repec.org/paper/tuftuftec/0780.htm

petitions when it looks like women just don't like to compete? Additionally, is there a better way to recruit female cybersecurity professionals?

The answer to both questions is quite possibly yes. In reference to the Deloitte women's-only hackathon, when it comes to women and competing, culture or environment really matter. When women are in a room full of women, they're more likely to compete, and when they're in women-only environments, they do better in competitions.[6]

The case for nurture when it comes to women putting themselves forward for tournaments and competitions is strong, which leads me to studies surrounding single-sex schooling for girls. It's claimed that when girls are educated in a single-sex environment it can favour their competitiveness, their likelihood of choosing subjects considered more male, and their academic achievements. This is of particular interest to me, not because I was educated in a single-sex school from when I was ten to sixteen years old, but because I've been witnessing what may or may not be a trend amongst cybersecurity women. Without making any deductions, as they could be false, I'm researching this, and as this is still ongoing, if you want to help, you can.

If you're a woman go to https://www.surveymonkey.co.uk /r/3CGKZ6W.

If you're a man go to https://www.surveymonkey.co.uk /r/R2BXNC8.

Educational studies' findings do indicate that when girls are placed in a co-educated environment, they may be under more pressure to maintain their gender identity, which may lead them to conform to boys' expectations of how girls should behave so they're not socially rejected. Therefore, if behaving competitively is

---

6. http://web.stanford.edu/~niederle/NV.JEP.pdf

perceived as being a masculine trait, then being educated alongside boys might result in girls making less competitive choices.

This is certainly what Alison L. Booth and Patrick J. Nolen from the University of Essex wanted to test. Using a controlled experiment with students who were almost fifteen years old from publicly funded British single-sex and coeducational schools, they examined the role of nurture in explaining the reason why women shied away from competition. Studying the choices made by the girls from both types of schools when they were given the opportunity to enter a tournament, they uncovered significant differences between the competitive choices of girls from single-sex and coeducational schools. Moreover, when the girls from a single-sex school were randomly assigned to mixed-sex experimental groups, they behaved more like boys.

Consequentially, the researchers concluded that the reason why the average female avoids competitive behaviour more than the average male is not on account of their gender, but due to social learning – in other words, nurture.[7]

Not every country has a single-sex schooling environment, and I'm not suggesting that it's fundamental in order for a girl to want to complete. In Sweden, there are no single-sex schools, but the country is progressive when it comes to gender equality. Interestingly, too, when a study was performed there with children aged seven to ten years old, there appeared to be no difference in competitiveness.[8]

Other work also suggests that gender may be attributed to nurture. In 2009, Gneezy, Leonard and List looked into the role of nurture, and compared subjects from two distinct societies – the patriarchal Maasai tribe of Tanzania and the matrilineal Khasi tribe

---

7. http://legacy.iza.org/en/webcontent/publications/papers/viewAbstract?dp_id=4027
8. http://legacy.iza.org/en/webcontent/publications/papers/viewAbstract?dp_id=4027

in India. They found that in the patriarchal society, women were less competitive than men, just like the results from studies using data from Western cultures. However, in the matrilineal society, women were found to be as competitive as Maasai men.

What we can learn from all this research is that when it comes to attracting women to cybersecurity through competitions, the environment really matters. With this in mind, I investigated the gaming world and the work that's being done there to attract and identify female cybersecurity talent.

As Jay Abbott, Managing Director of Falanx Cyber Defence and Chair of the Competitions Board at the Cybersecurity Challenge UK, remarked, 'The big thing missing from bringing talent into the industry is actually engaging the talent where they live, which is in the games world.' He's right, particularly when it comes to women, as I discussed in Chapter 6. Research shows that the gender split is now fairly even amongst adults, teenagers and children gamers. The gaming environment enables people who are interested in cybersecurity to be brought together in a fun way. And, they can either compete individually, where they're identified or not, or in teams that are mixed or women-only.[9]

The Golden Rules

- Women dislike competitive environments more than men, even when they're more able than men, unless you provide conducive situations and environments
- Women are more willing to compete when they're placed either in teams, or in women-only environments, or for jobs which are seen to be oversubscribed and desirable

---

9. http://www.wired.co.uk/news/archive/2015-10/01/cyphinx-cyberse curity-game

- Confidence matters and sponsors can encourage more women to compete, particularly when they're high-performing talent

A checklist for hackathons, competitions and challenges

✓ **Are your hackathons or competitions held in appealing, non-threatening environments?** If you're going to attract more women into cybersecurity then you need to ensure they feel comfortable, included and safe.

✓ **Are you using gaming environments for competitions and challenges?** As the gender split is now fairly even amongst adults, teens and children gamers, the gaming environment enables people who are interested in cybersecurity to be brought together in a fun way. And, they can either compete individually, where they're identified or not, or in teams that are mixed or women-only.

✓ **Are you holding women-only hackathons or competitions?** If you do, you'll attract more girls, teens or women and they'll also do better.

✓ **Are you holding mixed gender hackathons or competitions and if so, are you allowing females to pick their co-participant?** If you are then this will increase their self-confidence and willingness to compete. However, it may also decrease males. Consider the ramifications of doing so.

✓ **Are you ensuring women are encouraged by their sponsor?** Women are more likely to compete when their sponsor has signalled that they're doing well, especially highly talented women.

✓ **Are you ensuring you're telling women job applicants how many apply for your jobs?** Desirability matters more to women than tougher competition.

Challenge Three: Retention

12. Cultivating Workplace Culture

- Workplace happiness
- Communication, including humour
- Workplace flexibility
- Workplace policies
- Work-hard, play-hard cultures
- Collaborative, open and inclusive cultures
- Creating a culture of equal pay and promotion

I knew something was up when Megan emailed and asked if I'd have time for a coffee when I was next in town. As we chatted, she told me that she was thinking of resigning from her new role as a Senior Risk Officer at a large bank and leaving cybersecurity altogether. She was miserable, dumbfounded at the culture of her new workplace, and tired of it all.

As she described her environment, my heart sank.

'Jane, you'd think that this organisation was perfect judging from all their activity and PR. I know that they're committed to gender diversity, are meeting their targets for women, and are trying really hard to improve things for women in the organisation, but it's just not working out for me here. I was in a meeting the other day and, as usual, I was the only woman present. More senior managers surrounded me, as did junior executives. When I brought forward an idea, one of the more junior executives scoffed out loud. Quite frankly, I was shocked. I found it hugely inappropriate, and it was embarrassing for me. However, I didn't have the energy to confront him on this, and I'm tired of having to do this – of having to be resilient and of having to think how can I handle this without coming off as the bad guy.

'It's ironic just saying that word, but in all seriousness, I'm fed up of being alone, a minority in the workplace, and not being supported. At no point did any of the senior managers who were present step in to call him out. His behaviour was tolerated, and it certainly signalled to me, and everyone else in that meeting, that this type of behaviour is an acceptable norm for the company, and deeply ingrained in their workplace culture.'

After listening to Megan, I had to consider whether she was overreacting or right to be feeling like this. I couldn't know for sure, as I hadn't been in the room with her. But nonetheless, having chatted to thousands of men and women in cybersecurity from all over the world about their workplace culture, I could be certain of one thing – situations like this for women in cybersecurity are typically the standard, and not the exception, which isn't good.

In my opinion, no one should feel like Megan does at work. It's detrimental to someone's health, their family, and the organisation they work for. What Megan had described to me was workplace culture, and despite what appeared like commendable efforts by her employer, it sounded like there was room for improvement.

For days after, all I could think about was the retention challenge, and how to keep highly educated and trained women in cybersecurity, or entice them back to work when they'd had a career break. It really bothered me, for I knew that if this didn't happen, nothing would change. Women in cybersecurity would still be leaving in greater numbers than they would be joining. They'd still continue to be a minority, suffer gender discrimination, and the progress we'd need to make together, as an industry, to combat our threat actors would not occur.

I knew from studies that workplace stress increased voluntary turnover by almost 50%, as unhappy employees registered with recruitment agencies, declined promotions, or resigned.[1] With this happening, it was clear to me that retention provided the best outcome for all parties, for when women remained in the workplace, they could avoid the stress that went with changing jobs, and organisations could avoid the substantial turnover costs associated with recruiting and training new cybersecurity professionals. Additionally, they'd dodge lower productivity, lost expertise, further resignations from staff, who may be under increased pressure whilst covering another's workload, and higher exposures to attack.

But, putting all these benefits aside, I also knew from experience that happy people at work perform better and increase profits.

Workplace happiness

When Gallup performed a 142 country study on the state of the global workforce, it discovered that only 13% of employees were psychologically committed to their jobs, and that this could be costing companies billions.[2] In the USA alone, this was estimated to be setting the economy back $450 to $550 billion annually, as disengaged employees resulted in 37% higher absenteeism, 49% more accidents, 60% more errors and defects, 18% lower productivity, 16% lower profitability, 37% lower job growth, and 65% lower share price over time.[3] In the UK, Oxford Economics reported that the cost to replace an employee was £30,614, and for more senior

---

1. http://www.stress.org/workplace-stress/
2. http://www.gallup.com/services/178517/state-global-workplace.aspx
3. http://www.gallup.com/services/178514/state-american-workplace.aspx

employees the cost would increase multiple times.[4] Looking at employee happiness another way, economists at the University of Warwick in the UK evaluated 700 participants across four different experiments, and found that a happy workforce could actually cause a spike in productivity of up to 12%.[5]

Shawn Achor, the author of *The Happiness Advantage*, and a former psychology professor at Harvard University, is someone who also advocates the paybacks.[6] In an insightful TED Talk, he described how the human brain works better when a person is feeling positive. According to Shawn, when people are feeling happy and thinking positively, they've a tendency to be more creative, better at solving problems, and more effective collaborators working towards common goals. Furthermore, when they've created strong social networks and good relationships with their peers at work, they're better at staying engaged and performing under stress.[7]

When he studied 11,000 employees, leaders, and physicians at Ochsner Health System, a large healthcare provider, Shawn found that effective social support led to not only more satisfied employees, but also to more satisfied clients. To establish this conclusion, he educated all Ochsner's employees about the impact of social support on the patient experience, and then asked them to modify their behaviour by using the '10/5 system'. All they had to do was to make eye contact and smile when they came within ten feet of another person in the hospital. Then, when they came within five feet of another person, they had to say, 'Hello.' He found that by modifying their conduct in this small way, they achieved

4. http://www.oxfordeconomics.com/my-oxford/projects/264283

5. http://www2.warwick.ac.uk/newsandevents/pressreleases/new_study _shows/

6. http://www.inc.com/jessica-stillman/happiness-makes-your-brain -work-better.html

7. http://www.ted.com/talks/shawn_achor_the_happy_secret_to_better _work

more unique patient visits, a 5% increase in patients' likelihood to recommend the company, and a significant improvement in its medical-practice provider scores.

Creating a culture of happiness through social interaction and connection internally can help with retention, but it's not the only thing that can be done. Coming back to the conversation I had with Megan, the second thing I couldn't help but think about was that most of the time men don't deliberately set out to make women feel miserable in the workplace. However, trouble often arises through poor communication, and this includes humour.

Communication, including humour

Men mock, tease, joke, and use banter a lot, and most of the time when they're hurling insults at one another, they're just fooling around. Often it's a sign that they've a strong bond with each other. I can't tell you how many times I heard my penetration testing team call each other names, and how bitchy I once thought they were being. You see women don't tend to do this with one another. When they throw an insult, it's because they mean it.

Humour is complex, particularly when we work globally, with different cultures, genders and age groups. What's acceptable to one demographic may not be to another. And, according to research, men and women have different types of humour, as they process it in different ways. Although both men and women are funny, the way they use humour with one another can often result in tension, as each gender takes offence at something the other has found funny.

Deborah Tannen, an American academic, and Professor of Linguistics at Georgetown University in Washington, D.C., has studied this extensively, and she believes that men and women use language, including humour, to achieve different goals. She claims that men use conversation and negative humour, such as joke telling, one-liners, slapstick, and banter for one-upmanship, social status, or to demean others. Women, on the other hand, use conversation, compliments, and humorous stories to help them establish closeness with others, and gain mutual support. Although there are always exceptions, research has consistently indicated that these trends exist.[8]

That said, when Martin Lampert of Holy Names University and Susan Ervin-Tripp of the University of California, Berkeley, analysed fifty-nine conversations, they noticed something else that was going on when men and women used humour in each other's presence. Whilst men were more likely to tease and use one-upmanship humour with other men, they teased them significantly less when in the presence of women. Furthermore, in mixed company, women teased more than men, and directed their teasing towards the men. The type of humour associated with gender roles reversed as the women became less self-deprecating, whilst the men laughed at themselves more.

Martin and Susan concluded that men reduced their levels of teasing with women because they were concerned they might deter them, whilst women became more assertive around men to offset feelings of vulnerability, and to position themselves as equals.

Although this could signal progress for women in cybersecurity once they stop being a minority in the workplace, just knowing this won't help those who find themselves in a situation like Megan's. Instead, they need a practical means of dealing with it right now. Sometimes when women in cybersecurity speak to me about these situations, and ask what's the best way of dealing with them, I'll recommend that they laugh it off, make a witty retort, or deal with it tersely and directly, but it really does depend on the situation, and what's been said. It won't help men, either, for what more conversations made me increasingly aware of was that men too were suffering

---

8. http://repository.wellesley.edu/cgi/viewcontent.cgi?article=1323&context=thesiscollection

in the industry. They didn't know how to handle the situation, and were often just as tired of it as women were.

To illustrate what some men are feeling, I'll use John as an example. He's a Professor who teaches Computer Science at a North American university. He's also a huge champion of diversity, and recently told me about an incident that left him feeling deeply uncomfortable.

'I was teaching a class and one of my male students openly belittled one of my female students. I didn't say anything when it occurred, but I did discuss it with the female student straight after. I told her that I'd be speaking to the male student immediately, that his behaviour wouldn't be tolerated, and that he'd have to apologise to her, and the class, when we next met. However, the female student requested another way forward. Instead, she asked me if she could handle it herself. I agreed, she sorted it out, and there haven't been any more occurrences in this class.'

To many, this approach might seem like the wrong thing to do, as the rest of the class had witnessed the behaviour, but were unaware that it was being dealt with. However, in my view, if both parties were happy with the outcome, which they were, and no more instances occurred, then the solution worked. It also empowered the female student. She felt she didn't need her Professor to step in and sort this out, as she was perfectly capable of doing this herself.

And, this is where the problem can sometimes lie – the expectation. The strategy that the female student used worked for her, but Megan wanted another to step in and deal with her colleague's bad behaviour on her behalf, even if it was another man. Unfortunately, without clarity, no one knew how to handle Megan's situation, or even that there was a problem. And the same thing will continue to happen, and more women will resign, or leave the industry completely, unless it's dealt with.

What's important for all parties is that they feel able to communicate how they're feeling without any fear of being labelled as a troublemaker, or someone who's overtly sensitive. Humour is fun and it can really bond a team, but if a woman is on the receiving end of a remark that they find offensive, they'll feel isolated and alienated. Women must consider whether they're being super sensitive too, and if they're not sure, then they need to check with others who may have witnessed what went on. If it still appears offensive, then it needs to be dealt with as soon as possible.

Managers need to be aware that women don't always have the same appreciation of banter as men do, so it's a good idea to steer the type of humour so it's inclusive. Also, if there's an instance of banter or humour that's clearly inappropriate, this needs to be managed. I find the best way to do this is not to make a big deal of it, but to bring it up during an employee's induction when they start. The team will then understand what's acceptable, and what's not.

The same thing goes for profanity, or making sexual remarks about a woman. It's disrespectful, and if you witness this, speak up. I'm fairly hardy, but when a CISO I knew continually used a particular word in a meeting, I had to say something. I dealt with it swiftly, told him that using the word offended me, and politely asked him to stop. He did, and I think the men in the room were grateful that I'd said something, for many didn't like him using it either.

Sexual harassment

Unfortunately, women in cybersecurity can be subjected to sexual harassment. Sometimes it's discreet and at other times it's blatant. Having spoken to thousands of women and read numerous blogs, I've discovered that there's a trend for some companies and countries to offend more than others. Furthermore, few women confront this when it occurs, preferring to turn a blind eye or to leave the workplace instead.

Some experts reason that sexual harassment in the workplace occurs because of sexual tension and desire. Others believe it's more to do with power. When Professor Jennifer Berdahl performed a study of college campuses and workplaces, she discovered that masculine women actually reported higher levels of sexual harassment than feminine women, and it was more common in male-dominated workplaces. She proposed that it was not on account of desire. Rather, it was to punish women who violated feminine stereotypes. Men policed women, and by doing so ensured women conformed to a specific form of femininity that they'd defined culturally.

Corporate cultures can be hostile environments for women in cybersecurity as some are still built around male bonding and facilitated by the sexual objectification of women. Client entertainment after work can involve lap-dancing clubs and some trade shows, particularly in the USA, hire booth babes – a practice Europe hasn't seen for well over a decade.

In 2015, RSA took action to address this by banning booth babes from their 2015 conference in San Francisco. Linda Grey of RSA Conferences said they wanted to '..make security professionals feel comfortable and equally respected during the show.'

Founder and CEO of CyberSN and brainbabe.org, Deidre Diamond, who's been in technology for over 20-years believes now is the time for change. She says her problem is not with having attractive women on stands at trade shows. Rather, it's to do with them not being trained to understand the basics of the cybersecurity products they're representing. It's why Deidre set up #brainbabe and STEAM-Con Connection, which educates STEAM students of all genders on cybersecurity products and services and then connects them to conference booth jobs. Having been hired as an entry-level employee — with a liberal arts degree as a Sociology and Criminal Justice double major — and trained to lead and create cybersecurity software organisations, she believes the community needs to expand its awareness of what it means to be in cybersecurity. By better informing others in regard to what it means to be in cybersecurity she's sure the cybersecurity industry can reap the benefits of a more diverse cybersecurity workforce.

Workplace flexibility

Technology has delivered so many benefits and is changing the way we work. For example, we're working longer hours, communicating with more people, in different time zones and countries, and with multiple technologies. Remote access means we're now working from home more, too, and as a result, fewer companies are insisting that their employees are present in the office every day. Many cybersecurity professionals I know work from home when they want, and simply commute into the office for meetings, or to fulfil projects. Some consultants even work from global locations that they choose to live in.

Fifteen years ago, this was how it was for all the penetration testers I employed. I allowed them to work from anywhere they wanted so long as they could get online. As a consequence, they worked from Australia, Spain, France, Sweden, Finland, Portugal, Bulgaria, Ireland, Thailand, South America, North Africa, and South Africa, and technology made it possible. I thanked them when they went above and beyond, provided an environment that was attractive for them, along with the tools they needed for work, and a means to communicate with the team so they didn't feel isolated. It was incredibly pioneering at the time, yet it made perfect sense to me. Work could continue, staff retention was high, recruitment was easy, everyone was happy, and performance boomed.

What this also showed me was how valued workplace flexibility was for my team, and as a result how it became a key differentiator in terms of my consultancy's recruitment policy. It also made me think about how the workplace is rapidly seeping into our home-lives, how it's becoming an extension of the workplace, how our work-life boundaries are no longer fixed, and how much of a good thing this is going to be for everyone, not just for women in cybersecurity.

I'll explain why.

A regular day for me looks like this. Each day I'm up at 6am dealing with emails, getting ready for work, and making breakfast for my children. I take them to school at 7am, either head into London, which is a four-hour round trip, for meetings or to deliver work, or back home for offline or online meetings with clients, prospects, and business partners. Then, on most days, I'll return to collect my children from school at around 4pm. Working away from home is more challenging. On the days when I have to be in London before 9am, or if I've to stay late, I'll organise a taxi for the children.

When I get home at around 5.30pm, I'll feed my children, help them with their homework, do some household chores like washing or cleaning, and then I'll hold more meetings online, typically via Skype or Zoom with those who are just starting their days. My day doesn't stop until late evening when I answer more emails and social media messages, and write blogs or proposals.

The point that I'm making is that the work gets done. It doesn't matter that I'm a woman, or a mother, or a single parent, or working in an office or remotely from home. What does matter is that I'm able to provide an income for my family, do the work I love, serve my clients well, and be there as a mother for my children. Over the last nineteen years, I've been both an employer and an employee in cybersecurity, and as a woman who works full-time, has three children, no spouse or home help, I can honestly say that juggling it all has been, and still is, extremely hard. I've made sacrifices as, no matter what anyone tells you, you can't have it all.

When you've got children and you work full-time, you've got to manage long working days that sometimes involve time away from home, along with school drop-offs, pick-ups, sick-days and holidays that can range from fourteen to twenty-two weeks per year depending on the schools you've placed your children in. To compensate for my childcare arrangements, and as I'm a global business owner, I'll typically be found working late into the evening, and on some weekends.

This is my choice, and I'm no superwoman – I want to make

that very clear. Thanks to changes in the way that we work, I've managed to find a way that suits my lifestyle. All it requires is for me to work for myself, and have a team of associates, and business partners whom I can call on regularly.

Samira, my virtual PA, is the team member I rely on the most. She books appointments for my children, organises handymen so my house can be maintained, and manages my work diary and travel arrangements. She's there as an emergency back-up, too, for times like when my teenage son, Ethan, missed his train, and subsequently the taxi I'd arranged for him. As I was unavailable to take his call because I was onstage, chairing an event, Samira sorted it out.

To get the most out of a workforce, let alone increase the proportion of women within it, it makes sense to consider workplace flexibility, or new ways of working. For employers, this means defining the expectations clearly and having systems that are set up to support this. For employees, especially parents, it means being crystal clear about what type of schedule works best for them and their family, along with their professional goals and the benefits they can provide to the employer. Women in particular need to communicate these so others, who can affect their career navigation, don't make assumptions based on typical female stereotypes. It means verbalising they're committed, and loyal to their employer; visibly demonstrating their ability, communicating their willingness to return to work after having a baby, or to travel and be away from the home, and to go for promotions or new assignments that will stretch them – if that's the case.

Workplace policies

Being a working mother in cybersecurity isn't as straightforward as many would like it to be. Not only do you have to assess what type of career you want, what type of employer you want to work for, or whether you want to be the employer yourself, you've also got to assess whether it's affordable, as childcare provisions are expensive.

Where I live, the average cost for a nursery place is £11,000 (net) per child, per year, and if you're in London you can add another £3,000 on top.[9] Affordability isn't the only issue, though, as places are competitive, and typically there's a waiting list.

I've spoken to countless mothers in cybersecurity who've struggled with this. To solve the issue, some have chosen nannies, which are even more expensive, or au pairs, as they're a cheaper option. However, both are only viable solutions when accommodation can be provided for them, often along with a car if you're not in a city. Getting women in cybersecurity to return to work after having a child has to be desirable for them, but it also has to be practical, make economic sense, and fit in with their country's culture.

India serves as a perfect example, with many women leaving the workforce once they marry or have children. I referred to this in Chapter 3. Japan is also similar. According to the Japanese women I interviewed, although it enjoys huge technology development in most fields and a highly educated workforce, Japan is very traditional, and practical difficulties exist for women when it comes to combining their careers with motherhood. Childcare is hard to come by, and whilst nurseries are affordable and good quality, they're oversubscribed, and nannies are costly. As a result, the levels of attrition for women soar to 70%, and few return to work after giving birth.

The workplace culture in Japan is tough for women. Typically, flexible working policies are rare, organisations aren't family-friendly, employees work long hours, face-time is valued above performance, and drinking rituals after work are an expectation.

But, Japan and India aren't the only countries with cultural challenges. Life for working mothers in the USA is harsh too, and Jessica Shortall, a strategy consultant and social entrepreneur, wrote

---

9. http://www.dailymail.co.uk/news/article-2288839/Sending-child-nursery-expensive-private-school-cost-time-place-doubles-decade.html

about this in her book, *Work, Pump, Repeat: The New Mom's Survival Guide to Breastfeeding and Going Back to Work*. She detailed how 40% of working mothers in the USA are sole or primary breadwinners, 88% don't get paid leave, and the Federal Family and Medical Leave Act only allows them to take twelve weeks of unpaid time away from work.

According to the OECD, this makes the highly populated, advanced superpower one of only two nations in the world not to guarantee paid maternity leave.[10] Instead, providing paid family leave falls on individual companies, or state governments like California, which is one of only three states in the USA to have such a programme.[11]

Devoid of any firm data for the numbers of women in cybersecurity who leave not to return, I can only share with you data from the tech field, which comes via research from Kieran Snyder, the CEO of Textio. In 2014, when she collected stories from 716 women who'd left the tech industry, she found that 68% cited motherhood as a factor for leaving and not returning, and 10% said it was purely on account of the maternity leave policy. Through her research, she discovered that some were forced to be on call whilst on leave, or return early, and when they did return, many didn't have a set place to express milk, which made it inconvenient and awkward. These were women who didn't want to leave the tech industry; they just wanted to recover after giving birth.[12]

Returning to work within a few weeks of having their babies has a profound effect on women's health and their family's wellbeing. Statistics show that the shorter a woman's leave after having a baby, the more likely she is to suffer from depression and anxiety or to

---

10. https://www.youtube.com/watch?v=SJyE4okoQyA&feature=youtu.be
11. http://paidfamilyleave.org/news-room/blog-posts/do-you-know -about-paid-family-leave-lots-of-californians-dont.
12. http://fortune.com/2014/10/02/women-leave-tech-culture/

commit suicide. Yet, returning to work early is exactly what many working mothers in the USA are doing, and that's even when they're given a choice and are at the top, setting the workplace culture and acting as role models.

Take Marissa Meyer, the CEO of Yahoo. She returned to work two weeks after giving birth to her twin girls, despite the company having a very generous maternity policy. Sheryl Sandberg did something similar, and Baroness Karen Brady, a well-known English sporting executive, politician, television personality, newspaper columnist, author, and novelist took three days' leave with her first child as she had a manager to fire. I too repeated this pattern, stopping work the day before giving birth and returning to work just two days after my last two children were born.

In hindsight, it's not something I'm proud of doing because I believe in leading from the top, and know that practices such as these can send a clear signal to women in a team that if they want to take their full maternity leave, perhaps management isn't for them. I also know that operating in this manner is damaging – ask any working mother who's been subjected to it. What we need is better solutions and win-win scenarios across the world for working mothers and families, and at all stages of their children's development, as it can be just as hard when children get older.

Thankfully, in many parts of the world, new mothers and their employers are supported with statutory maternity programmes provided by their governments. Increasingly, too, new fathers are being supported, which really helps to avert discrimination towards mothers and retain them in the workplace. This forward thinking approach establishes new workplace cultures, and communicates to the workforce that when an organisation chooses to revaluate and put family ahead of work, there's no disadvantage.

Women with children in cybersecurity thrive when there's a workplace culture like this. They know they're needed, are worth investing in, and will go above and beyond for a team and manager who are in full support of a healthy work-life balance. They'll worry less about being judged and excluded from challenging work or cool projects because of family commitments. And then a fantastic workplace culture is formed with strong bonds of connection, loyalty, and support.

But, many organisations aren't stopping there. They're extending workplace flexibility policies to all employees, which is the best solution of all, as then parental discrimination can be ended. Whether an employee has a child, parent, pet, or just prefers to work more flexibly, they believe it shouldn't matter. This is a people issue, not one of gender.

Fujitsu gets this. Working with the UK and Ireland division, it's setting out a new strategy, as it understands that the benefits of attracting and retaining women are more than just a numbers game. It knows that the improvements it wishes to see in its workforce will be underpinned by a culture where women can be completely themselves, achieve their potential, and contribute fully to the success of the company.

Management Consultant and Distinguished Engineer, Sarah Armstrong-Smith, told me how Fujitsu is actively strengthening gender inclusion and has a number of activities planned for this year, some of which include offering workplace flexibility through its Agility Passport scheme, and promoting more female role models via its Stand Out programme.

'Stand Out is a diversity and inclusion initiative that highlights people who stand out for all the right reasons – both in terms of their professional achievements and their inclusive behaviours. Torchbearers are nominated to lead the way, and they're given a platform for three months to share their stories internally and externally so standards and aspirations are raised. Collectively, our aim is for the Torchbearer Network to show the real value of diversity to our business, and inspire others to follow in their footsteps.'

Like Fujitsu, EY has some progressive workplace policies. Whenever I met with their employees, past or present, junior or partners, men or women, within their cybersecurity division in the UK and Ireland, they all conveyed how committed EY is to encouraging their employees to fulfil their family obligations without any fear of compromising their careers. They told me how the company recognises the benefits of building a better working world, and how it's established diversity and inclusiveness networks to help their employees develop career pathways whilst maintaining healthy personal lives. It also has support networks like the Working Parents' Network, Professional Women's Network, and Cross Generation Network. Additionally, it offers flexible work arrangements, like reduced work schedules, career breaks, and seasonal work schedules, and depending on the role, it can often arrange flexible working hours, or work-from-home initiatives.

Organisations that operate in this manner are paving the way for more women to enter and remain in cybersecurity. They're changing the default rules that govern work for women and men – the baseline expectations about when, where, and how work will be done in cybersecurity. As a result, they're reaping the rewards. In fact, EY has estimated that it achieved benefits of £15 million per year when it opted for a new shift in its policies across 10,000 UK employees.

Workplace culture changes like these are impressive, but perks don't have to be reserved for large corporations. The rise of entrepreneurship sends a powerful message that a company is fun, progressive, and competitive. Furthermore, entrepreneurship can lead the way for change in the workplace. And, if childcare provisions are offered, it's a totally viable route for working parents in cybersecurity, and a joint responsibility which isn't exclusive to working mothers. This would be liberating for many men, too, as increasingly they're sharing the childcare responsibility, seeking better work-life balances, and want to spend more time with their children.

Duo Security understands this and it may explain why they've been so successful at retaining such a diverse workforce. Out of

400 employees, 20% are minorities. Duo epitomises best practice when it comes to workplace culture in cybersecurity, and the reason why boils down to the value they place on people. From day one, their founders' goal was to 'build better security, not just more' and that's why they obsessively focus on people and the user experience someone has when they interact with their brand. They've built this philosophy into the fabric of their culture and it extends to every touch point of their brand, whether it's from one of their employees interacting with them from within their organisation, or from a client or partner outside of it.

Branded as 'the most loved company in security', every employee at Duo makes a difference, and can pursue their unique ideas about how to build a great business. They pride themselves on having an open, collaborative environment where people do great work, learn a lot and have fun.

Having built an environment such as this, getting people who share their values is crucial for Duo, as everyone enables one another, and the atmosphere is of family. Although not everyone likes the idea of co-workers being friends, Duo encourages their employees to socialise together, for example, they go on outings or organise picnics where they can bring their family and friends – and to look out for one another. The company actively listens to their employees too, for they know that this is where they'll find out what's working and what's not, which is particularly important when the business is scaling so rapidly. All feedback is acted upon whether it's to do with the design of their physical workspace (desk spaces, chill out zones etc.), their workflows, or how they communicate with each other. They appreciate the impact of environment and how it affects performance. Equally, that a healthy, happy, performing workforce can only be achieved by taking time out of work to recharge.

Work-hard, play-hard cultures

Improvements in culture can make an enormous difference to the way that every cybersecurity professional operates in the workplace, not just women. One to tackle proactively is the work-hard, play-hard culture – that ruthless, macho competition to arrive early, stay late, work harder and party, which remains prevalent amongst many cybersecurity organisations and consultancies, yet has been shown to increase turnover rates and absenteeism, and stifle performance and profits.

The unspoken old-fashioned rule for managers, or anyone aspiring to be one, is that if you leave before a certain time, you're not committed to your job, and promotion will be unlikely. The pressure is particularly noticeable for women, especially if they're mothers or carers. In environments such as these, many women either accept the reality that if they won't conform to expected standards their careers will be stifled, or overly compensate by working harder, staying later, and adopting more of a male persona. They'll try to fit in or otherwise they'll hide their family arrangements. As one newly appointed female cybersecurity professional told me recently, 'I can't even tell my team members I'm a mother for fear I'll be judged and ostracised.'

Whilst this is alarming, from having visited many countries in the world, and interviewed many cybersecurity professionals, I see some countries forging healthier approaches to workplace cultures. In an increasingly connected world where smartphones enable everyone to work around the clock and not switch off, creating a workplace culture that ring-fences an employee's free time is challenging. It's particularly problematic for us in cybersecurity, as incidents occur at any moment, and many professionals are expected to be on call. However, some countries are managing this better than others, and it's largely on account of legislation.

According to the OECD's Better Life Index, Denmark has the best work-life balance of the twenty OECD countries studied. On average, only 2% of Danish workers work more than fifty hours per week, compared to 13% in other OECD countries.[13] Other countries are also encouraging their workforce to disconnect in an attempt to lower stress and improve their employees' work-life balance. They know that working excess hours doesn't improve productivity in the long-term.[14]

From January 2017, French companies with more than fifty employees have had to guarantee them a 'right to disconnect' from their emails outside of office hours. Germany has set laws that forbid managers to contact employees when they're on holiday, and Japan, Spain, and South Korea are also implementing changes.[15]

When it comes to socialising after work, which is often expected if you're going to fit into any team, many women in cybersecurity don't participate. They've told me that if they're not excluded, which is rare, they've usually got family commitments, or have felt too apprehensive to attend. Being the odd one out – the token woman – isn't fun, especially when heavy drinking sessions often ensue, and the chances of being subjected to an initiation ceremony when you're new to a team are high. If women have partaken in these in order to bond with the team, they've usually ended up having to replicate the scene from *Raiders of the Lost Ark* when Marion out-drinks the men at the bar. Whilst after work socialising is great for 'building rapport with the guys' or 'team building' providing you're not pressurised to drink more than you wish to, in most cases it's off-putting for women.

Collaborative, inclusive and open cultures

The only way to improve things for women in cybersecurity and the industry in general, is to create collaborative, inclusive, and open

---

13. http://www.oecdbetterlifeindex.org/topics/work-life-balance/
14. https://www.alternet.org/story/154518/why_we_have_to_go_back _to_a_40-hour_work_week_to_keep_our_sanity
15. http://time.com/4620532/countries-work-life-balance/

workplace cultures. This is especially relevant when women join cybersecurity from another field, for example, law or technology, as often they're labelled as outliers and ostracised by their male co-workers. Women from all over the world have told me that many of their male peers will work hard to undermine them, and they'll use bullying tactics such as intimidation.

One woman's story was typical. She said, 'Some of my male co-workers deliberately use technical jargon because they know I won't understand it. Then, they'll delight in telling me that I'm not technical, and suggest that perhaps cybersecurity isn't for me. I find it irritating, and small minded.'

Behaviour like this can go on for years, and be directed at junior executive all the way up to CISOs, until the woman stands up for herself and proves she's just as capable as the men are, or far better, which is often the case, or leaves the profession completely.

Daksha Bhasker, who works for a Canadian telecommunications and media company as a senior network security architect with the network technology development team, has spoken and written about this before. When I spoke to her, she brought up how unique cybersecurity is because effectively it's built on a culture of exclusion and a community of secrets – secret knowledge, classified information, association with dark hacker communities, trust circles, and other secret resources. She told me how hard it could be to navigate your cybersecurity career, as information is guarded and not widely accessible. As a result, networks of trust form.

She said she'd seen women in cybersecurity strive for acceptance, integration, and equal participation in these trusted networks, yet be excluded simply because they didn't fit the typical profile. In other words, they weren't male. She didn't believe that government security clearances made any difference, either.

All that happens is that women don't advance sufficiently or into core security roles. Instead, they're relegated to security roles that are essential, yet ancillary, for example, administration, project or programme management, business development, marketing, or communications. I'm not surprised anymore when women tell me they've become dissatisfied due to these challenges, or why 56% leave mid-career and choose professions where upward mobility is more achievable.[16]

Conduct like this must be stamped out, for it's affecting the way the industry performs and advances. This will not only help to form a culture that's good for gender diversity, but will be of benefit for the whole team, as collaborative cultures improve success. Knowledge hoarding, silo mentality, and one-upmanship wastes collective brainpower.

Daksha elaborated on this, and told me about a study that was performed by the US military. Entitled 'Women in Battle: What Women Bring to the Fight', the study looked at the US military's decision to integrate women fully. Although the article served to expose the flaws in two persistent objections – the presence of women in combat units erodes the vital bonds that develop between men; and women put men at risk, as they're physically weaker – it did uncover some findings that are interesting in terms of performance. The study found that 'groups are collectively more intelligent than individuals on a range of simple to complex tasks – and that collective intelligence increases as the percentage of women in the group increases.'

The researchers attributed this to a trait they called 'social sensitivity' which is all to do with how well a person reads the emotions of other people. According to them, this ability leads to more collaboration within groups, and women tend to score more highly than men in this category. The study also revealed that when a

---

16. https://www.scmagazineuk.com/rsa-women-breaking-the-glass
-firewall/article/537541/

single person or a small proportion of the population dominated a group's conversation, the group became collectively less intelligent than those in which communication was evenly shared. Additionally, groups with more women tended to have a more even communication distribution pattern. With firm data, the military concluded:

Women provide a vital contribution to critical and creative thinking and decision making in our national security apparatus. This capability is unnecessarily missing in many military units where currently there are no women.

Although this report concentrates on the military and a connection between women and performance, it's not the only one to make the connection. Catalyst Information Center published 'Why Diversity Matters', which includes multiple studies to demonstrate the link between diversity (including gender) and corporate success.[17] [18]

This may be why there's been a global drive to increase the number of women Directors and Board Directors. In 2006, Norway became the first European country to pioneer this when it introduced a 40% quota for female Directors of listed companies. It came into force in 2008 with stiff sanctions, such as dissolving companies for non-compliance. Since then gender quotas for boards (with less severe sanctions) have been imposed in Belgium, Iceland, Italy, the Netherlands, and Spain. Further afield, Malaysia has enforced a 30% quota for new appointments to boards, and Brazil has a 40% target for state-controlled firms.

But not every company needs quotas to make changes. Bank of America is an organisation that's leading the way when it comes to

---

17. https://odeo.hq.nasa.gov/documents/DiverseProblemSolvers_TAGGED.pdf
18. http://www.catalyst.org/system/files/why_diversity_matters_catalyst_0.pdf

designing open and inclusive workplace cultures. With over 208,000 employees globally, award-winning for its diversity achievements, it's razor focused on attracting, retaining and developing diverse talent. As a result, it has strong representation at all levels. For example, more than half of its global workforce is female and more than 40% of their U.S. workforce is racially and ethnically diverse. Chairman of the Board and CEO Brian Moynihan leads from the top and the culture is permeated throughout the organisation, supporting everything that makes their employees unique, and providing resources to help them grow professionally and personally. As a caring organisation, it recognises the whole employee, not just the one who shows up for work. It encourages on-going education and awareness so its employees can learn from each other, plus have candid dialogues – or courageous conversations as it calls them – about the issues that affect their employees in the world at large, and amongst their communities, appreciating that feelings don't disappear when people come to work.

When I spoke to Leslie Henry, VP and Specialist for Data Systems and Security in the Chicago, U.S. office, she told me how having worked at the bank for twelve years as a middle manager, she was encouraged into cybersecurity. 'What became apparent was that they didn't just want my skills, they wanted my voice too. Although I wasn't from cybersecurity, right from the start they welcomed me into the team and told me that I was in charge of my own career. I'm sure that's why they're always so open to listen to any ideas I have, and implement the ones they believe are worthwhile. For example, like the time I was able to design and introduce a risk reward template that streamlined risk analysis and assessment. My managers have challenged me and pushed me in order to help me develop and as we're a close-knit team and socialise together we have a lot of fun in the process.'

As a lesbian and African American, Leslie belongs to the LGBT Pride network within the Bank and notes that it has more than

17,000 allies and out-of-work members, including the Chairman/ CEO. She also considers herself to have been fortunate to have such strong leadership whilst in the cybersecurity team, not just from her CISO Craig Frolich, but also from three other female African Americans, which she's found particularly inspiring. Yet, she says what she enjoys the most about the Bank, and sees as its greatest differentiator, is that the culture is supportive of people rather than of minorities. 'Bank of America is where I feel I can be my authentic self. Their policy is to be culturally additive, by concentrating on the culture a potential employee can bring to the organisation, rather than the target skill.'

With eleven employee networks, a variety of development and learning programmes that help drive a culture of mutual respect, and promote teamwork and positive engagement at every level of their company, plus enterprise partnerships that share their common goal of driving inclusion this certainly seems to be the case. Leslie adds, 'Although they do so much, they're never complacent. They always want to learn more, do more and improve.'

Learning from Bank of America, there are several actions we can take if we're to create a collaborative, open, and inclusive culture. The first is to define the mission, vision, and what we stand for. Although this will vary for each company or cybersecurity department, the best way you can deliver this is via a manifesto, or departmental manual.

Whichever method you choose, ensure that it encourages all employees to speak up if they're experiencing discrimination in the workplace, and to notify an ally, ideally one who has some influence within the organisation. Additionally, as a leader, if you witness an incident, you must call it out, otherwise the culture will be set.

Competition is something that I've talked about throughout this book, and that women are more likely to dislike competitive environments compared to men, and deselect them, regardless of their ability.[19] Given the fact that women are often penalised for displaying traits that are in opposition to their gender stereotype, for example, being too assertive and speaking up, which can cause them to be rated 14% lower compared to men, who are rewarded with 10% higher ratings, it's vital to create workplace cultures where women are heard, and are not having to fight for their ideas to be recognised.[20]

Having more female leaders throughout an organisation obviously would help to reduce this, as people would become more accustomed to women contributing and leading. However, that will take time. Until then, there are some practical things that you can do.

The first thing you need to be aware of is that sometimes it may not be as simple as men ignoring a woman's voice in the room. It may be that men haven't heard a woman's voice. Men hear differently to women, and as their voices affect the brain differently it's more difficult for them to hear female voices. Men actually have less acute hearing than women, and this difference becomes more pronounced the older they get. For example, girls will be distracted by noise levels that are approximately ten-times softer than levels that will distract boys.

A study at the University of Sheffield discovered that whilst both men and women process voice sounds in Wernicke's area, in the left cerebral hemisphere, men only tend to process male voice sounds there. They save female voice sounds for the auditory portion of the right hemisphere, which is where they process melody lines or background music. As women listen with both hemispheres they're able to pick up more nuances of sound and voice tonality, for example, crying or warning tones. But, as men listen with one hemisphere primarily, they're less able. Therefore, if you're a woman

---

19. http://web.stanford.edu/~niederle/Niederle.Vesterlund.QJE.2007.pdf
20. https://www.nytimes.com/2015/01/11/opinion/sunday/speaking -while-female.html?_r=1

in a room of mostly men, make sure you speak more loudly, lower your pitch, keep it even, and ensure you end sentences with a lower inflection.[21]

Armed with this knowledge, the other thing you can do is to ask all team members to lead or present in turn at meetings. This takes the focus off women and may even help the whole team with their communication and presentation skills.

If you're leading a meeting and you notice that a woman's idea has been stolen, you can step in to credit her. If you notice that women in your team aren't speaking up in a meeting, ask them for their opinion. Tell them you'd like to hear from them.

When I worked at the NCC Group, this was what my Managing Director did in a management meeting when I first started. He noticed that all the male Directors were getting airway, and that I hadn't contributed. He knew I had an opinion, and ensured my voice would be heard. He also gave me several Group projects that would stretch me in terms of my skillsets, plus increase my visibility within the organisation. I had the support of my CEO, too, who made it clear I should inform him if anyone stood in my way.

Listen out for the language that's being used to describe a female member of the team. If you notice someone calling a woman *forceful, bossy, abrasive, strident,* and *aggressive* when she's leading, or *emotional* and *irrational* when they disagree with something, ask them what's leading them to say that, and whether they'd be saying the same thing if that person were male.

Check this in performance reviews, too. In a report performed by Kieran Snyder on whether there was a difference in how high performing men and women were described in tech companies, she concluded there was. She complied 248 reviews from 180 people, 105 men and 75 women. They came from twenty-eight different tech

---

21. http://arlenetaylor.org/sensory-preference-pas/7444-gender-hearing -differences

companies comprising a range of large to small. She found that out of the reviews, about 71% contained critical feedback. However, the percentages were not evenly distributed – 58.9% of the reviews received by men contained critical feedback compared to 87.9% of the reviews received by women. Although both men and women were given constructive suggestions, women were repeatedly criticised for being *bossy, abrasive, strident* and *aggressive* and told to pipe down.[22]

When it comes to promotions, question what's valued, truly needed, and whether you're defining leadership in accordance with an old-fashioned, less progressive, aggressive management style.

Finally, it's worth bringing up the physical design of the workplace environment as this helps to display a collaborative and inclusive culture. Many companies think that all they have to do is offer ping-pong or snooker tables, and gaming stations such as Xboxes, and a kitchen filled with snacks and drinks in order to keep their talent happy. But, as people are sociable, providing as much space for thought and discussion or asking the women in the team for feedback on what would appeal to them can be effective means of displaying and facilitating collaboration.

Creating a culture of equal pay and promotion

If female cybersecurity professionals are to be retained in the workforce then it's time to pay them the same as their male peers. The fastest way to ensure a woman exits a company is by letting her find out that she's not being paid the same amount as her male colleagues, who are doing exactly the same job. Although I've read one report that states how women in security are being paid more than men, the 2017 Global Information Security Workforce Study

---

22. http://fortune.com/2014/08/26/performance-review-gender-bias/

does not agree.[23] It reveals the inequality in terms of the pay gap, and women whom I've spoken to about this concur.

Whilst writing this book, during one week alone I heard from three senior leaders who reported issues. Isabelle, a Director in a cybersecurity software company, told me that she'd recently found out that she was on two pay grades below the men who reported to her, and that she wasn't in line with the other Directors. When she brought this up with her line manager, another woman, she was told that HR wouldn't allow her to be on the right pay grade as the jump would be too extreme. She told me how this had made her feel undervalued, unmotivated, and abused. Additionally, she'd be looking for another job if HR didn't make it right.

Bob, a senior leader from a large financial organisation, noted the same issue when he was making an offer of employment to a woman. He told me that HR wouldn't offer anyone more than a certain percentage increase even if it were their market rate. Camille, who works for an insurance organisation relayed how she had to receive a job offer from another company and resign in order to be re-employed and receive a pay increase. However, upon re-joining she was denied the higher tier job title that the other company was offering. And Stephanie, a senior cybersecurity leader from an energy company, told me that her employer had said that he was giving the promotion to her male colleague just because he had a family to raise.

Practices like these are worrying, and are why some organisations are losing top female cybersecurity talent, especially at the middle management and junior VP levels. It's also why globally men are four times more likely to be in C-level positions, four times more likely to be in executive management positions and nine times more likely to be in a managerial position. If women

---

23. https://www.scmagazineuk.com/women-in-security-earn-up-to-30-more-than-men-finds-report/article/535369/

in cybersecurity are continually passed over for promotion or not paid fairly, when there's no penalty for moving jobs frequently, as there are in other professions, it's hardly surprising why they resign and seek other employers.[24] Or, why they get fed up and leave the industry at dramatically higher rates than women in other fields, or switch to other occupations.[25]

To improve the situation, assess the data and formally audit your team. Establish whether your male and female team members with the same qualifications are being paid the same amount, and receiving promotions and raises at similar rates. If there are disparities, investigate. Track your retention rates, too, and again break these down by gender. You may even want to consider publicly releasing these as many organisations do along with further data, for example gender comparisons between performance evaluation, promotions, and so on, as a useful means for measuring change, accountability, and competitiveness.

Change is only going to happen when more leaders drive this. Many managers need training, mentorship, and supervision whether they work for large corporations or small start-ups. Often, they're unaware of human psychology, their unconscious bias – which amounts to 87% according to $(ISC)^2$ 2017 GISWS report, and what drives performance.

To wrap this chapter up, if an organisation is to retain more women in cybersecurity, then it needs to make sure it's got the basics, like pay, equal. It has also got to offer more than attractive salaries, working from home arrangements, flexi-time, and perks such as gym memberships. Women, along with men increasingly, value

---

24. http://www.catalyst.org/system/files/The_Myth_of_the_Ideal_Wor
ker_Does_Doing_All_the_Right_Things_Really_Get_Women_Ahead
.pdf
25. https://academic.oup.com/sf/article/92/2/723/2235817/What-s-So
-Special-about-STEM-A-Comparison-of-Women

workplace wellbeing over material benefits, and this is achieved by creating a happy, healthy workplace culture that rests on a few major principles.

The Golden Rules

- Helping women to feel included and like they're fitting in is hugely important
- Policies and procedures must become people issues
- Organisations need to create workplace cultures of happiness, as simply offering workplace flexibility isn't enough
- Women can empower themselves and boost their own happiness at work
- Employers must be aware that progress ensures happiness and offer it to women
- Organisations need to be clear about their policies for intimidation, discrimination and victimisation, and take action immediately
- Encourage knowledge hoarding to be reported and called out as unacceptable behaviour.

Checklist for workplace culture

✓ **Have you created your mission, vision and values statements and ensured your employees or team know and live them?** When you can clearly and transparently communicate what you want from your business or department and why you'll not only inspire your employees or team, but you'll also give them something to be proud of and demonstrate just how much you care.

✓ **Have you clearly communicated to your employees or team their job descriptions and what you expect from working together?** By setting clearly defined boundaries, you'll create trust and a more agile company.

✓ **Do your employees or team feel you're approachable and that they've got a voice?** When you allow your team to give you feedback, voice concerns, and make suggestions for improvement it will help to guide company policy.

✓ **Have you given your employees or team some level of autonomous decision-making?** Empowerment increases morale and productivity.

✓ **Do your employees or team feel valued?** You don't have to spend a fortune to show you care about your employees or team. You can do this by saying 'thank you', or by publicly recognising someone, or by incorporating some new policies, procedures or fun activities, for example, bring your dog into work, or team picnics etc.

✓ **Are policies uniformly enforced?** Everyone must adhere to the policies for a failure to do so will only display inequality and resentment amongst your employees or team.

✓ **Do you and your leadership team practise what you preach?** You're a role model so you must show integrity and abide by the policies you set. Failure to do so will lose you respect and jeopardise the whole culture. In fact, you'll run the risk of setting a culture known for insincerity.

✓ **Do you encourage learning and development?** Training modules and events can help your employees or team to become better informed about the issues each minority faces and how together you can help promote an inclusive working environment. By encouraging your employees or team to expand their knowledge and skills in work-related areas you show you care, are committed to them and appreciative.

✓ **Does your company have employee networks?** This is simply an extension of encouraging learning and development.

✓ **Have you committed to unconscious bias training for all**

employees? Everyone is biased and the more your employees or team understand how to recognise their biased approaches or the language they use, the greater the chance you have of reducing it.

✓ **Do you have a diverse leadership or a women's executive programme?** This should serve to engage, develop, retain and support career advancement of high potential talent.

✓ **Are you resilient, adaptable and innovative?** Failures are learning lessons, and sometimes new rules or policies will be implemented that won't work. Being open to change, innovation and continuous improvement demonstrates humility and good leadership.

13. Career Navigation

- The merits and pitfalls of mentoring and sponsorship
- What is a posse?
- The value of networking

My heart broke as I handed my daughter over to Jo, the nursery owner. It was April 2002, she was five months old and my third child. Up until that point she'd been with me whenever I made calls and did team or supplier meetings.

Once again, I was living up to an expectation of being an unstoppable force in my penetration testing firm. I'd finished work the day before giving birth, and returned, with her in my arms two days after. My mother didn't approve, warning me that my health would suffer. Feeling invincible, though, I ignored her.

My team was relieved, for it signalled business as usual. Having played it safe for the last seven years and plateaued in terms of revenue, I knew we were at a turning point. Despite having a newborn, a fourteen-month old, and a ten-year old, I felt that if ever there was a time to change gears and reaccelerate growth in the business, it was now.

The business had done well. It was now a multi-million dollar firm that had grown within two years without any seed capital. And although I'd established a lifestyle business that was fitting in with my family, this had not been my intention. I was ambitious, and had set out from the start to create an asset which could be sold within five years for no fewer than ten million pounds. Now behind schedule, I knew that if I was going to hit my goal, which was achievable, I had to get a move on. That meant taking more risks, and one of those was signing up to exhibit at Infosecurity Europe, the UK's leading information security event.

Investing a substantial amount in this, I set to work. I worked with stand designers to create our look, and devised a solid marketing and PR campaign, which my marketing team implemented weeks before the three-day event. Then, every staff member, bar our accountant, worked on our exhibition stand during it. I ensured everyone could pitch well, would sell in a proactive consultancy manner, and was charged with passion, belief, and excitement.

By the end of the event, it looked like our hard work was going to pay off. We'd attracted reams of qualified leads, and having followed them up straight after, we'd received verbal orders for two very large deals within a few weeks. As each client needed a fast turnaround, we recruited immediately, and it was then that things started to go wrong.

My business's bank manager backed out of a loan that they'd virtually rubber-stamped; several large clients went under or had their funding pulled; another client was yet to pay; and a large order was put on hold. Although the business had a good sales order book, it now had a cash flow problem, no reserves, and creditors were chasing us. It was totally exposed, and I was frustrated at the situation, extremely stressed, and unsure if it would survive. With a bank charge against my house, failure looked likely.

Yet it was at this point that I found my mentor. His name was Mike, and he was my business's landlord.

As he'd always shown an interest in what the business was doing, and we were on good terms, I approached him for advice as soon as I discovered the mess we were in. In his sixties, he had shared many stories with me over a four-year tenancy, and I knew him to be kind, measured, and extremely shrewd. He'd told me about how he'd built, sold, and acquired a multitude of businesses during his lifetime, and how he'd encountered his fair share of failures and successes – both in terms of his career and personal life. Given my predicament, I couldn't have dreamt up a better mentor, for he took me under his wing and from that point on helped me to turn around a failing company.

The first thing he did was to point me in the direction of recovery practitioners, and tell me to investigate other choices aside from insolvency. He was right, as there were choices. We could sell the company for a pound, secure jobs for three of our employees and make the rest redundant, or we could fight for our business and try for a company voluntary arrangement (CVA).

Having shed many tears, and weighed up the risks, I opted for the latter. I knew that a CVA would be tough, that few businesses succeeded, and that the arrangement could only progress if it obtained its creditors' backing. So, I phoned or met each one, explained the situation, and eventually gained their support.

Then the hard work began. Mike passed no comment, but as I was his newly appointed protégé, although neither one of us has ever used a term like 'mentor' to describe our relationship, he taught me some business basics, like budgeting. Lessons like these continued ad hoc for the next two years, and he held me accountable for every plan that I made. He also set me work, checked it, tested me on my understanding of it, and introduced me to his network and trusted key contacts. Throughout all of our meetings, he encouraged and empowered me, and I've much to thank him for, particularly as he did this freely.

Within two years, my company had not only survived, but it had become more profitable than it had ever been. Fifteen years later, Mike and I still keep in contact, and I update him on what's going on in my life.

The merits and pitfalls of mentoring and sponsorship

Mentoring is defined as a relationship in which a more experienced or knowledgeable person helps to guide a less experienced or knowledgeable person. Sheryl Sandberg, the COO of Facebook and author of *Lean In*, has written and spoken extensively about mentoring. She believes that if you have to ask someone to mentor you, then they're probably not your mentor, and advocates teaching women to excel so they'll attract a mentor, rather than teaching women to find a mentor so they'll excel. Her reasoning for this is that all the latter does is keep women dependent on others.

Being committed to empowering others, I'm inclined to agree with her, especially as this is what happened to me. Additionally, I know what it's like to be a mentor, and to be asked to do this regularly. Unfortunately, whilst I value mentoring enormously, there's something about the process of being asked to be a mentor that feels awkward. I put it down to the fact that when you mentor someone, it's because you see potential which you believe is worth investing in. You also know that it's a reciprocal process, and that your mentee will have just as much to teach you as you'll have to teach them. Both participants profit, and that's why it has to be a natural process of selection, or purposefully engineered via a structured programme.

Mentoring is also a commitment, so I've a tendency to feel stressed whenever I'm asked to mentor someone. Being short on time, I know that somehow I need to fit this in amongst my work, other mentees, and family commitments. It's daft, really, as I've always got time to help someone, but it's why I prefer not to use a term to describe the relationship, and why I'm quite casual about it.

For example, I'll say something like, 'Just email me or give me a call if you need my help. I'll be there for you.' This works for me as I can give advice sporadically, when needed, as opposed to regularly every week or month. Interestingly, there's been research which suggests that this type of informal mentorship can yield greater results than formal mentoring. In a study, Belle Rose Ragins from the University of Wisconsin, Milwaukee and John Lin Cotton from Marquette University examined the effects of the type of mentoring relationship and the gender composition of the relationship on mentoring functions and career outcomes reported by 352 female and 257 male protégés. They discovered that protégés of informal mentors viewed their mentors as more effective and received greater compensation than protégés of formal mentors. However, whilst they received more career outcomes than non-mentored individuals, they also found there to be few differences between non-mentored and formally mentored individuals.[1]

With so much activity around mentoring, I've been curious to examine whether it can help us to retain more women in cyber-security. Looking at a 2010 World Economic Forum report on corporate practices for gender diversity in twenty countries, I saw that mentoring programmes are extremely popular, for 59% of the companies surveyed said that they offered internally-led mentoring and networking programmes. Moreover, 28% said they had women-specific programmes. Yet, to date, I've rarely come across anyone, let alone a woman in cybersecurity, who's being mentored through a formal programme. Knowing how frequently I'm asked to mentor, I was surprised by this, as there seems to be a need.

But, does mentoring really matter? This was something that Lillian T. Eby, Tammy D. Allen, Sarah C. Evans, Thomas Ng, and David DuBois examined in schools, academia, and the workplace. They concluded that the overall magnitude of association between mentoring and outcomes, such as behavioural, attitudinal, health-related, relational, motivational, and career, was relatively small.

---

1. https://www.bu.edu/sph/files/2012/01/Ragins_Mentor-functions-and -outcomes.pdf

Their research highlighted the need to play down what are sometimes seemingly unrealistic expectations about what mentoring can offer to mentees, institutions, and society at large. Additionally, they cautioned scholars, practitioners, and policy makers not to overestimate the potential effect of mentoring and to think carefully when developing programmes. Mentoring may or may not be the best or only solution to a particular problem.

Their findings provided guidance on the types of formal mentoring programmes that stood the greatest chance of success and the outcomes that you could expect from mentoring certain groups. In general, attitudes (e.g. towards work satisfaction, school, or career expectations), interpersonal relations, and motivation/involvement may be the most easily influenced by mentoring. However, they found that mentoring might be less useful for health-related (e.g. substance use, psychological stress and strain) and career outcomes (e.g. promotions, or salary increases). Concentrating on the type of mentoring, they found that in the academic field, mentoring may be most useful for improving performance and attitudes towards school, but be less effective for withdrawal behaviour. Similarly, in terms of the workplace, mentoring can enhance helping behaviour, situational satisfaction and attachment, and interpersonal relationships, but be less likely to heighten job performance and deter withdrawal behaviour.[2]

What's clear from the research is that we can learn from mentoring programmes that are in existence, which will help us to retain more women in cybersecurity. Mentoring is of benefit, but only when the expectations are realistic. If you're hoping that mentoring can retain women in the workforce, or in further education, or get women promoted into leadership positions, it may not be the best solution. However, if you want to coach or advise women so they

---

2. https://www.ncbi.nlm.nih.gov/pmc/articles/PMC2352144/

feel better about the jobs they're doing, then it may be perfectly suitable.

This is what Catalyst, a leading NGO that has a mission to expand opportunities for women and business, found when it surveyed more than 4,000 employees who'd graduated from top global MBA programmes. Through analysis, it noticed that women typically had more mentors than men, and that their mentors were different. Firstly, they coached or advised more than those of their male peers, and secondly, they were less senior and less influential within their organisation. Those mentoring men, however, took a more active role in advancing their mentees' careers by getting them visibility, putting them forward for jobs, and vouching for their ability. They also negotiated on their mentees' behalf for interesting projects, promotions, and pay increases. In other words, they sponsored rather than mentored.[3]

Catalyst also discovered, in another report, *Leaders Pay It Forward*, that more women than men were helping to develop the next generation of leaders. It turns out those women who were once identified as high-potential talent, and mentored, coached, or sponsored in their careers tend to pay it forward. And, there's a positive financial return on their investment when they do. The report found that their careers advanced and their compensation grew. In fact, they received an extra $25,075 in additional compensation over two years.[4]

However, when it comes to women and mentoring there's a warning. When Herminia Ibarra, Professor of Organisational Behaviour and the Cora Chaired Professor of Leadership and Learning at INSEAD, examined both mentoring and sponsorship, she

---

3. https://hbr.org/2010/09/why-men-still-get-more-promotions-than -women
4. http://www.catalyst.org/media/paying-it-forward-pays-back-business -leaders

discovered expectations were not being well met, as high potential women were being over mentored and under sponsored. As a result, talented women weren't being linked to sponsors who were highly placed within their organisation, and subsequently weren't being promoted into leadership roles. This is why she recommends a company defining the objectives of the programme it is implementing.

As a rule, she advises that when the objective of a programme is career advancement for high potentials, mentors and sponsors should be selected on the basis of influence within their organisation. However, when the goal is personal development, mentors and mentees should be matched to one another in accordance with good chemistry.

This is what IBM Europe is doing with sponsorship. Its programme is designed for senior women below the executive level and aims to promote selected participants within a one-year period. Each sponsor is tasked to raise their protégé's profile, promote them to decision makers, and find them internal projects that will fill in the company's skills gaps. Failure to obtain a promotion is viewed as a failure of the sponsor, not of the protégé.

Sponsoring certainly has many benefits. According to Catalyst, effective sponsorship is absolutely critical to accelerating a woman's career. It helps women who are working hard and playing by the rules to get noticed and promoted. No longer are they overlooked for prestigious assignments and big promotions. It enables women to make broader and more strategic contributions to their organisations, plus it circumvents gender stereotypes and the double bind – where women are penalised for exhibiting self-promoting behaviour which is considered acceptable in men. Sponsors are able to recognise and reward their protégé's talent and speak up on their behalf.[5]

---

5. http://www.catalyst.org/system/files/sponsoring_women_to_success
.pdf

Sponsorship can be seen as a triple win, as it also benefits sponsors and their organisations. The report found that sponsors described a deep sense of satisfaction that came from investing in their protégés, sustaining talent within their organisation, learning new skills that could augment their own careers, and establishing reputations as caring leaders. Committed teams and a 'pay it forward' culture benefit the organisation too, as employees feel more valued and supported. Importantly, though, sponsorship increases employee engagement, retention, talent development, and the strength of the talent pipeline.

Whilst sponsoring can offer many opportunities for women, it's not a silver bullet for the retention challenge. Sponsorship still has to be earned and sponsors still have to be attracted. Women who are keen to advance their careers have to build effective personal brands and make their skills, strengths, and work known in an authentic manner, which is something I'll be discussing in the next chapter.

What is a posse?

In addition to mentoring and sponsoring, there's one other thing that can help more women in cybersecurity to be retained in the workplace, and that's the posse. The posse is a small group of people, roughly no more than fifteen, whom you can count on when the going gets tough. You may have known them for years, worked with them, studied with them, and either see them regularly or not very often, particularly if they live in another part of the world. You'll be able to assemble them quickly when you need to, and they'll have some of the same expertise in common so they'll be able to understand one another and add value.

When I was in Sydney speaking at a panel event at an Australian multinational bank, I was reminded of the value of a posse when I heard one of the keynotes from an Executive Manager of Digital Assurance. She told the audience how she started in cybersecurity and how badly her career had begun. Being talented and having been recruited alongside three men, she was earmarked as a high potential. With her qualifications, she outshone the others.

However, when she was given projects to complete, she said she failed spectacularly. This led to her becoming increasingly withdrawn. Her manager was dumbfounded and considered letting her go when her performance further deteriorated. When she gained a new manager, he too was confused when he experienced her deliverables. But, rather than fire her, he decided to change his approach.

Instead of giving her a whole project, he chopped it down and gave her bite-sized chunks. To his relief and hers, she excelled. He continued with this approach and gradually expanded the size of the chunks he was giving her. Within a short space of time, she was able to complete a whole project and deliver it to a high standard.

When this young woman examined what had gone on, she said she was unaware that the other three male recruits had also struggled with the projects they were given. However, because they socialised and discussed the work together, they were able to figure things out as a collective group. Unfortunately, she felt isolated and as if she had no one to go to. Being on her own, she was unable to determine what her manager wanted. Had she had a posse, though, she could have contacted them immediately and asked for their help.

My posse is made up of a variety of different types of people. Some are within cybersecurity and others aren't. For example, French born Neira Jones is in cybersecurity, fintech, regtech and payments. She has more than twenty years' experience in technology and financial services, working for companies like Barclaycard, Santander, Abbey National, Oracle Corp., and Unisys. She's a market influencer, sits on public and private company boards and trade organisation committees. She is regularly invited to advise organisations of all sizes on payments, cybercrime, information security, and digital innovation. When I was asked to speak at AISA a few years ago, she was the person I contacted to ask whether 'someone like me' could do this. She was also the person who helped me create a speaker's rate card when I kept being asked to speak at events.

My brother is also someone I turn to regularly. Having been in cybersecurity for almost as long as I have, he's a useful sounding board. Knowing me in-depth obviously helps.

Ali Stewart from Ali Stewart & Co isn't in cybersecurity or technology. She's a masterful executive and leadership coach who's taught the highly acclaimed Liberating Leadership system to leader-developers both in the UK and throughout the world. Ali is someone I turn to for communication advice and use when I'm proposing communication consulting.[6]

Ernesto Moreno is another trusted member of my posse. He's also outside of cybersecurity, but he's an experienced consultant, leadership coach, speaker, and entrepreneur. He's measured, has razor-sharp insight, sees the big picture, and when I need advice for my business, I turn to him. If he sees me heading in the wrong direction or procrastinating with my 'busyness', he calls me out, which I always value.[7]

Marcus Ubl, a co-founder of Verve Rally, is someone else I consider in my posse. In the last decade, he's built and sold three businesses and has a particular interest in technology. Like Ernesto, he's incredibly astute, particularly when it comes to systems and operations.[8]

Having a posse is imperative, but there's a drawback that's worth being aware of. Unless you've purposefully crafted one that's diverse, like I've done, they can often think and approach things in the same way. If you have a challenge that's complex and requires innovative thinking then you may need to draw from a bigger community. This is where weak ties can come in handy.

---

6. http://alistewartandco.com/
7. http://ernesto-moreno.com/
8. http://marcusubl.com/#Home

The value of networking

Weak ties are typically associated with finding jobs and the work of the sociologist Mark Granovetter. Until his research, most people believed that jobs were found through strong ties – personal connections with friends, family, or peers at work. However, what Mark discovered was that the primary source of job leads came from weak ties – distant acquaintances, or friends of a friend. It turns out that people rarely refer their close connections for jobs because they're either worried that it will reflect badly on them if it doesn't work out, or because they're more likely to know of their close connections' faults and weaknesses, which they believe could interfere with being a good employee.

But, this wasn't all Mark discovered. When it came to information, having a loose and diverse network of acquaintances enabled people to tap into much wider sources of information and expand their thinking. By having a network of likeminded contacts that operate in the same circles as you do, you rarely learn anything new. However, when you're able to access a wider community, you can access different types of thinking and sort out challenges with confidence.[9] [10]

The Golden Rules

- Mentoring is useful for personal development or entrepreneurship
- Sponsorship is an effective solution for an employee's career progression
- Whether you choose mentoring or sponsoring, be clear about what type of relationship you want and your expectations

---

9. https://www.cs.kent.ac.uk/people/staff/saf/share/great-missenden/reference-papers/Weak%20Ties.pdf
10. https://sociology.stanford.edu/sites/default/files/publications/the_strength_of_weak_ties_and_exch_w-gans.pdf

- Form a posse of about fifteen people who know you well and whom you can contact for advice
- Join a community so you develop weak ties and a larger network for big ideas.

A checklist for creating sponsors/mentors/posses/networks

YOUR POSSE. Look back over the last two to three years and list the people you've turned to when you've needed advice or help about advancing your career. You may have gone to them to discuss important work matters, bounce ideas, get support for important projects, or for advice on how to evaluate new career opportunities. They'll be available quickly and you'll be able to count on them.

YOUR SPONSORS. Look back over the last two to three years and list the people who've been actively sponsoring you. Who's sung your praises, helped you elevate your profile, made introductions, provided useful resources, or suggested projects that can fill in skill gaps?

YOUR MENTORS. Look back over the last two to three years and list those who have helped you with personal development. These people may have counselled you or advised you to read particular books, attend events, or learn new skills. They don't have to be in cybersecurity.

YOUR NETWORK. Look back over the last two to three years and list the groups or networks you belong to. Make a note of how often you show up for their events, and what you get out of these events when you do.

14. Personal Branding

- The importance of personal branding and influence
- What holds women back from creating a personal brand?
- How can women create an effective, authentic personal brand?
- The importance of voice and linguistic style
- Creating credibility and content.

As far as I was concerned, I'd just opened Pandora's box. It was July 2011. A few months previously, I'd left the NCC Group, the first job I'd had in over a decade. I had no idea what to do next, and was at an event trying to figure things out.

I heard Tony Robbins and Richard Branson speaking about their journeys as businessmen, authors, and philanthropists, and I was hoping they'd inspire me. Being a fan of both, I wasn't disappointed, but it was a talk by an internet marketing coach that actually moved me into activity.

He was pitching online branding, and whilst I knew how to do this for a company and with the help of designers, I didn't have a clue how to do this for myself. It actually shouldn't have mattered, either, for I'm a big believer in outsourcing and playing to your strengths. However, for some strange reason, that year I'd set myself a goal to build my own website. Unsurprisingly, by the end of his talk, I'd convinced myself that I needed to learn much more, and I signed myself up for his two-day training programme immediately.

By the end of those two days, my head was spinning with the possibilities of what I could do next. With my newly gained knowledge, I set to work on building my personal brand. I wanted to test what I'd been taught and that it worked, so I began with Twitter, promising myself it would be a better experience than my first attempt with social media three years earlier. At that time, a client from a well-known retail brand had connected with me on Facebook, and asked me out. Unfortunately, when I thought I was replying to his message privately and letting him down gently, I soon discovered I wasn't. Instead, I'd managed to post my message directly on to his timeline for all to see. It was hugely embarrassing, especially as I didn't realise what I'd done immediately.[1]

Thankfully, Twitter proved straightforward. Within eight weeks I'd amassed 2,000 followers, and that was purely by implementing the lessons I'd learnt and sharing useful content.

Seeing its potential, and enjoying it, I continued with my learning. I read whatever I could about social media, communication, networking, and personal branding. I also tried lots of different techniques, tested many platforms like LinkedIn, YouTube, Facebook, Pinterest, and Instagram for their usefulness, and spent thousands of pounds on training courses. It was hugely beneficial, for over the years I've attracted clients, partners, analysts, and journalists, and I've been able to help a lot more people.

Then, in 2016, Influencer50, a company that IBM, Google, Microsoft, Walmart, Oracle, Salesforce, and Virginia Tech University use, acknowledged me as a top fifty influencer in cybersecurity in the UK. And, in 2017 IFSEC Global named me as the third most influential person in cybersecurity in the UK.

---

1. http://simoncoulson.com/

The importance of personal branding and influence

The reason why this matters is because in today's world, influence is becoming increasingly important. Influence is driven by expertise and credibility on subject matter and the relationship between an influencer and their followers.

An influencer is someone who has the power to reach audiences, who the market is listening to, and who's influencing buying decisions. They're not necessarily those who are on social media or shouting the loudest, so sometimes they can be hard to identify. Typically, though, they're trusted subject matter experts, have a large following, and can be relied on for original thought leadership, which their network is hungry for. They also lead with passion and curiosity, drive action amongst their followers, foster communities, and are connectors.

In his book *The Tipping Point*, Malcolm Gladwell explores the concept of connectors – people who possess a specific gift for bringing the world together and an intrinsic and natural gift for making social connections. He argues that these agents of change play a major role in determining social trends and phenomena.

Whilst influencers are significant, being one is not something that everyone aspires to. However, having an authentic personal brand, which all influencers have, needs to be, as the way we work is changing. For women in cybersecurity this is vital, as studies find that self-advocacy is better for your career than working hard.[2]

Those who create a strong personal brand that evokes who they are, what they stand for, and how they're different to everyone else are going to attract better opportunities. Even though there are reports of a skills shortage in cybersecurity, professionals, particularly women, aren't going to be assured an interview for a job,

---

2. http://www.catalyst.org/knowledge/myth-ideal-worker-does-doing-all
-right-things-really-get-women-ahead

or the job they want, or promotion unless they de-commoditise themselves – in person, on paper, and online.

Despite goals to increase the numbers of women in cybersecurity, competition is going to be fiercer than ever, and everyone is going to have to work harder. To impress hiring managers (internally and externally) or gain opportunities as an entrepreneur, everyone is going to have to become more visible, and create a memorable experience in the minds of those they interact with. It's going to be the main way to get doors to open to new opportunities, and enable the recognition that will take many to new levels of success.

This past year, I'm certain that I wouldn't have achieved all that I have done if I hadn't crafted a strong, authentic personal brand, and built a valuable network across multiple social media platforms like LinkedIn, Twitter and YouTube. Although I've always attracted cybersecurity professionals, as they've trusted me for career help and guidance, having been identified as an influencer, I'm now attracting more companies as they're placing emphasis on trust and impartial advice, and my income is increasing. By becoming visible, connected, credible, and valuable on an inner circle – where I am now – I get to hear about the many good opportunities that are being shared between a few people, instead of being on an outer circle where there are a few opportunities shared between many people. This makes business so much easier, for I'm consistently gaining exposure as I'm invited to speak at or chair events; attend exclusive dinners with other influencers; contribute to books, reports, industry standards or certifications; and feature in the media. Having an effective personal brand allows me to effect change, act as a role model for other women in cybersecurity and pay it forward. Social capital has become a very valuable form of currency.

What holds women back from creating a personal brand?

When it comes to personal branding and women in cybersecurity,

I've noticed several things that are going on regardless of company, level, or location. The first is that many women aren't visible, either online or offline, or both. Many women in cybersecurity will tell me that they don't like social media or self-promotion, and believe that doing a good job should be enough to get them acknowledged and promoted.

In an ideal world, it would be, but in the world we're living in, it's not, and it's important for women to be playing by the rules of the game. The rules of the game dictate that there are two kinds of work – visible work and invisible work, and that only visible work results in promotion or being allocated interesting projects or assignments. Men know this and apply the rules. They're far more comfortable speaking about their accomplishments publicly, and advertising their worth to their clients, peers, and bosses.

The second thing I've noticed is that when women in cybersecurity become visible through public speaking events, they're typically not making the most out of the opportunity. I'll give you an example.

About a year ago, I attended an event in London that was being run by one of the Big Four. I was attracted to it as it had a fantastic line up of speakers and panellists who were talking about topics I was interested in. I was also helping one of my mentees, Olivia. I'd brought her along as I was encouraging her to network with more women in the industry, and teaching her how to do this as she found it difficult. I could see that, like so many other women, she had a misconception about networking. Many think it's all about taking and creating self-centred connections in support of career advancement. Networking is actually about giving, sharing, and helping people, and this is something that many women enjoy and do naturally.

The evening started with a keynote speech from a female CISO, followed by an insightful panel discussion with some leading professional women working in the industry, and a special guest speaker, who'd worked as the Deputy Director of Cyber Defence Operations at GCHQ. It was slick, over 100 professionals attended, and I found it insightful. The speakers were human, witty, and unpretentious. I liked them a lot, and Olivia was impressed.

However, what I noticed was that none of the women were particularly visible online. What this signalled to me was that they either didn't care, or didn't understand the value of personal branding. They came across as being inaccessible and unfriendly, which I'm sure was unintentional.

As I sat in the audience wanting to spread the word about how amazing they were, I first looked for the event hashtag, and discovered there wasn't one. Then I looked for the women online. Unfortunately, I couldn't find them on Twitter, and when I found them on LinkedIn, I noticed that their profiles were incomplete and that they weren't engaging fully with their network. I remember shaking my head at the time and feeling so disappointed.

By not having an effective personal brand and working it fully, women in security are simply and unknowingly conforming to their gender stereotypes and the roles society expects them to fulfil. If we're to change this for women in cybersecurity, open up more opportunities for them, end the gender pay gap, and help them to be more fulfilled in the workplace, then we have to take action. We have to teach them how to build an effective personal brand and ensure they implement the lessons. Learning is earning.

When I speak about this at events or train CISOs and aspiring cybersecurity leaders on how to build a personal brand, I usually start by letting them know what personal branding is, and that branding is happening all the time, whether they like it or not. I'll explain that in essence it's what people are saying about them when they're not in the room. For example, in an organisation, if a woman comes across as being quiet or too caring, it's likely she'll be branded as being passive or weak, and unsuitable for leadership positions. If she's too open to learning new things, she may be branded as naïve or a disrupter; and if she's too ambitious, she may be branded as being aggressive and someone no one wants to work with.

Considering all of this, women in cybersecurity must take control of their personal brand, for the fact of the matter is that information about someone is typically only a few clicks away. People are looking at each other all the time, and when they do, they're making quick judgments about them. A strong personal brand can give women in cybersecurity more confidence, and it can open up more opportunities. Furthermore, it can deliver returns for the organisation they work for, for example, more productivity; easier recruitment; and more effective relationships with employees, clients, and partners.

How can women create an effective, authentic personal brand?

When I'm teaching a class about how to develop a personal brand, I always start with getting my students to consider their objective – why is it good to have a strong personal brand, what do they want from it, and what will success look like for them? Their objectives could be anything – engaging with journalists so they get more press; obtaining increased status as they're up for an award; winning new clients for a piece of work; securing new jobs or projects that may fill in a skills gap; or speaking at events. I then get them to consider the avatar – in other words, the profile of their ideal target market. We work through a detailed exercise until they can clearly identify exactly what their target audience looks like, where they reside (online and offline), what content they'll consume, how they like to consume it, plus what their problems are, and what they're aspiring for.

Then, we look at the students' channels, and assess their own profiles. I let them know that when someone Googles their name, the first page of results is how the world sees them. If they don't show up, then the world will see them as being a nobody. I ask them therefore to check if it's clear what they do, what they're good at, and whether testimonials can be found about their work.

I also get them to think about their style, body language, and how they're communicating on email or by phone. I find the easiest way to do this is by analysing well-known figureheads within cybersecurity, and outside. Finally, if there are women in my class, we'll talk about voice pitch and linguistic style plus all the nuances around interruptions, asking questions, and apologising. These are really important as the wrong pitch can make them sound less competent, trustworthy, educated, and employable. The wrong linguistic style can reduce their influence, and affect their career development within an organisation.

The importance of voice and linguistic style

To gain authority, women are often advised to pitch their voices lower, and experts have discovered that over the past fifty years, women's voices have dropped significantly as they've entered the workplace and tried to fit in. Once women's voices typically registered a full octave higher than men's, but today they're just two-thirds of an octave higher. Although this may help women to become heard, what's happening right now, particularly for millennial women in the USA and the UK, is that a new fashion of speaking is emerging and it's tempering progress. Vocal fry, a guttural growl at the back of the throat, has joined more traditional young-women voice mannerisms such as run-ons, breathiness, and question marks in sentences, known by linguists as uptalk. Unfortunately, these new voice styles are also seeping into women's written work, which can further affect their organisational influence.

When it comes to linguistic style, research suggests that women need to combine likeability and competence in order to be influential. In a study on nonverbal behaviour, gender and influence by four leading researchers, participants were asked to view a videotape of either a male or female colleague delivering a persuasive message using a high-task, dominant nonverbal, social, or submissive style. Those using the high-task style spoke relatively fast with few hesitations; they maintained neutral facial expressions, relaxed body postures, moderate eye contact, and calm, moderate intrusive hand gestures. Those who used a dominant style had louder, firmer, angrier voices; they maintained more eye contact and had stern threatening facial expressions, and stiff, backward leaning postures. The social style meant using a pleading tone of voice, friendlier facial expressions; those using it leaned in more and displayed moderate, calm hand gestures. The submissive style was all about using the softest, shakiest, slowest voice, with hesitations and stumbles.

Aside from the submissive style, all worked but not as equally for some genders as others. For example, when the dominant style was used, whilst both men and women were disliked, women were disliked more. The same was true for the high-task style. When women used this men found them less likeable, more threatening, and less influential than when other men used it. The only style that didn't penalise women was the social style, for it mixed masculine and feminine traits.[3]

Deborah Tannen, whom I referred to in Chapter 12, has been researching the influence of linguistic style on conversations and human relationships since 1974. She's found that communication isn't as simple as just saying what you mean. As language is a learned social behaviour, what matters most is how you say what you mean, and this is different for each person, in accordance with his or her cultural experience. She's seen how ways of speaking learnt in childhood affect judgments of competence and confidence in the workplace, and how this affects who gets heard, gets credit, and what gets done.

She believes how we say things matters, for this helps us com-

---

3. https://www.researchgate.net/publication/232524267_Nonverbal _Behavior_Gender_and_Influence

municate not only what we mean, but interpret what others mean, and make evaluations. Yet, unless we're preparing for a job interview, or presentation, she's found that people rarely think about their linguistic style – their choice of words, use of jokes, stories, questions, apologies, pauses, pace, pitch, turn-taking, indirectness, and directness.

Looking at turn-taking is important, as women are often accused of not speaking up during meetings. Just the other day a senior male cybersecurity leader, who advocates diversity said to me, 'The problem with women is that they need to be more like men. They need to speak up more in meetings.' But it's not as simple as this. Firstly, women don't need to be like men, and secondly, assertion should never be allocated to men alone.

The simple act of a person speaking and another responding requires a subtle negotiation of signals, for example, how long you take to pause and when you speak. It sounds straightforward, but cultural factors such as country, or region of origin, and ethnic background, as well as gender all have an influence.

When it comes to women, researchers have found that not only do they speak less in meetings – 75% less – but also they're left out of the conversation more often than men. As women typically wait for a pause in a conversation and then speak, rather than talk over the top of others and interrupt, this has been shown to affect the quality of meetings, and the decisions that are taken afterwards. Furthermore, this speaking pattern has been found to irritate men.

When Kieran Snyder, whom I mentioned in Chapter 12, decided to measure interruptions in meetings in the tech industry she discovered that although people interrupted a lot, overall men interrupted more than women. In fact, men were almost three times as likely to interrupt women as they were to interrupt other men. And although women appeared to continually interrupt each other, they almost never interrupted men. Finally, the more senior the speaker, the more they interrupted.[4]

Her findings imply that women have to learn to use interruptions in order to advance their careers, particularly in male-dominated tech settings like cybersecurity. Additionally, women need to understand that there are two types of interruptions. The first type is as a means to encourage, whereas the second type is to assert power. Whilst language communicates ideas, with linguistic style it negotiates relationships and power hierarchies. If you're a woman and want to measure how many times you're interrupted (manterruption) you can now do so via the Woman Interrupted application.[5]

When it comes to who gets credit for an idea, women in cybersecurity can increase their odds by using certain pronouns. The easiest way for them to achieve this is by simply owning their ideas and using 'I' as opposed to 'we'. Although it sounds easy to do, the challenge that most women have is that this will feel unnatural and risky. The reason why is because in almost every culture women have been taught from an early age not to brag or show-off. At school, most will have learnt that if they want to be popular and not ostracised from their peer group they'll have to downplay their achievements. They'll also have to avoid ways that make them stand out from others.

When it comes to asking questions, these too can send signals about competence and power, which women, being intuitive, can often pick up on. If only one person in a group asks questions, he or she has a higher likelihood of being judged as less competent or negatively evaluated. Although both genders in cybersecurity run the risk of being put in a one-down position, humiliated and

---

4. http://www.slate.com/blogs/lexicon_valley/2014/07/23/study
_men_interrupt_women_more_in_tech_workplaces_but_high_ranking
_women.html
5. http://www.womaninterruptedapp.com/en/

lectured, for women, as a minority, this is higher. One senior cyber-security woman told me about her experience and how debased this had made her feel. Learning from this, she now only asks questions in a group setting where she feels safe with the power dynamics of those present.

Like interruptions and questions, apologies have a tendency to be regarded differently by both genders. According to a study in the *Journal of Psychological Science*, women use apologies because they have a lower threshold for what constitutes offensive behaviour.[6] Men, on the other hand, are more attuned than women to the status implications of using them, for apologies can mean putting them in a one-down position, or admitting to being in the wrong.

Creating credibility and content

I teach my students the important rule that perception is reality, and that reality counts for nothing. Furthermore, that from this point on they have to become the bait. Their job is to attract opportunities, as they're now a brand, their profile is a tool, a door opener, and it needs to represent them well if it's going to work for them around the clock. As a result, they need to invest in it accordingly.

This means they have to review their headshots, as these are the first things people look for online. A professional headshot differentiates people immediately. It will work much like a logo does for a brand, and it allows them to become more easily recognisable. After this come their bios and headlines, which will have to be eye-grabbing and crafted in accordance with the nuances of the social media platform they're using. My students' goal from all of this activity is to be remembered positively.

In terms of content, my students have got to feed their network from now on, know exactly what they want, and be consistent.

6. https://web.stanford.edu/~omidf/KarinaSchumann/KarinaSchumann_Home/Publications_files/Schumann.PsychScience.2010.pdf

It's no good doing this every now and again, as that doesn't make them appear dependable and trustworthy. As everyone's hungry for content, especially visual content that's emotionally appealing, the students have got to be reading, watching, and listening to the same things that their target market and influencers are. Then they need to share this content across their social networks and attribute it to the original source, even if that means sharing a competitor's content. Reaching out to their market and engaging with them in this way is vital, as is commenting on posts, blogs, tweets, and answering questions. By contributing to a conversation that their target is already having, and sharing content that they'll find useful, the students add value to their network.

Creating a personal brand requires much effort, particularly the content. Although some individuals will outsource the whole activity to marketing agencies or internal departments if they work in large organisations, I never recommend this as a strategy, even when writing isn't their skill or time is limited. All this does is set an individual up from the start to be untrustworthy, which in security isn't a good thing. If they don't create their own content, their network will know.

Finally, in order to complete their personal branding and further differentiate themselves, individuals need to volunteer for projects at work and outside of it, for example, at universities, schools, and charities. And participate in panels and speaking events.

I find that once women in cybersecurity learn that personal branding is not about self-promotion, bragging, or chest-pounding, but about giving value, sharing knowledge, praising and acknowledging others, expressing gratitude, developing relationships, and becoming known as the source for certain subject matter, they embrace it more fully and excel. To inspire them to take action, I also let them know a couple of extra things. The first is that in numerous studies, it's been reported that women have high emotional intelligence (EQ) scores, which is a key ingredient in relationship building, and often a better determinant for success in the workplace, leadership, and personal excellence than intelligence (IQ). In fact, a study showed women's EQ can be, on average, four points higher than men's, and they generally score higher on self-management, social awareness, and relationship management.[7]

The second relates to the way women's brains work. In a study, Dr Ragini Verma, a Professor from the University of Pennsylvania, and her colleagues, examined the neurological connections in the brains of males and females aged between eight and twenty-two. Their research suggests that men's and women's brains are wired differently, and that on average women are actually better at connecting the left and right sides of the brain than men. Additionally, male brains may be optimised for motor skills and spatial ability, and female brains for memory and combining analytical and intuitive thinking.[8] Although the research makes many sweeping generalisations and plays to gender stereotypes, it could be good news for women as personal branding involves both logic (defining the objective, target audience, platforms, etc.) and intuition (understanding the target audience's needs, how to engage, communicate and build relationships, etc.). That said, it's important to bear in mind that the brain is not hardwired or fixed. Rather, it is very plastic and develops in accordance with how it is used, and in relation to social and cultural factors, which I've mentioned in earlier chapters.

7. https://www.td.org/Publications/Blogs/Management-Blog/2013/06/Emotional-Intelligence-Is-Key-to-Our-Success

8. http://www.livescience.com/41619-male-female-brains-wired-differently.html

The Golden Rules

- Influence is becoming increasingly important as influencers affect buying decisions
- If women are to gain influence they need to mix masculinity and femininity traits and use a social style to communicate
- Personal branding matters for women in cybersecurity, as it helps ensure their talent isn't overlooked
- At its core, personal branding is a shortcut to what you represent, so women must think about what they want to become known for
- Personal branding must be created and implemented by each individual, rather than outsourced
- Women have higher EQ scores than men, and their brains are wired differently, yet, both male and female brains are plastic, and develop in accordance with how they are used and in relation to social and cultural factors

Checklist for personal branding and influence

The five Cs:

✓ CONSIDER. Have you defined your objective and set your goals? Why are you creating a personal brand? What will success look like for you? Have you completed an avatar exercise so you know who your target audience is, where they reside, what problems they have, what they aspire to, so you can establish how you might help them?

✓ CHANNELS. Have you performed a gap analysis on your social media channels? How are you showing up? Can you be found? Are you presenting yourself professionally and optimising your opportunities? Have you had professional headshots taken, and are they consistent across all the social media platforms you use? And are you showcasing your uniqueness and charm?

✓ CONTENT. Are you sharing content that you think will be useful to your network? This might be other people's content and/or your own. Remember effective brands fulfil a need and provide a service that others want.

✓ CONNECT. Are you reaching out to connect with your target audience and your market influencers?

✓ CONSISTENT COMMUNICATION. Are you engaging with your network when others reach out to you and being consistent with your efforts? Does your target market know when they'll hear from you?

15. Personal Growth

- Resilience, grit, and toughness
- Exposing failures
- Confidence and the imposter syndrome
- Self-efficacy
- Fake it till you make it
- Presence
- Perfectionism and procrastination

Every now and again one of my friends will post something on my Facebook profile that they think I'll enjoy. That day I'd been sent a video and a story about a lobster. Narrated by a Rabbi, he spoke of how the lobster is a soft, mushy creature that protects itself from predators by encasing itself with a rigid shell. Confined by the capacity of this non-expanding shell, its growth requires pressure and discomfort. Once a year, when its shell becomes too restrictive and painful, the lobster makes for a rock formation, hides from predators, casts off its shell, and remains there until it grows a new one, a few sizes larger.

When it emerges, its shell is soft and offers little protection, as it takes a while for it to harden. At that moment, the lobster is vulnerable, yet this pattern is repeated indefinitely over the course of its potentially long lifetime.

The story of the lobster is relevant, for it can teach us many things in regards to retaining women in cybersecurity, particularly in regards to continual growth in the face of adversity. The lobster cannot change the way it's been made; it has to accept this. It grows only because of pain. Driven by discomfort, which is too much to bear, it can't go to a doctor, nor can it self-medicate. In order to survive, it has to grow, and that requires taking action, having self-belief and courage.

Self-belief + courage + vulnerability = strength.

Women in cybersecurity are obviously not lobsters, but I do believe they need to be encouraged to embrace discomfort in order to fully develop their careers. Furthermore, they may have to become their own biggest supporters in the process of doing so. Whenever I've spoken to senior women in the industry, they've always told me how their careers have grown because they've encountered some discomfort, and taken action on things that might have scared them and resulted in failure or a less than perfect outcome. They've also never been ready, but they've embraced the opportunity each time it's occurred.

My career has certainly followed this pattern. I remember starting out. One of my first office jobs was a three-week assignment, doing data entry for a technology company. My friend, who put me forward for the job, told me it was easy, and no experience was necessary. However, without any experience of computers, I can tell you that I was absolutely petrified. As ridiculous as this seems now, at the time I was doubtful I could do it, but as I needed the money, I agreed, and then worked hard to convince myself I'd be fine.

The only way I got myself to that job was by repeating a simple mantra over and over again: 'I can do it, and I'm going to do it, I can do it, and I'm going to do it…' It was like a scene from the Disney film *Dumbo*, when a train puffs up a steep hill singing, 'I think I can, I think I can,' and then when it reaches the top and is on the decline, it continues, 'I thought I could, I thought I could.'

When I arrived at the office and began calling companies and entering data, I obviously found the job to be a breeze. I clearly had nothing to fear. However, had I given in to my fear and not gone, I wouldn't have expanded my comfort zone, started a cybersecurity consultancy, and had my children, Ethan and Anja.

Fast forward a decade, and I encountered a similar experience of discomfort when I was employed as an Associate Director of Operations at the NCC Group. By that time I had much more experience, yet I still questioned my ability. At one point during my tenure, in addition to my main responsibilities, I was given the opportunity to lead a multi-million pound SAP project for the Group, and at another point I had to ensure my office became ISO9001 certified. My Directors believed I had the ability, insisted I rose to the challenge, and before I knew it, the projects were mine.

Once again I was scared, stressed, and deeply uncomfortable about doing each project for fear of failure, as I had no experience. But, I mustered up some courage, believed in their judgment, and as I'd built good relationships internally, I told myself I'd be OK, as I could just reach out to my peers for help and advice if I needed it.

What I didn't know at that time was that my response was actually typical of a woman coping with stress. Whilst everyone goes through periods of stress in his or her life, women deal with it in different ways to men. For a long time, researchers have claimed that the fight-or-flight response is the typical physiological and behavioural human response to stress. However, recent research suggests that whilst men might respond to a stressful situation by using the fight-or-flight response, for example lashing out, or avoiding the issue, or bottling up their emotions, women generally turn to the tend-and-befriend response.[1] This means that women are more likely to nurture and protect those around them in order to promote safety and reduce distress, whilst forming social alliances, which can aid the process. This is particularly useful in cybersecurity particularly during breaches when effective incident response and crisis management is called for.

The reason why women cope with stress differently to men boils down to the way the female body functions, for example, the way women use oxytocin, in conjunction with their reproductive hormones and endogenous opioid peptide mechanisms. In a study by Laura Klein and Shelley Taylor on the relationship between friendships and stress, they discovered that women are actually genetically hardwired for friendship because of this. When life becomes stressful for women, they seek out friendships with other women as a means of regulating their stress levels. Women need to talk about their emotional experiences, too, and to process what's happened, and what they might do going forward.[2]

Researchers also suggest that they cope better than men when it comes to prolonged periods of stress, because the protective effect of their reproductive hormones can block the negative effects on the brain.[3] Women therefore have an advantage, particularly when their networks are intact and built strategically.

But what happens when women pluck up the courage to deal with a new assignment or a job that stretches them and it doesn't work out? How do we ensure that they're encouraged to pick themselves up, try again, remain in the company, or in the industry? The answer is by teaching women how to become more resilient, gritty, and tough; by supporting them through their learning with

---

1. http://www.healing-arts.org/healing_trauma_therapy/Biobehavioral _Responses_to%20Stress_in_Females.pdf
2. http://www.anapsid.org/cnd/gender/tendfend.html
3. https://www.ncbi.nlm.nih.gov/pubmed/10941275

mentoring; and by sharing other women's successes and failures, through real-world stories of change, so they don't feel isolated.

Resilience, grit, and toughness

Let's start with resilience, and a story. A few years ago I was hired to train a team of unhappy, non-performing male cybersecurity sales executives. As soon as I entered the training room, I knew I was in for trouble, as their body language signalled resistance and defiance. Arms were folded, legs were spread out wide, and chairs were being tilted back.

Although I tried my best, my delivery was completely off-kilter, and I was so bad that I wasn't invited back to do any more work for the company. I couldn't blame them, either. It was an expensive learning lesson, and as I was so mortified by the whole experience, I vowed never to repeat that again.

Instead of giving up, though, and deciding that training wasn't for me, I upped my game, and learnt about how to teach groups of people. I also viewed the experience as a positive learning lesson, and was grateful for it. Then, when I trained my next group, as nerve-racking as it was, I found I excelled. I was happy with that outcome, as my hard work had paid off, and thankfully, because I've got high standards, believe in continuous improvement, have determination, grit, and resilience, I've excelled ever since.

Resilience is all about building toughness and recovering as quickly as possible from setbacks. If we're to retain women in cybersecurity, we need to ensure they're more resilient than ever. The good news is that women already have a high capacity for resilience, and once they understand this, I believe they'll become more confident and able to deal with whatever the industry is going to throw at them. Women don't need to become battle-axes, or more male-like, or anything other than themselves in order to succeed in the workplace. But, they do need to understand their standards, what's in it for them, have a network of supporters to cheer them on and advise, and be able to use creativity, guile, and empathy.

Teaching women to have more grit is slightly harder, as this is to do with strength of character, and it's questionable as to whether this can be learnt. Some believe it can be, as it's associated with having a growth mindset and believing that your ability to learn can develop with effort.

According to Angela Lee Duckworth, an American psychologist, author, professor and expert on grit and self-control, it's about having passion, commitment, and perseverance for very long-term goals. It's also about having stamina, finishing what you start, rising from setbacks, wanting to improve and succeed, undertaking sustained and sometimes unpleasant practices in order to do so, and working really hard to make your dream or mission become a reality.

In order to have grit, women need to understand why they do what they do, and this has to matter. They need courage, which can be taught, for it's concrete rather than abstract. When they have a dream or mission that they're passionate about, if it's important enough to them, they'll learn to strengthen. Typically, it's a trait associated with visionary leaders and entrepreneurs.[4]

Exposing failures

Now let's look at failures. Ask any successful woman in cybersecurity whether they've failed multiple times during the course of their career, the answer you'll likely get is a resounding, 'Yes, lots.' However, what typically happens is that they keep their failures private. It's understandable, too, as exposing their mistakes makes them stand out more, increases their vulnerability and sometimes gets them fired.

Until recently, I adopted the same approach, not speaking or writing about my failures, or 'learning experiences' as I prefer to call

---

4. https://angeladuckworth.com/

them. However, I now believe that in order to help more women in cybersecurity, this needs to change. If we reveal our vulnerabilities, we can empower all parties.

I'll give you an example. A few months ago I was invited to speak at a bank. My talk was about overcoming adversity. I was slightly nervous about what I was going to talk about, but nonetheless I wanted to share fully, so I could help more people.

I spoke about how I'd grown a cybersecurity consultancy from nothing, but also about how I'd lost almost everything – my relationship, business, career, children, and home, and the steps that I'd taken to rebuild my life. As I became human and vulnerable, rather than some kind of superwoman who's always succeeded and manages a career and family, the audience opened up and a healthy question and answer session ensued.

One very senior woman spoke about how she too had suffered, and how she was finding it hard to cope with the practicalities of being a single parent who worked full-time. She asked for advice, and I was able to provide her with a solution that could help her immediately. I felt good being able to help her, and encouraged as she had the confidence to speak up and felt safe in doing so, and she felt good about being helped.

Confidence and the imposter syndrome

Confidence is hugely relevant, as all too often women are plagued by a lack of self-confidence. Typically, this reveals itself in multiple polarising forms, from the imposter syndrome to a lack of perceived competence. The imposter syndrome is where a high-achieving, successful person feels undeserving, guilty, or like a fraud; is uncomfortable when being praised for their accomplishments; and believes that it's only a matter of time before they're found out for who they really are – imposters, with limited abilities. The syndrome is extremely common, particularly the higher up in management a person goes, and it isn't exclusive to women. However, it's often regarded as being so, as men don't tend to talk about it for fear of being socially ostracised when they come clean about failing to conform to their male stereotype – confident, assertive, and so on.

There are ways to handle this. As we're discussing women, the first thing you can do is to let women know that it's normal, and they're not alone – lots of people suffer from it. The imposter syndrome doesn't discriminate. Every CISO or subject matter expert (SME) I've ever met has doubts about his or her skills and abilities. But, they're liked, respected, and competent, so let them know this.

The second thing you can do is to ensure that women aren't comparing themselves to other people, or themselves. Whilst most people know the former, many don't know about the latter. Comparison is the thief of joy, but it's important, especially for high achieving women who are driven, as they will typically benchmark themselves and want to see progress.

I learnt all about this more recently, when I tried to do something new which I should have excelled at, but instead consistently failed. This was perplexing, and being a high achiever I found it to be a new and unpleasant experience. Failing wasn't something I was used to, particularly when I was working hard and had put time into it. It was only when a friend stopped me in my tracks after I broke down in tears about it that I understood.

He said, 'Stop comparing yourself to yourself. You're not the same person you were then.'

Remind women that they're human, evolve, and even if some things feel like a step backwards, they're always progressing. Few people talk about this, though. Instead, they'll say, 'So long as you're moving forward, that's OK' or 'Fail fast, fail forward'. But, learning and development don't work like this. Sometimes you do move backwards, and that's to be expected.

Whenever I'm training on this, I use the analogy of an elastic band. When it's pulled back, it shoots forward at speed, so I encourage my students not to give up, but instead to prepare for fast growth.

The third thing you can do is to get women to build a new habit. Women need to learn how to accept a compliment, and utter a 'thank you' as a natural response whenever it's given. To begin with, it's highly likely they'll feel uncomfortable whenever this occurs, as the natural response will be to brush the compliment off, downplay it, credit circumstance or other team members, but with practice it will become easier.

The same thing will occur when you get them to talk about their achievements and successes, which is important, particularly as women have been conditioned not to brag. Ideally, you'd want them to do this with failure – their learning lessons – too, as women habitually blame themselves for these, but women won't disclose failures unless they feel absolutely confident that they're safe to do so without suffering a penalty. Then you can move on to enhancing self-efficacy and perfectionism.

Finally, consider whether women really have an issue with confidence or if it's actually more to do with the way they see risk. As they're a minority in cybersecurity due to their gender, and have more of a tendency to be risk averse than men, is it any wonder that women are not raising their heads, pushing themselves forward, speaking up, and going for promotions more often? Being the odd one out, these things make them feel vulnerable, and, therefore, more at risk. Only by helping women to feel more supported, and less at risk can we help them to transform.

Self-efficacy

Albert Bandura, an early cognitive psychologist, coined the theory of self-efficacy. According to him, it's about 'the belief in one's capabilities to organise and execute the courses of action required to manage prospective situations.' There are many reasons why people believe in themselves and feel a sense of control, but what's of interest is what we can do to enhance this amongst women in our field.

Helping women to embrace a challenge or new task, and succeed at it, without taking the task over, we lead them to greater feelings of self-efficacy. It's important they take up the new task, as avoiding it can undermine and weaken self-efficacy. By encouraging, gently nudging, and convincing them to perform the new task and stretch themselves, just like I was stretched at the NCC Group, you'll empower them.

Although your belief in them will help them to believe more in themselves, whenever I'm training on this I always bring up the quote by Henry Ford: 'Whether you think you can or whether you think you can't, you're right.' This helps my students get into a positive state of mind, then they'll realise that they own this; they have the power.

Shadowing someone works to empower them, too, especially if they're similar to you, as they'll be able to relate to you, and it will increase their beliefs that they can master the same skill as you. Finally, by providing constructive feedback frequently, you'll help them to overcome any self-doubt.

Vanessa Pegueros, who's currently teaching a master's degree course 'Leading and Managing Enterprise Information Security' for the Information School at the University of Washington, and is the CISO of a successful SaaS company enabling digital transformation, agrees. She told me, 'I'm the first one in my family to go to college, and I paid my way through it. I've changed jobs eleven times during the course of my career, which for someone of my age is quite unusual. But, I had to do this in order to pursue my goals, as I wasn't prepared to wait.

'Whenever I experienced a roadblock in my career, or was discriminated against, or not recognised, I'd usually blame myself first, and then I'd pick myself up, and move on. The older I got, the faster I became at this, as I learnt to have more compassion and forgiveness for myself. I saw everything as a learning lesson. Sometimes I understood the lessons quickly, and other times it took me a few years, but I was always grateful for them, felt in control of my career, understood that failure was OK, and that it was just part of success.'

The conversation I had with Vanessa was enlightening, as she brought up another point that has a bearing on women in work. She said she'd seen women in the industry not knowing how to recharge themselves, and become drained and despondent. She told me how she'd watched her sons play sport, learn how to lose, and then recover, compete, and win again.

'Men play more sports than women, and they learn how to do this.'

She has a great point. The gender difference in sport is marked, and in a 2014 survey of thirty-seven countries, researchers found that four times as many men play competitive sports than women. Participating in a competitive sport can prepare women for the workplace, which is not a meritocracy.[5]

Fake it till you make it

The second way that confidence manifests itself amongst women is when they consistently underestimate their skills. They don't put themselves forward for new jobs unless they're certain they're qualified for them; and avoid asking for pay rises, speaking at events, and voicing their opinions in meetings.

Men don't do this. Whenever they're asked to take on more responsibility, they'll typically respond with, 'Great. When do I start?' Women will usually answer with, 'Do you think I'm ready?' It turns out that men are substantially more overconfident than women. They'll take on more risks, are more optimistic when taking on risky situations, and are particularly overconfident in areas where they're expected to have expertise.

Research also suggests that it's impossible to be non-biased when it comes to self-evaluation. In a meta-analysis of nearly 100

---

5. http://time.com/4322947/men-women-sports-evolution/

samples, men consistently rated themselves as being effective leaders, despite ratings that suggested otherwise.[6]

According to more studies, women are also so concerned about how others perceive them that they'll overlook their successes and build up flawed pictures of their careers. And, this keeps them stuck. It also risks their future in our industry, as unhappy employees won't be driven to produce their best work, and nor will they remain.

One of my favourite ways to deal with this is to get women to learn the 'fake it till you become it' approach. It was Amy Cuddy who first introduced me to the concept. A few years ago, I found her online, delivering a TED Talk, and by the end of her speech I was in tears. I could relate to her story and message in so many ways. My elder son, Tom, was gifted like her, had also suffered a head injury, and it had taken him two years longer to complete his degree. Whilst she talked about the imposter syndrome, it was how our body language can shape whom we are that really grabbed my attention.[7]

Having performed much research, she found that by holding your body in high-power poses for short periods of time, for example, two-minutes, you can summon up an extra surge of power and sense of wellbeing when it's needed. What happens during the process is that this stimulates higher levels of testosterone (the hormone linked to power and dominance in the animal and human worlds) and lower levels of cortisol (the stress hormone that can, over time, cause impaired immune functioning, hypertension, and memory loss).

By making the body more expansive, like animals would do for dominance (big because they're in charge, or small and enclosed because they're not in charge and can hide their vital organs), women can increase their feelings of power, have a greater tolerance

6. https://www.apa.org/pubs/journals/releases/apl-a0036751.pdf
7. https://www.ted.com/talks/amy_cuddy_your_body_language_shapes _who_you_are

for risk, and improve their performance during presentations, job interviews, or participating in a class.[8]

I've certainly tried this. Before every presentation I give, I find a quiet place to stand, put my hands on my hips, and expand my chest like Wonder Woman, breathing, envisioning, and preparing. I also tell myself that I own that stage, and to go knock it out of the park. I find it works, but there are other subtle power poses that women can use. For example, a prop, such as a whiteboard, allows them to reach out and rest a hand on it, and, therefore, take up more space, or spreading elbows wide on a table or desk.

Whatever method a woman chooses to use, the important thing for them to understand is that everyone forms opinions of one another in accordance with how much they trust, like, respect them, and view them as competent. However, a powerful connection of warmth can override competence, and this is often underestimated. Women have to connect with those they're communicating to before they can get buy-in to an idea, or lead a team, and if they want to move up the ranks in a company, they need to be able to demonstrate presence.

Presence

As a woman's career progresses, she'll discover that everyone has technical competency, but not everyone can communicate or has presence. Presence is the way you carry yourself, and how you convey yourself when you communicate in meetings and conversations.

The expectation for leaders is that they'll be self-confident, decisive, and assertive. Their poise will typically communicate this, as will their tone of voice and business attire. Women in cybersecurity must learn how to work this. Too often, I meet capable women in the industry, but they've got weak handshakes, aren't standing up straight, and speak timidly. This just keeps them down, for it sub-

---

8. https://www.ncbi.nlm.nih.gov/pubmed/20855902

tly communicates that they don't feel equal and are a subordinate, even when they're amongst peers and are not. Furthermore, they can often appear too helpful, polite, humble, and non-opinionated.

Train women how to state their opinions firmly, backing them up with strong rationale, and how to ask thoughtful, strategic questions so they can move on from just being nodding heads when others share information. Finally, ensure they're mindful of the language they're using. Their choice of words will reveal how confident they're feeling, and others will pick up on this.

Although Dr Carol Dweck, the author of *Mindset*, didn't research gender, she did investigate what prevented students from achieving their potential. She concluded that it came down to their mindset, and how it was developed. Advocating a growth rather than fixed mindset, which I briefly mentioned earlier, she outlines four strategies for creating one.

First, exercise your brain, for it works like a muscle, and through training it can be developed. Second, use the word 'yet', as language shapes actions, and whilst it's OK to be honest about your limitations, you must tack a 'yet' on to the end of any affirmation.

I'll give you an example of how this might work for us in cybersecurity. If I encountered someone who was about to present to their board on the state of their organisation's security, and they were feeling apprehensive, I'd be OK with them saying, 'I can't speak the language of the board...yet.'

Third, affirm variables that are in your control, as when you affirm effort, you'll typically get more effort. So, instead of saying things like, 'You're really good at communicating to the board,' it would be far better to say, 'I love the strategy you used when you communicated to the board,' or, 'I love how hard you tried.'

Fourth, surround yourself with other growth mindsets, so you don't revert back to old habits and become lazy. Risk and growth require work, and often people make excuses as to why they can't grow, change, or make a difference. My CISO Mastermind Club offers this as a solution.

Perfectionism and procrastination

Perfectionism and procrastination are two sides of the same coin, and time and time again we hear these traits hold women back. Having a daughter and two sons, I've witnessed this first hand by how my children have handled their homework. My elder son, Tom, went through a phase of just not doing his homework. He simply couldn't be bothered, and would sooner play computer games. He accepted he'd get into trouble, and knew he could only do this for so long, so he made the most of it.

My younger son, Ethan, has always worked hard, and handed in his homework. He gives it his best shot, and knows that if it's not good enough then at least he can look himself in the eye and say he tried. But my daughter, Anja, won't hand in her homework unless she's entirely happy with it. If she's unclear about something, she won't even start it. She'd sooner serve a penalty – a detention – than be judged on something that didn't meet her standard, or was wrong. And, even though I'll coax her to do it, and explain what's going on, I can often feel like I'm wasting my breath. Thankfully, I know that I'm not, and that through perseverance she'll make progress.

Perfectionists typically hold themselves up to an impossibly high standard. They subconsciously feel that when they're submitting their work, people aren't actually judging it. Rather, they're judging the perfectionist's worth as a person. That's why it can be hard for them to start and complete projects.

Whenever I've encountered a perfectionist in my team, I've worked hard to build their confidence. This means giving them regular feedback, encouraging them to change their mindsets on how they look at failure, or a less than perfect outcome, and sometimes breaking down their tasks into more manageable milestones. I've also helped them to understand where to put their effort, as some tasks require a high attention to detail, but many don't. If they can understand which ones do, they'll be able to manage the time they put into them better, and their energy.

I also get them to analyse their feelings regarding projects or tasks. If they're putting them off, then they need to look at why, and think about whether they need to ask for help. Finally, I'll teach them strategies for jumping when they're not ready to, and often these will come via stories, as everyone learns better that way.

Here's one I use every now and again.

A few years ago, I was found by a broadcast agency that had just launched a new initiative called the Broadcast Ready Expert Women, as part of the overall Expert Women campaign. This was after a journalism school lecturer called Lis Howell saw that 80% of the experts on the news were men, and that this wasn't mirroring working society, she felt she had to change this. So, she presented a pledge to British broadcasters that 30% of the experts on their programmes should be female. Some wouldn't sign it and developed their own internal expert women initiatives to address the problem, but the likes of, *Channel 4 News*, and *Sky News*, signed it immediately.

When Kerry Hopkins, the Founder of Broadcast Ready Expert Women, presented the initiative to about fifty hand-selected female experts, all of whom had been interviewed as subject matter experts, and were ready for TV appearances, she spoke about the challenges of getting women to step forward.

She said, 'Women, unlike men, lack confidence, and if they don't believe they can do it or know enough, they won't step forward to be on the news.' She then told of how men would just jump at the opportunity to be on the news, even if they didn't know that much about the subject matter. They'd catch a taxi, speed dial one of their colleagues who did know for an explanation, then they'd wing it on TV and often perform well.

I paid attention, and when a major British broadcaster called to speak to me about DARPA's Cyber Grand Challenge at Black Hat in

2016, and going on an iconic national radio programme, I decided to rise to the challenge. I told them I was just about to go into a meeting, and asked if it would be possible to call them back in an hour. When they agreed, I got straight on to Google, checked a few things, and phoned someone in my posse to ensure I was correct with my thinking. I then called them back. Much to my relief, they'd decided to change their programme schedule, and I wasn't needed. However, by this time I knew I was ready.

The Golden Rules

- Encourage women to believe in themselves more, and to understand that failure is part of success
- Empower women to take charge of their careers, and enlighten them about the fairness of the workplace
- Inspire women to stay committed to their decisions, but flexible in their approach
- Teach women how to recharge themselves, so they can fail, pick themselves up fast, and move on
- Ensure women understand about how confidence is displayed verbally and non-verbally, and teach them how to work on their words, tonality, and body posture
- Build confidence
- No one is ever ready, no one ever knows it all, so women must learn to jump, have faith in their abilities, and have people around them who they can reach out to if they get stuck.

Checklist for personal growth

- ✓ **Are you expanding your comfort zones regularly?** Doing this will not only help you build your confidence but also your skillset.
- ✓ **Do you finish what you start and do what you say you're going**

to do when you said you'd do it? This is all to do with integrity but it can often relate to expanding comfort zones. Typically, people avoid doing things not because they're lazy but because they're uncomfortable. Everyone moves towards pleasure and away from pain.

✓ **Do you know why you do what you do?** When you know this, you'll establish your purpose or direction.

✓ **Have you created a plan, dream board or dream diary?** These activities will help you to focus your mind and achieve your goal. They're also fun to do. Some will recommend sharing these with others to increase your odds of achieving them, whereas others will argue this will decrease your chances. Whatever you decide to do, remember you can use old school techniques or apps to help you.

✓ **Do you share your successes?** Sharing your achievements publicly may seem a bit narcissistic, but studies have shown that publicly sharing these motivates you to accomplish more. Providing you're not only sharing your wins, you're also indirectly breaking down barriers, giving permission for other women to share theirs, and for this to be seen as an acceptable practice for women.

✓ **Do you keep a daily journal?** Life is a roller coaster and often you have to come to your own aid. Writing empowers and can also facilitate any healing process that you're bound to have to go through at various stages of your life. Keeping a journal enables you to make sense of most things, and provides you with an emotional release where you can vent about issues related to work or the home.

✓ **Are you building new, healthy habits?** There's an old saying, 'How you do anything is how you do everything'. Habits reveal who you are so ensuring you're building healthy habits that support your objectives is important. They set a foundation, a tone for your life. They can also make you more efficient and eliminate wasted time, and replace motivation.

✓ **Have you made an achievements list?** Often, it's easy to forget how much you've achieved as you're caught up in the busyness of life. Compiling an achievements list can remind you of how far you've come and that small steps lead to quantum leaps. It can also improve your confidence and self-esteem too. Start at the beginning, from as early as you can remember.

✓ **Have you made a failure or learning lesson list?** This helps you get used to seeing failures as learning lessons and also how you deal with them.

✓ **Do you surround yourself with other growth mindsets?** Jim Rohn claims that we are the average of the five people we spend the most time with. Take notice of this and mitigate the risk of others pulling you down or stealing your dreams and aspirations.

✓ **Are you mentoring others and paying it forward?** This helps to empower you and build your confidence. As it's a two-way process you'll also learn from your mentees plus, according to a report by Catalyst, *Leaders Pay it Forward*, paying it forward pays back. They found that it not only benefits mentees but aids career advancement and compensation growth for those providing the assistance – an extra $25,075 in additional compensation in two years.[9]

✓ **Are you being mindful of the language you use?** For example, if you can't do something ensure you add 'yet' onto the end of your sentence. Better still and where possible, spin the language so you're referring to it in the positive.

---

9. http://www.catalyst.org/media/paying-it-forward-pays-back-business-leaders

Thanks for reading Part Two. Now you know more about the challenges and how important a change agent you can be. If you've not taken our pledge yet go here: https://bit.ly/in-security-pledge.

You can make a difference.

PART THREE
Taking Action

16. Through The Looking Glass

- Women's treatment of women in security
- Men's treatment of women in security
- Creating division
- Corporate social responsibility
- Jam today, not tomorrow

A few years ago, I was at a business seminar and the speaker opened the event with a story. It was about a boy, an old man, and a starfish, and it went like this.

Once upon a time, there was an old man who used to go to the ocean to do his writing. He had a habit of walking on the beach every morning before he began his work. Early one morning, he was walking along the shore after a big storm had passed, and found the vast beach littered with starfish as far as the eye could see, stretching in both directions.

Off in the distance, the old man noticed a small boy approaching. As the boy walked, he paused every so often, and as he grew closer, the man could see that he was occasionally bending down to pick up an object and throw it into the sea.

The boy came closer still, and the man called out, 'Good morning! May I ask what it is that you are doing?'

The young boy paused, looked up, and replied, 'Throwing starfish into the ocean. The tide has washed them up onto the beach and they can't return to the sea by themselves. When the sun gets high, they will die, unless I throw them back into the water.'

The old man said, 'But there must be tens of thousands of starfish on this beach. I'm afraid you won't really be able to make much of a difference.'

The boy bent down, picked up yet another starfish, and threw it as far as he could into the ocean. Then he turned, smiled, and said, 'It made a difference to that one!'

The story of the starfish serves to remind us of our task ahead, and that every small action to improve gender diversity in cybersecurity can result in a favourable outcome. Furthermore, it moves us forward.

When I started this book I had a commitment to investigate further, the courage to stand up and speak at events about it, and to try and improve things.

The work that I've done since then has tested me; it's literally consumed my life. Every waking hour, aside from coaching or consulting with my clients, has involved speaking at events about the topic, researching, travelling to meet new contacts, and interviewing them about what they've seen, experienced, or think about women in cybersecurity. I've learnt and grown so much, seen countries that I'd only dreamt of visiting, and met some incredible professionals in cybersecurity.

Women's treatment of women in cybersecurity

Up to the point of writing this book, I was unaware that I'd experienced gender discrimination and bias, for when you run your own company you're often fairly shielded. Since then, I've certainly encountered some, but nothing in comparison to what many women are contending with. Sadly, however, the greatest gender bias I've felt this past year has come from women, which has surprised me.

It began as soon as I launched my Kickstarter Project and fundraising activities for the publishing of this book. Shamelessly pitching, I went after the low-hanging fruit – women who'd spoken to the press repeatedly about the gender issue, or who'd received awards for helping other women, or who'd set up women in security networks. As they knew how tough it was to navigate their careers in security when facing a multitude of obstacles and bias, I naively thought that they'd be eager to help. However, whilst some did help, I'm sad to say that most did not.

Instead, I experienced criticism, name-calling, or sabotage, which usually took the form of them saying they'd help and then doing nothing. I also saw how many were exasperated with the old gender diversity argument, and wanted to distance themselves.

At first, this upset me, and then I became angry at their lack of integrity. But, now I realise why they may have behaved like this, and also how wrong it was of me to expect them to help. The work of Joan C. Williams and her book, *What Works for Women at Work* has helped me to understand this enormously.

Firstly, we're all human. Men don't support men just because they're the same gender, so it wasn't fair of me to expect this of women. Helping another person has nothing to do with gender. It's to do with being a decent human being, buying into a mission, sharing common values, and making it a priority.

Secondly, we work in an industry where there are so few women that this can lead many to conclude – rightly or wrongly – that there's only room for one woman to claim the spotlight or a job at the top. It's entirely predictable for women to be insecure and intensely competitive, particularly those in large corporations where the workplace cultures often support this type of behaviour. Queen bees, female misogynists, or 'bossy pants bitches' are just symptoms of gender bias in the environment and, like every industry, we have them in cybersecurity.

Thirdly, women are under intense pressure to judge each other. They're being scrutinised all the time, and their identities and personal styles come under constant attack. There's no right or wrong way to be a woman in cybersecurity. Women don't have to be a cyber punk with coloured hair, tattoos and piercings, or wear hoodies and black lace-up boots, or stilettos and designer suits. Women don't have to take on a masculine persona, or shy away from their femininity in order to thrive. They don't have to talk like a techie, either.

Women in cybersecurity can dress and speak however they want, be whatever they want to be, and will be accepted for it. Their identities as women are not at stake. Cybersecurity is a tolerant and fun profession, and accepts the square pegs that don't fit into the round holes.

Fourthly, many women don't have as much power to change things as I originally thought. Many are still navigating their careers, biased behaviours, and office politics. That doesn't make it right for them to ignore someone asking for help, or to treat another woman more harshly than they would another man, or to toughen women up in the same brutal ways they were when they first started out. Instead, they'd be advised to recognise that all women are different, and have diverse experiences, which makes them an asset to the team, and our industry. Furthermore, through collaboration, and adopting an abundant attitude, we can all become more effective.

Finally, when it comes to distancing themselves from other women, or the whole gender diversity debate, many women might be doing this because they suffered discrimination early on in their careers. Or it might be because being politically savvy enables them to maintain their power in their workplace. Many are just surviving.

Men's treatment of women in security

When I look at how men have supported me, I now know that I

was biased in my view, for I was less judgemental of them from the outset. That doesn't feel good, but I'm telling you how it is. Unsurprisingly, therefore, I was encouraged. Ignoring a few misogynists, some of whom are blatant, I found men genuinely want to address this issue and they recognise the benefits of having a gender diverse cybersecurity workplace and ecosystem. They also recognise that some of the issues that affect women affect them too.

I spoke to one CISO called Ryan, who told me how he'd taken paternity leave, and found that his job had been advertised in the process. Had he not logged in to his place of work to share a baby photo whilst he was off on leave, seen this, and reapplied, he'd have been out of a job when he returned. Men also have daughters, and they're keen for them to remain as open-minded as possible about a career in technology, and not to experience inequality in the workplace.

There are still issues, especially when it comes to sexual harassment, particularly at conferences, but I've only ever heard these come from the USA. Unlike the rest of the world, and despite campaigns to address booth babes, they still exist at conferences there and unfortunately, there are reports that men are sexually harassing women – groping, verbally insulting, inappropriately hitting-on them, or suggesting that women are only there to help men out.[1]

I heard how 2016's DEFCON, which has a mainly male black hat and white hat audience, maintained a less-than-enlightened attitude towards women. During Hacker Jeopardy, the oldest contest of the event, scantily clad women served drinks to the contestants, and at one point placed a sex toy resembling a male sex organ on the speakers' platform whilst questions were being asked about male

1. http://motherboard.vice.com/read/female-hackers-still-face
-harassment-at-conferences

sex organs. Despite a women hacker, called Banaside, competing, nothing was said, but she did go on to win the contest. Ironic.[2]

Some women turn a blind eye to this and are prepared to put up with it. But, Emily Crose isn't, and spoke to me about her experience. She recalled how in 2011 she'd taken her wife to the conference, and how one of the goons (conference volunteers), had shamelessly solicited to see her wife's breasts in front of her in exchange for a hole in her DEFCON goon bribe card. In 2012, a participant and San Francisco journalist called KC tried to solve the problem by creating Creeper Move cards. Red, yellow and green cards were created and if someone displayed inappropriate behaviour such as harassment, they were given a red or yellow card depending on the severity of the offence. Green cards were given to those who demonstrated respectful behaviour.[3] Unfortunately, these cards had no effect on the culture of the convention, and were scrapped in 2013.

Having witnessed the 2016 affair, she's saddened, as she remembers DEFCON being built with fun in mind, and bringing something new and creative to achieve that end.

'Women in security shouldn't have to put up with this. We shouldn't have to worry about being targeted or exploited in this manner if we attend.'[4]

Although the contest caused a stir, particularly on Twitter, DEFCON is trying to change, and the organisers are keen to welcome more women. In 2016 the event had a record turnout, and as a result more women competed in challenges. The RooTZ event, which teaches hacking skills to children between eight and sixteen years old, was reported to have a gender-neutral attendee ratio. DARPA's

---

2. https://metacurity.com/are-women-hackers-making-headway-defcon -sends-mixed-messages/

3. http://geekfeminism.wikia.com/wiki/Creeper_Move_cards

4. https://medium.com/@emilymaxima/when-will-defcon-stop-being -a-massive-sexist-cringe-fest-cd9d58ccb549

Cyber Grand Challenge Final Event, where automated cyber reasoning systems competed in a ninety-six-round game to capture the flag, also featured three teams with female members. And, there was a two-day TiaraCon to advance the careers of women in cybersecurity.

Creating division

Today's political climate is fuelled with division, and when I began talking about the challenges we face regarding women in cybersecurity, one woman told me that simply by using the words 'gender diversity' that was exactly what I was doing: dividing. That was not, and is not, my intention. Although I chose the words deliberately for inclusivity reasons, I now realise that whenever they're used, the perception is 'women-only'.

Women-only groups are useful for all the reasons I've mentioned in this book. However, not every woman wants to join one, and men must be included and feel part of this change if we're going to transform. The UN's HeforShe campaign advocates this, and encourages women to solicit support from men.

Men's support must be canvassed, and the best place to start is with those in leadership positions. Male cybersecurity leaders must be encouraged to support women more often, and given guidance on how to build meritocratic cultures. Women must also support and champion their participation.

This is what happened at PayPal in 2016 when Women@PayPal sponsored a gender equity panel without any women participating. The panel was titled 'Gender Equality and Inclusion in the Workplace: a Conversation with our Male Allies'. Although it caused uproar online, it demonstrated support, and how male allies are facing up to the problem of gender equity and coming together to discuss it in a public forum.[5]

It also reveals how men and women can support one another and exemplify decent human behaviour. One female senior leader in Australia did this for me last year. When a Director from a major brand attacked me unnecessarily on LinkedIn, she took a screen shot and informed the company where he worked. She knew its brand advocated gender diversity, copied me in on her email, and we received an appropriate response.

More support like this needs to happen whenever discrimination is witnessed. It's another reason why I advocate building a community of kindred spirits with people who believe in the same mission, and who can build their networks flexibly however they choose. The emphasis needs to be on people.

Corporate social responsibility

Corporations can help too. They have a responsibility to the groups and individuals they can affect, for example, their stakeholders (customers, suppliers, employees, communities, shareholders, financiers, etc.), and to society at large.

One of the best ways I've seen this done recently is by a corporation putting pressure on the supply chain. More frequently, I'm hearing how large global tech organisations are asking their suppliers for diversity percentages whenever they go out to tender for cybersecurity solutions. When more organisations follow their lead, this will then become a business driver rather than a nice-to-have.

Jam today, not tomorrow

As you can see, I believe in taking action. The reason I wrote this

---

5. http://www.usatoday.com/story/tech/news/2016/04/25/paypal
-defends-all-male-gender-equity-panel/83497400/

book was to ensure that the gender divide in cybersecurity ends, and right now.

A few years ago, I was one of two women who were invited to attend Infosecurity Europe's Advisory Council meeting. The objective of the meeting was to discuss the key challenges and issues that needed to be addressed in the conference programme, and to guide its programme development and speakers for the 2016 show.

I suggested several topics, which were met with interest. One of those was gender diversity in cybersecurity. Yet, the event Director decided not include this topic because she felt there was no solution. She raised a fair point, and as I said that I'd be able to provide her with that solution for the next year, I asked if we could revisit it.

We are now at that point. If organisations want to increase their gender diversity in cybersecurity, achieve more success, mitigate their risks, things need to change. For women and men to achieve more satisfaction in the workplace, and produce better strategies for combatting cyberattacks, things need to change.

This book is not about jam tomorrow. It's not about more talking, as that's already gone on for far too long. This book is about jam today, and taking action. As a leader, by implementing the strategies I've written about in this book, you can improve the situation for women in security, for your organisation, and society at large.

The Golden Rules

- Don't be overwhelmed by the task ahead – small steps make a difference
- Be aware of bias, particularly if you're a woman dealing with another woman
- Gender diversity is a people issue, and everyone benefits
- Call people out whenever you experience gender discrimination
- Don't just talk about the issue of gender diversity, act it out
- Allow male leaders and allies to help

17. A Call To Arms

According to the 2017 Global Information Security Workforce Study, the figures for women in cybersecurity continue to stagnate. Women globally are estimated to represent 11% of the cybersecurity workforce, are more likely to experience discrimination, feel more under-valued by their employers, and earn less than their male peers. Men are nine times more likely to be in managerial positions and four times more likely to be in executive management. Yet, women in cybersecurity, on average, have higher levels of education.

This is disheartening. Cybersecurity has the potential to offer so much for women. As an industry, it's dynamic, well paid, future proofed (as much as any job can be), and a diverse discipline. It requires many skills, from technology to analysis; business to risk management; strategy to creative thinking; communication to people management. Women are naturally predisposed to all of these skills, and I believe through diversity of thinking and experience we can get much better outcomes in cybersecurity when women are included and diversity is more evenly balanced.

Whilst this book has only concentrated on gender diversity within cybersecurity, my aim is that it can lead the way for all diversity, and improvements within our industry so we become stronger and better at dealing with our adversaries and the cyber threats that face us.

Like many minorities, women have unique abilities and add huge value to the cybersecurity industry. However, unless we radically improve our efforts to attract, identify and retain them, we'll miss out. Some of the challenges I've written about in this book can be addressed quickly, and others will take much longer – years. That said, we must not be discouraged. Can we change things? Yes, we can, but only if we take action to level the playing field. This means we need to start with equity, rather than equality. Equity is about giving everyone what he or she needs to be successful. Equality is about treating everyone the same. As girls and boys, and men and women, in many parts of the world, have different barriers to overcome in order to achieve the same results, we need to allow for this.

I believe that there's no better time to take action to address this than now. I've pledged to improve my unconscious bias, to become a visible, accessible role model and to shine the light on others who step up and help. Furthermore, I'll continue my work to mobilise an effective cybersecurity workforce, and create more equality for women within it. I can't do this alone and that's why I now request your help.

This book is not a drill. It's a call to arms, and the task I need you to participate in will be challenging. It will also require stamina and toleration for learning lessons, as the issue won't be solved overnight. Many times, you may feel like giving up, for there will be those who'll ridicule you and obstruct your efforts along the way. Don't despair. Keep going, for there will likely be those who'll surprise you, and offer tremendous help.

Remember this is fundamentally a people issue that we're solving. It's my belief that men and women in cybersecurity can achieve more together than by being the sum of the parts. No one gender is better than another, but we are different, and that's OK as this makes us strong. Furthermore, small steps and tiny tweaks in everything that we do to improve the inequalities that all genders are facing in cybersecurity will lead to quantum leaps, big changes, and better outcomes.

I therefore ask you to help me with this mission of improving gender diversity in cybersecurity. Be as mighty as a drop in the ocean, for as Mother Teresa said,

We ourselves feel that what we are doing is just a drop in the ocean. But the ocean would be less because of that missing drop.

No matter how small a change you make, it will have an effect, particularly when focused.

When we demonstrate that many fantastic opportunities exist for all people in cybersecurity, including women, we can create a more resilient, diverse workforce, bring about lasting change for all genders, and impact improvements for the greater good of cyber-security and humanity, worldwide.

To keep this dialogue open and us supporting one another, I created the IN Security movement and IN Crowdd, an exclusive cybersecurity community that's open to women and men who believe in diversity and helping one another. I invite you to join me there at https://bit.ly/in-crowdd.

Please visit www.cybersecuritycapital.com too, as this site exists to help you reach your career goals and support women in cyber-security. There, you can gain access to new resources for learning and development; find out about networking opportunities at IN Security events; and read, watch or listen to inspiring stories for empowerment.

Finally, please take the IN Security pledge at https://bit.ly/in -security-pledge and become an IN Security Ambassador.

The most successful people always take action within twenty-four hours. I hope you're one of them.

Acknowledgements

This book arose out of a want, a need, and a desire. It wouldn't exist if it were not for all the men and women in cybersecurity who recognised the challenge, wanted it solved, and believed in me. You made this book possible, and your contribution is greatly acknowledged. I thank you with all my heart. You are my heroines and heroes.

I'd also like to thank my sponsors. In the order that they came on board: Duo Security, ZoneFox, Bank of America, Stott and May, Digital Shadows, Fujitsu, BP, Reliance ACSN, and the NCC Group. Within these companies, there were some key ambassadors who worked hard to make the sponsorship possible. I'd like to thank Stephen Sparkes from Bank of America, Sarah Armstrong-Smith at Fujitsu, Lauren Goodwin from BP, and Lauren Chiesa from Resilience ACSN who immediately committed to sponsorship or were tireless in pushing for it. I'd also like to shine a light on Simon Oxley, Melanie Oldham, Andrew Martin, Bill Woodcock, Oliver Gilkes, Gary Hayslip, James McKinley, and Meg Layton who backed me and made a significant financial contribution. You've shown your integrity, how much you care in terms of moving the needle on gender diversity in cybersecurity, and I'm indebted to you.

Thank you to the men and women who gave me their time for

interviews and told me their stories in person, over Skype, or via private messages on LinkedIn. I can't name you but you know who you are. Furthermore, thank you to those within my network who connected me to people they thought could help. Chris Olive went above and beyond, but I'd also like to acknowledge Tim Anderson, Ray Stanton, Alan Jenkins, Ian Moyse, Charlie Timblin, Lizzie Clarke, Andrea Burns, Mo Cashman, Lesley Kipling, Carmina Lees as they also helped. And, to Tom Berry at Made by Chameleon, who offered great advice in terms of writing style, and connected me to journalists whom he thought would be interested in the story.

Writing a book has required me to summon up a huge amount of courage, and for that reason I'd like to thank my publisher Rethink Press, and the founders, Lucy McCarraher and Joe Gregory. I owe Lucy so much, as she told me I'd be crazy not to write this book when I initially asked whether I should. She also recommended I work with Rethink book coach, Debs Jenkins.

Debs has been there to support me every step of the way. She helped me plan the structure of the book, came up with cool ideas, checked my writing, held me accountable for meeting the time-scales I'd set, and built my confidence. The fact that she is a woman and a former coder proved hugely valuable, but so did her liking for dogs, cats and horses, and having a similar sense of humour through which we instantly connected. Joe guided me on this journey, too, and came up with a brilliant title. You've all helped ensure this book is of value to its readers.

On that note, I'd like to thank my beta readers, Arno Brok, Clive Room, Vicki Gavin, and Jivika Govil, plus my marketing assistant Becky Ashton, as they worked to extremely tight deadlines, and at the drop of a hat. Your feedback was priceless and I was proud to implement it all.

To Tarah Wheeler, who inspired me to start this book as a Kickstarter project. To #WomenInTechChat, who allowed me to use their photos for my Kickstarter project, website, and other social media. Additionally, to the industry non-profit organisations and those from within them who offered help, for example, Soraya Viloria Montesde Oca from BSides London, Vicki Gavin from the Women Security Society (wss), Joyce Brocaglia from the Executive Women's Forum (ewf), Jacqui Loustau from the Australian Women in Security Network (awsn), Magda Chelly from Woman in Cyber, Stephanie Aldridge from Cyber Security Challenge, Deidre Diamond and Veronica Mollica from #Brainbabes, Tony Clarke and Eoin Keary from owasp Dublin, Jacqueline de Rojas from techUK, Dalim Basu from bcs North London, and Adrian Davis and Brian Higgins from (isc)^2 emea.

To the journalists who interviewed me and featured me in their online magazines, including but not limited to Tony Morbin and Tom Reeve from SC *Magazine*, Joe Pettit from *Tripwire*, *Dropbox Business Blog UK*, *IDG Connect*, and *eForensics Magazine*. And to Sophie Hodgson from Aspectus for co-ordinating the PR and launch of the book.

To the long line of powerful women in my family who've inspired me to work hard, have courage, speak out, and pursue something I believe in. I'd like to start with my great grandmother, Jane, whom I didn't know, but whose name I took. Whilst writing this book, I learnt that she too was a single parent and did a 'man's job', painting wheels during the First World War so she could support her family. She fought to keep this job when the soldiers returned from war, and won.

To my granny, her daughter, who inspired me to be 'tough as old boots' and always told me I was doing a 'good job'. This memory has kept me going when I've felt like giving up.

To my mother, her daughter, who's been my greatest champion, and has reassured me with advice like, 'You can do this ... and you'll be good enough when it really matters.'

To my daughter, Anja, who's joined me for much of this journey, and who inspires me every single day.

Acknowledgements

To the powerful men in my family, too: my father, brother and sons Tom and Ethan. You've witnessed what this book has required of me, have put up with my obsession over it, the sacrifices that we've had to make as a family, and have challenged me with my thinking. Thank you for being great male role models, for believing in fairness and justice, and walking the talk.

Finally, thank you to you – my readers – for reading the book and any resulting support you give.

The Author

Jane Frankland is an award-winning entrepreneur, author, speaker, and consultant. She is one of the top 50 influencers in cybersecurity in the UK. Jane has nineteen years' worth of experience in the industry, has built and sold her own global penetration testing firm, Corsaire, been an SC Awards Judge for Europe and the USA, and held senior executive positions at  several large PLCs. Over the years, through her companies, she has been actively involved in OWASP, CREST, and the Cyber Essentials Scheme, and served as a Board Advisor for a CISO forum with over 170 senior cybersecurity leaders.

Jane believes in strengthening cyber space with an optimised, gender diverse cybersecurity workforce. Through Cyber Security Capital she helps cybersecurity leaders and entrepreneurs deal with the challenges they face in their careers and businesses. She does this via IN Crowdd, a global community she's created that stands behind a mission to connect, inspire, train and empower ambitious cybersecurity professionals.

Jane has a BA (Hons) from Loughborough University and is a Fellow of the Institute of Sales & Marketing Management (ISMM). She is a mother to three children, has a Weimaraner dog, a black and white moggy, and several chickens. The question you'll hear her ask the most in business is 'What's your objective?' and her favourite quote is 'Stay hungry. Stay foolish. Love what you do!'

Our commitment to diversity and inclusion

At Bank of America, we're committed to making financial lives better through the power of every connection.

We're focused on attracting, retaining and developing diverse talent. Women make up more than half of the Bank's global workforce including many in key roles on our cybersecurity team. Diversity and inclusion strengthens our company so we can better meet the different needs of our employees, customers and communities.

We continue to focus on being a great place for people to work, where everyone has the opportunity to achieve personal success.

Learn more at
bankofamerica.com/ inclusion

Connect with us: 🐦 @ BofA_News

Changing the face of security: it's time to make Jane Bond a reality

It's like a scene out of James Bond. A luxury hotel in the Alps has just had its systems disabled. A group of hackers has taken over its security, locking all the hotel's guests out of their rooms. The hotel is powerless. But for you? Your work has just started.

You work in cyber security. No two days are the same. On a Monday morning, you're defending a bank from online attacks. By the afternoon, you're finding gaps in a global retailer's security policy. You're outsmarting hackers. You're protecting people from the murky underworld, where figures in dark rooms try to expose personal, private information.

And all the while, you're building an exciting career in a fast expanding industry. You're learning more about the internet, and about how people tick. You're getting into the brains of hackers, and sussing out their next steps before they do.

But in cyber security, we can't protect anyone without the best people. The challenge? Well, as the saying goes, 'insanity is doing the same thing over and over again and expecting different results'. Men traditionally dominate the industry. People recruit from the same 'old boys' network. The shortfall of STEM skills is significant. And there's little diversity – only 10% of those working in information security are women.[1] So, how can cyber security companies expect to stay ahead of hackers, when they themselves don't think and act differently?

Well, at Fujitsu, we do. Women are the driving force in our cyber security business. Women make up 40% of our UK security leadership team. And women lead key transformation and infrastructure projects, such as the recent set up of our online portal by our female graduates.

We know that to stay ahead, we need the best talent.

[1] (ISC)2's 2015 Global Information Security Workforce Study

Fujitsu's cyber security teams: a case study

« I was inspired to join the security team by a woman in a senior position. And since I first started, a lot has changed. I remember the first external conference I went to – I could count the number of women on one hand. It's a lot better now. Many more women are building careers in security, but we've still got a long way to go.»

Inderjit Birak, Managing Security Consultant

« There's no denying it – security is a male-dominated industry. And I certainly felt under a lot of pressure to prove myself when I was younger. But this just motivated me to be the best. I'm now recognised as a subject matter expert, and I'm co-chair of the Fujitsu Women's Business Network.»

Sarah Armstrong-Smith, Managing Consultant & Fujitsu Distinguished Engineer

Pump up the Volume!

ONCE UPON A TIME, NOT SO LONG AGO, THE WORLD WAS QUITE A DIFFERENT PLACE. THERE WAS A TIME WHEN WOMEN STRUGGLED FOR EQUALITY, FOR RESPECT AND FOR RECOGNITION THAT THEIR QUALITIES AND SKILLS WERE AS VALUABLE AS A MAN'S.

TODAY OUR DAUGHTERS BEGIN THEIR CAREERS OBLIVIOUS OF THAT PAST WHERE MANY OF THEM WOULD HAVE BEEN TREATED AS SECOND CLASS. TODAY OUR SISTERS, OUR MOTHERS AND WIVES ARE LEADING COMPANIES REPRESENTING A GOOD PROPORTION OF THE C-SUITE POPULATION ACROSS THE GLOBE. THEY WORK ALONGSIDE MALE COLLEAGUES WHERE THERE EXISTS MUTUAL TRUST AND BELIEF IN EACH OTHER, WHERE THE STRENGTHS OF BOTH WOMEN AND MEN ARE PERFECTLY COMPLEMENTED, WHERE A DIFFERENCE IS RECOGNISED AS AN ASSET AND WHERE A VOICE IS QUITE SIMPLY A VOICE.

IT'S HARD TO IMAGINE A WORLD DIFFERENT TO THIS, HARD TO RECOGNISE WHY IT TOOK SO LONG TO EVOLVE INTO A TIME WHERE YOUR SEX WASN'T DISCRIMINATED AGAINST. WE'LL ALWAYS REMAIN CURIOUS AS TO WHY IT TOOK SO LONG FOR US TO RECOGNISE THE POWER OF EQUALITY. THANKFULLY, NOW THAT PAST IS STUDIED IN HISTORY LESSONS FASCINATING OUR CHILDREN WHO WILL NEVER UNDERSTAND HOW IT COULD POSSIBLY BE, THAT ONCE UPON A TIME THERE WAS SUCH A THING AS INEQUALITY OF THE SEXES. THEY ASK US, "BUT WHY DID PEOPLE THINK BOYS WERE BETTER THAN GIRLS?" THEN THEY SAY, "THAT'S RIDICULOUS."

THIS IS A SPEECH THAT WILL ONE DAY BE GIVEN AT A GIRLS' SCHOOL GRADUATION CEREMONY. WHILST WE MAY WONDER WHEN SUCH A DAY WILL BE, THE MOST IMPORTANT QUESTION IS, HOW DO WE GET THERE? WHAT DO WE NEED TO DO? WHILST THIS IS A QUESTION FOR SOCIETY, WE BELIEVE THAT OUR RESPONSIBILITY AS A COMPANY STARTS BY DRIVING CHANGE WITHIN OUR INDUSTRY. WE CERTAINLY DON'T HAVE ANY ANSWERS YET BUT WE ARE SEARCHING – WE'RE ON THE PATH.

THAT PATH IS SURPRISINGLY LONG AND STEEP, IT'S CERTAINLY NOT STRAIGHT NOR IS IT OBVIOUS. IT SEEMS THERE ARE ROCKS WE MUST MOVE OFF THE PATH AND THERE ARE PARTS WE MUST BUILD. AS WE WALK THIS PATH, WE MUST MAKE IT WIDER FOR OTHERS TO JOIN UNTIL ONE DAY IT IS NO LONGER A PATH BUT THE GROUND WE WALK ON – WHERE ONE DAY IT WILL BECOME OUR FOUNDATION.

OUR FIRST STEP IS SUPPORTING THIS BOOK – BEING PART OF THE FORCE THAT PUMPS UP THE VOLUME OF THIS CONVERSATION. WE CONSIDER OUR SUPPORT OF THIS MISSION AS THE BEGINNING OF OUR JOURNEY IN PROMOTING EQUALITY – PAGE 1 OF OUR STORY.

Specialists in IT Security Management

bp

"At BP we strive to create an inclusive workplace where everyone is able to deliver
to their maximum potential. By being inclusive we embrace diversity. By bringing
more women into the cyber security industry, the industry as a whole can realise
these incredible benefits."

Simon Hogkinson
BP's Chief Information Security Officer

Chichi Abraham-Igwe
Risk Management
Lead

*"I value the courage of
forward thinking and
diversity"*

Michelle C. Duyongco
Red Team Lead

*"Being confident
and visible are key to
encourage and draw
out other females to
the field"*

Emma Leith
Head of Digital Security
& Risk

*"It's a really exciting and
varied career choice and
one where women can
easily make their mark"*

Vidya Jeyachandrabose
Digital Security Project
Manager

*"I contribute towards
making BP a secured
company by managing
security project delivery"*

Christine Maxwell
Director of Governance, Risk &
Compliance

*"We have successfully recruited a
number of great females into the
BP security team with a near 50/50
Leadership team"*

Rajinder Purewal
Governance Policy & Reporting
Lead

*"I've contributed towards introducing
new ways of thinking and solving
problems by providing a different
view point/mindset towards security"*

Lauren Goodwin
Digital Security & Risk
Officer

*"It is critical for women and men
to promote diversity of all forms
to enable BP to thrive while
remaining secure and safe"*

Printed in Great
Britain
by Amazon